Fractured

Fractured

Living nine lives to escape my own

Ruth Dee

HODDER &
STOUGHTON

First published in Great Britain in 2009 by Hodder & Stoughton

An Hachette UK company

1

Copyright © Ruth Dee 2009

A CIP catalogue record for this title is available from the British Library

ISBN 9 780 340 97897 9

Typeset in Sabon by Hewer Text UK Ltd, Edinburgh
Printed and bound in the UK by CPI Mackays, Chatham ME5 8TD

Hodder & Stoughton policy is to use papers that are natural, renewable and recyclable products and made from wood grown in sustainable forests. The logging and manufacturing processes are expected to conform to the environmental regulations of the country of origin.

Hodder & Stoughton Ltd
338 Euston Road
London NW1 3BH

www.hodder.co.uk

To my three children who make me so proud, my psychotherapist and care coordinator, without whom I would not be as well as I am today, and to my husband who I love so much.

Acknowledgements

I would like to thank the following people who have supported me and helped me to write this book:

My sister who has shown me both love and support. Hazel, who has been a great friend for the last fory-five years and helped with material for this book. Lynne and Marilyn who have also contributed material to this book. My care team who keep me challenged and moving forward. My local friends who have supported me through the writing process. Bob McDevitt, Rowena Webb, Helen Coyle and Kerry Hood at Hodder & Stoughton and Mel Dawson for all their help and advice.

Contents

Foreword

This book is a true story about me. I have Dissociative Identity Disorder (DID) or Multiple Personality Disorder (MPD), and this book will show you how it arose and affected my life as I was growing up. In order to provide a clearer picture of what was happening, I will briefly explain MPD to you.

MPD results from extreme trauma or severe abuse in early childhood. The extent of the trauma is such that the child is unable to cope with it and she disconnects the mind from the body – that is, she dissociates. During this dissociative process, thoughts, feelings, memories and perceptions of traumatic experiences can be separated off psychologically, allowing the child to function as if the trauma had not occurred. All children have this ability.

MPD is often referred to as a highly effective survival technique because it allows individuals enduring 'hopeless' circumstances to preserve some areas of healthy functioning. Over time, for a child who has been repeatedly traumatised, this defensive disconnection becomes reinforced and conditioned. Because the dissociative escape is so effective, children who are very practised at it use it whenever they feel threatened or anxious.

The dissociation from traumatic events can be as simple as completely forgetting the event – or the personality can separate into different parts. These different parts become the individual additional personalities, or 'alters', as they are often called.

When the personality has split into different alters, each one can take control of the host body. In my experience, they often do not talk to each other and some may not even know of the existence of others.

The person with MPD usually has no memory of what happens when an alter takes over – time passes as in a second but in reality hours or even days have gone by and they have no recollection of where they have been, what they have said or what they were doing.

An individual can have a few or many alters. I have nine regular alters ranging in ages from a year old, through early childhood and into early teens and adulthood. I say regular, because some have come briefly then left again and others, equally transient, might have arrived and departed without my even realising they were there.

Some people are known to acknowledge their alters by naming them. I never have. However, for the purposes of this book, largely to keep the alters clearly identified, I have decided to give them temporary names.

I have also changed the names of people and places, largely to protect my siblings, for, although I have respected their adult experiences by not encroaching on them, I have not been able to avoid reference to the childhood terrors we all of us faced. Furthermore, I have toned down the abusive language my mother often hurled at us for, even as the memory of her words still burn my ears, there is no need to scorch the pages of this book too.

My alters

My alters gather around me in a circle and always have the same positions. If we imagine that the space they occupy is a clock face, then from the very beginning there was a baby positioned at two o'clock. I'll call her Jill. She is chubby and has thin, wispy blonde hair that is a little patchy at the back. It looks like where she rests her head when she lies down, but I don't recall ever seeing her lying down. She cannot walk and can just about stand. When she attempts to stand, she always has her back to me. I watch her as she stoops and stands continuously in that sweet exploratory way that young babies do. She is clearly a desperately unhappy child and whenever I manage to get a brief glimpse of her face, I can see that her moist little mouth is turned down as she is preparing to cry. Other than her crying and shrieking, she never makes a sound. She doesn't babble or coo or make any normal baby-type sounds.

Beside her, at approximately 1.30, is a toddler, Sarah, aged between eighteen months and two years old. She too is chubby and blonde, but her hair is a little longer and clings to her head like a cap. She is very unhappy and, like Jill, other than her screams of distress, she never makes any normal 'toddler' sounds. In peaceful times, she sits quietly on the floor beside the baby.

At approximately 1.15 is three-and-a-half-year-old Jenny. Her fair hair is straight and just touches her shoulders, which she often scrunches upwards as though she wishes her head would disappear into them. When all is well, she too sits quietly on the floor. She is unspeakably unhappy and it is small wonder because she holds in her memories all manner of horrors. She is always frightened and has overwhelming feelings of hopelessness. She sits with her head forward, often looking at the floor or at her fingers, which she twiddles and twines around each other as though her life depended on it. Other times she would rock backwards and forwards like a fast-moving metronome. She would often say in her high-pitched baby voice that she wants to 'go to find heaven', by which she means that she wants to die. She thinks constantly of dying and I believe that came about because we always heard about unpleasant deaths.

When Mum was constantly moving house with me and my brother, I suppose the two youngest of my alters were there, but either I simply wasn't aware of them at the time or I was too young to appreciate their significance. They only pierced my awareness when I was a three-and-a-half-year-old tot. So from the age when most children begin to show a clear understanding of the implications of their environment, I recognised there were others and that they were there for me alone as only I could see them. What I didn't always know was when one or other had become me – that is, taken over my body – and because I wasn't aware, those periods of time were lost to me.

When we (my alters and I) are agitated about anything, these three little ones shriek inconsolably, increasing my levels of fear and distress even when there is no danger on the horizon. Anything could set them off. I could be feeling stressed because of the pressure of work, or someone's un-pleasantness, or any of a myriad of everyday things. They pick up on my anxieties, but not on the reason for them, and they immediately react, appropriate only to their function, but inappropriately for me.

Six-year-old Liz is next, at approximately one o'clock and she stands facing me. I see her most clearly of the alters and she is the most mature of those on that side of the clock face. Her hair is the colour of wet sand and her eyes are an unusual light hazel, which reminds me of a lion cub's. When she is preoccupied, she has the habit of taking her top lip between her teeth and looking at the floor with a small frown on her face. She has shed all of the baby fat and is a 'proper' little girl.

She wears a red dress with a pale-coloured cardigan and has ringlets in her hair. She holds the majority of my experiences from between the ages of six and approximately thirteen years old. Liz is an incredible alter. She comforts all of us when childhood is upon us – me, the two babies, and even two of the slightly older alters who sit on that side. It seems that her job was basically to keep us in a positive mind-set and to introduce an element of stillness, of calm, when something bad happened.

Even now, as a middle-aged woman with grown-up children of my own, childhood memories can overpower me, hurtling me back in time. When this happens, it is Liz who comes out to soothe the child in me. She is calm, indomitable, gets me to face whatever situation I am in and manages to keep us all calm too. Despite this, she too is depressed, and what I call 'logically suicidal'. By that I mean it isn't an 'I'm going to kill myself because life is so bad' suicidal thought, but rather, 'If life doesn't improve and we have tried everything we can, then death is the best option.' For me, that is a logically considered suicide because first she tries to work through the difficult times, all the while encouraging us all that we can do it. Indeed, several of us have been suicidal over the years, as we felt that death was preferable to living in such circumstances, but one or other alter (often Liz) always stopped us, as luckily that particular one was in a positive frame of mind and thought that, despite everything, life was worth living. It became clear to me that there had to be unanimous approval for so serious an action to be carried out and I realised that I wouldn't have been able to commit suicide *without their permission.* In this scenario, I suspected that they, collectively, had the power of veto.

When I think about her, I realise that, although Liz is only quite young, she probably had to have evolved to be the 'adult' individual I needed for my mental security, yet because of my age at the time she emerged (and possibly my distrust of adults also had some influence), she occupies a child's body and is indeed simply a rather mature child.

Although I sense her depression, she still manages to stay calm. I often heard her think, 'I am so afraid myself but I mustn't show it. It would cause such despair that Ruthie mightn't survive.' The first time I realised that in addition to everything else this was what she was quietly battling, I understood that I too must take some responsibility for keeping the others calm and I tried whenever I was able. I admire Liz greatly. Her quiet determination encouraged us and she always gave me excellent advice about how to deal with particular situations.

Don't give anything away. We can cope. Don't tell anyone anything.

I thought her personality seemed a lot like my own, so I tended to talk with her a lot.

Two other alters sit on the right of the clock face. They are the ones aged between seven and eleven years old and resemble each other enough to be twins, but because of the difference in age, they clearly are not. They are brown-eyed with dark hair and very fair skin that looks as though it would burn easily in the sun. Susan and Jessica sit together at approximately 3.30, facing the centre of the clock. They too are very frightened, but Jess has enough fight in her to show flashes of anger. They sit curled up, with their heads in their hands, which are laid on their drawn-up knees, clearly feeling very stressed. They hold all the information of certain events that were specific to one of my childhood homes and the debilitating fear they exude almost cripples them and me, for when they are agitated they simply cannot cope. Nor can I, because their fear makes me incredibly anxious, which in turn causes the three youngest children to scream disconsolately – which then acts to ratchet my anxiety up several more notches and a vicious circle of fear and despair sets in. Sue and Jess tend to talk through Alexis, another alter, particularly when they need to express anger. However, fear is their more dominant frame of mind. They need a lot of comforting because they are constantly thinking that something bad is about to happen.

During these times, even Liz would be overwhelmed with our need and I, as a child . . . I don't know how we coped. I suspect now that some of the hours I lost at various times then might have occurred as some other, perhaps older, unrecognised alter inhabited my body and used the time to slowly return us all to some kind of equilibrium. Or possibly we all simply vacated the premises, leaving my physical self to care for itself as best it could. I simply do not know. What I do know is that without Liz's struggle to keep us on an even keel my mind would have been completely destroyed.

My childhood alters had the effect of making me see myself watching my siblings, even though I believed I was physically in another room. Clearly I had dissociated and one or other of them had walked me to the door to see my siblings. Although I understood this dissociation much later, as a fifty year old, I don't really remember either dissociating or walking to the door. Afterwards, and when I was back in myself, as it were, I always used to think it was strange how I knew exactly what was going on with my brothers. I knew what was happening in their attic room when I was supposed to be in my bedroom downstairs. Watching them drew me into whatever events were taking place with them.

My alters would try to reassure me, tell me that everything was going to be okay so that, even as my distress mounted, I was reassured. By the time I was approaching puberty, there were five regular active alters in my life.

Alexis is a young teenager. She stands at the other side of the clock face, as do all the older alters, at between nine and ten o'clock. She was the angry one.

Several other alters meandered into my life in these school years and I had no idea exactly when they arrived or why, but I suspected that perhaps a few came to help with the stresses of school life, the exams, and just the general mayhem that many teenagers seem to have to experience, before wandering off again.

Adult alters also live within me. Kathy is the 'real' mother to my children and she also tends to mother the younger alters when they need it. She stands between seven and eight o'clock on the clock face. She arrived when my first son was born and took the pain of childbirth and its aftermath. I always felt comfortable with and in control of my children because of her invaluable help, and she allowed me plenty of time to enjoy them on my own. She is a very capable woman who is just the kind of mother I wanted to have, and has a huge capacity to accommodate children's needs. This allowed me to bring up my children without letting anyone see how much I was struggling to keep my life on an even keel. Liz, who continued to play a caring role for me in the background, tended to do so largely silently and with a stillness that kept me fairly stable most of the time, but I believe that Kathy probably helped her in this role too.

There are also other alters, particularly Jean, Carol and Val who went to work with me as needed. I was seen as a workaholic and I know I could manage the jobs I did because of these alters. They completely took over my professional and social commitments with a level of efficiency that allowed me to progress quickly up the career ladder.

There are also other 'minor' alters like Meg and Sharon, who come to help here and there. If I don't know what to say or do, an alter will take over. I therefore generally appeared to be functioning as a single, efficient person.

Not all of my alters worked to my good, however, and later in life others would emerge to give me grave problems. So, although for most of my life they were my salvation, my alters eventually led to my downfall. I needed them desperately and constantly talked to them all for comfort and to ask for advice regarding decision-making options. I am aware that my experience of MPD is unusual as it is considered unusual to see the alters, though of course I am not alone in having this visual experience.

Few people with MPD actually see their alters. They hear them but generally do not experience the pseudo-visual hallucinations that I have. By that I mean I see them but I know that they are not there. This is different from people who have hallucinations and believe that the people they see are really there (like the real-life character, the mathematician John Nash, subject of the film *A Beautiful Mind*).

As the older alters emerged, they seated themselves on the opposite side of the clock face to the youngsters. They also had the benefit of not being as loud as the younger ones. If I listened I *could* hear what they were saying or thinking, but as I grew older and realised just how different I was to other people, I tried very hard not to listen. I didn't know about alters then and I thought I was just mad.

Living with alters requires a great deal of flexibility and concentration. A problem I have is that when I talk about the past I often switch from one to another. As a result, my tenses get confused because I might move from one alter who is considering the topic under discussion from the present time to another who is stuck in the past. So when I switch, say into the six year old, I too am six and living in 1956. My details therefore are the details of that time, so that if anyone asked me for my address, for example, I would give the one I lived at then; I become that person at that time. If I then switch to another alter living somewhere else, I would 'correct' the address, but it still mightn't be the current one. As this was happening throughout my life, it was not surprising that the very few people who noticed something thought that I was 'a little odd'.

The problem is I don't need them any longer but couldn't stop their active participation in my life until a couple of years ago when, with the help of my therapist, I began to learn how to. Now they come to me much less often. I would have to be feeling very stressed or tired for them to come to the fore.

All my alters remain the age they were when they first emerged, and unfortunately they are stuck in the time of their emergence. So although the three year old, Jenny, emerged when I was a similar age, until quite recently – and I am now in my fifties – she remained a three year old, constantly reliving my past, but her never-ending present. It meant that when Jenny was distressed, the effect of her pain was to take me with her, so I too became very distressed.

It is only in the last year and as a result of therapy that began five years ago that the youngest ones have come to understand that time has passed and that they are no longer needed. They are now reintegrated with me; that is, they are no longer partially split off from the main personality that is my identity.

Multiple Personality Disorder can be a terrifying condition, for the sufferer and the people around them. It has been part of me for as long as I can remember and at times it has felt like a curse, but in fact I am certain that it has also saved my life. It has taken me years to come to a point where I feel I understand myself well enough to explain what it feels like to live with many selves. This is my story.

I

I am not alone

My name is Ruth Dee. I am fifty-seven years old and I have taken early retirement from the job I loved. I was an educator and I was passionate about my job. I rose through the ranks despite, and perhaps because of the demons that drove me. When I was at the pinnacle of my career, those very same demons derailed me. Everyone said how good I was, and I would like to believe them because teaching meant so much to me. So why did I retire? Well, that was not my choice. There were others involved. So many others. The helpful, the fearful and the angry both sustained and almost destroyed me.

I am sitting here with a cup of tea, reliving it all as I have been wont to do since my enforced retirement. As I sit and ponder, the others join me and soon we are all in reverie.

Sitting lost in thought is something I'm told I do a lot. Ever since I could remember, people have said to my parents, 'Your little girl is always thinking of something. I've been watching her for . . .' and they would tell my mother or father how long they'd been observing me, how still I sat, how when they spoke to me softly I hadn't heard, how they marvelled that their own children couldn't seem to achieve what I had, but were rather rumbustious and always putting their noses where they didn't belong.

'With that kind of concentration she'll go far.'

My parents would beam and take credit for my 'supposed' intelligence with words like, 'Good genes, you know,' or, 'Takes after me, I was always daydreaming too,' or, 'If you bring them up right, they'll always be a credit.'

Then there was the flip side, where a need to respond to my 'thoughts' occasionally caused me to speak aloud, and I might be observed talking to myself . . . again.

Sometimes someone might politely say, 'But is it really good? She seems so alone,' and my parents would laugh and respond, 'With her four brothers and sisters around, she is never really alone, so it is a good thing that she can make time for herself. It's good for her to be alone with only her thoughts for company.'

People rarely mentioned that I often talked to myself with an intensity that could have been disturbing to them. Perhaps they should have, but they didn't, and my life continued along its path.

They were right when they said that I would do well. As an adult, in addition to being a teacher, I had a promising, efficient and varied life as a wife and mother – three jobs I loved and worked hard to excel at. But they were very wrong when they said I was alone. I have never been alone, and I am not talking here of my three younger brothers and one sister. I have never known the peace of truly being by myself. I have never been able to shut off the chattering masses by excusing myself and going somewhere else – even if such a place existed. They were always with me.

I have never been alone, not since I was three and a half

years old and the world I knew – not a perfect world, never a perfect world – was blown apart, shattered into a billion pieces of sharp glass that would have slashed and gouged their way through my life with an even more destructive force if I had been alone.

I was not alone throughout my school years and, although that sometimes got me into trouble, no one ever really realised what was different about me. They probably just thought, every now and then, that I was a little odd.

I was not alone as I worked my way through college, into a good teaching job, up the career ladder and into a position of leadership.

I was not alone when I dated, fell in love, married, started a family, divorced, fell in love again and remarried.

I was not alone and my 'not-aloneness' acted almost always for my benefit, selflessly ensuring that I was tough enough to be a survivor at the most dangerous times of my disturbing life. It was something built in by nature – and in my own nature – to ensure that I would survive to find a good husband, reproduce and nurture my three young offspring until they were old enough to negotiate their own way through life.

I was never alone. Unseen by anyone else, the alters, my alters – my other selves – were there; always, always, always guiding me, protecting me and annoying me by wanting more of a share of my life than was safe for me to give them. I couldn't get rid of them, because they are me and I am them, bound tightly in a most intricate way. I have always had to struggle to keep them contained, to be in control – and, for a long time, I was successful.

Now here I am, a retired woman, sitting on my balcony. My wonderful husband Jamie is away somewhere and I've forgotten what it was he said he'd be doing. Or perhaps he spoke with one of my others who knows full well where he is and what he's doing, but she hasn't told me yet.

I am looking over to the street where a young woman has parked her car and is now releasing a baby from its special seat at the back of the vehicle. Holding on to her skirt is a small child, a girl in a pretty pinafore, perhaps four years old.

Pretty baby. Jenny's voice is young, as always. She hasn't aged since I first met her and she is just three and a half years old. *Pretty, pretty baby*.

I don't respond. I don't want to acknowledge Jenny is here because she has the power to take me back to my childhood.

The woman locks her car and, with the baby on her hip, takes the little girl's hand, crosses the quiet street and walks up the short drive to the house opposite. My neighbour, Kate, opens the door even before the young mother rings the doorbell; screeching loudly, she gathers all of them into her arms. I understand from the loud, excited comments that her daughter, who lives far to the north, has brought the grand-children for a visit.

As though Jenny had heard my earlier thought she says, *Takes us back, don't it?*

Jenny was never good at grammar, and she pronounces 'don't it' as 'doh-nit', but I don't correct her.

Takes us back, she repeats. She sounds a little plaintive, but still I don't respond, as poor Jenny was always scared and I'd learnt from past experience that if *I* pandered to her fear it often made it worse. There was just one who could soothe her.

The little girl across the way is shy, hiding behind her mother's legs, and the mother reaches down a gentle hand to draw her forward. There is a subtle shift in my perception. I can vaguely smell Pear's soap and baby powder and, as I stare, the little girl slowly transmogrifies into another – my only sister Mary, a frightened, screaming four year old. She changes shape and shrinks slowly. I watch, horrified, my mouth open, for although I have never experienced this vision in quite this way before, I know what will happen next.

Takes us back, don't it? Jenny is crying, becoming a little hysterical.

I turn to her, unbelieving, but my eyes are filling with tears and I can't see her. I blink them away furiously knowing, even as I do so, that I won't see her. When she is in this kind of mood, she sometimes hides from me, for her fears are not simply for her own pain, but my protection. I have tried in my turn to give *her* some kind of protection, but it doesn't work that way; the guilt eats away at me, but only Liz is able to soothe her. I find my gorge rising in response to Jenny's terror and try to call Liz to her, because when Jenny is in pain, I am in great peril. I fidget in anxiety, because although my adult self tells me there is nothing to fear, Jenny's panic reverts me to childhood.

I struggle to remain calm and to stay in the here and now. If I can do so, then I am an adult. I have always seen Jenny or Liz, Jessica, Susan or Alexis, Kathy, Jean, Carol, Sarah, Meg or Sharon, and many of the others and I have always been able to see myself through their eyes, though when I was a small child, I wasn't quite aware of exactly what was happening. The youngest of my alters have always been with me, though I did not see the first ones until I was three and a half years old. That was when I saw Jenny and two younger children, mere babies, for the first time. Even as I recall this, I feel Jenny enter and rejoin me, yet still maintaining a strong, separate presence – an astonishing feeling. Usually she or one of the others would arrive unannounced, without any preamble, and would be beside rather than inside me. If they were inside me it meant that they had taken over the host body, *my* body, completely.

J-just takes us back, don't it? Jenny's voice, apparently a stuck recording, is now a low murmur, as though by re-entering she has managed to find some calm, but it is more likely to be Liz's influence, for I now sense her presence as well. Since my childhood, six-year-old Liz has worked hard to soothe me and the younger alters and, as Jenny's panic diminishes, the vision I was seeing earlier returns to me. As I can still hear her saying, *takes us back, don't it?*, I realise that I am doing just that: slowly, reluctantly, inexorably, I am going back.

I am no longer looking at the scene across the road, but, even so, I 'see' Mary becoming smaller and smaller as the scene continues to play before my mind's eyes. In my reality I watch horrified as I, the older daughter, emerge as a young child.

I am not screaming. Neither is my three-and-a-half-year-old self. My small self is excited, because she (Ruthie) is in the car with her mum, dad and baby brothers.

It was a rare occasion. Daddy, who was away a lot, had come to visit us at the home Mum shared with us small children. Whenever he visited, he was lots of fun. He always smiled a lot, and when Mum was shouting and lashing out at Ruthie, which she tended to do a lot, he would stop her. Sometimes he would lift the little girl high, push his smiley face into hers, rubbing noses and he would say, 'Would you like to go to the park? I'll take you there in my chariot!'

We would always drive somewhere nice in the car: to the park, to the river, or just somewhere in the countryside. He would buy us dinner in places that smelt simply wonderful and then he would take us back home. When he left again, the magic would be gone. But not today, today my small self was excited. Daddy was here and we were in the car.

I am simply filled with foreboding – a warning of things to come. No such foreboding for her, and even if there had been, what could she have done about it?

We were going on a trip. Being with Daddy was a wonderful interlude in what was for both me and my mother, and possibly my baby brothers too, a stressful life. It seemed like a long journey, though I now know that it wasn't, and I kept asking, 'Are we nearly there?'

To which my father or mother would respond, 'Almost.'

I looked at the house we were approaching on a huge council estate. Not entirely sure why, I tensed as we drove up the long steep hill to it. A sense of dread filled me. I didn't really want to visit.

The car pulled up at the front door of a large three-storeyed house. It was old and painted white on the outside and the door was a dark colour. As I stared at that door, a memory of tall ceilings came to me. *There is a room on the top floor.* The thought shrieked through my mind. How I knew that, I was not sure. We got out of the car and Mummy took charge of the two babies while Daddy took my hand and led me to the front door.

Mummy took a key out of her purse and opened the front door. We went through it and I remembered that the dining room, to the left, had a fireplace and lots of dark brown furniture. My head swivelled as I took in the scene. To the right I knew was the front room, which we couldn't go into without Mummy or Granddad. Then I remembered. This was Granddad's house!

The front room was also full of dark furniture and there

were lots of cupboards with glass doors. Along the corridor a bit, and behind the front room was the day sitting room. *Gramma would be sitting on the settee in that room.* Again the thought arose unbidden. That room too was full of brown and there was a coal fireplace with a brown mantelpiece over it. I no longer wondered how I knew these things, because I remembered that I'd lived here before.

'Dad! We're here!' Mummy called out as I continued to look round me. My eyes strayed towards the stairs I could see. They led down to the cellar where the kitchen was. It had cream and brown cupboards and a door that led to the garden where a coal shed and the outside toilet were.

A man's deep voice rumbled. 'Come in, my dear!' and a strange fear overcame me even before I saw him. I raised my head and looked at the stairs leading to the floors above. They were very steep and I hated going up them.

My father gave my hand a tug. 'Come on,' he said.

We went into the front room, which fascinated me, for I'd only seen this room once before. It was full of people, none of whom I was familiar with, and I shrank nervously beside my father's trousered leg.

'Come on Ruthie. Don't be shy.' He looked down at me and smiled. 'Don't you want to see Granddad?'

I looked up at him and nodded slowly . . . carefully. Granddad I knew, but he wasn't there. At least I couldn't see him. I wasn't sure that I liked Granddad, even though he was always bringing me sweets and nice presents. Then there he was.

'Ruthie,' he said loudly as he scooped me up in his arms and swung me around for a moment.

I giggled, partly with fear, partly with pleasure and, at my mother's urging, hugged him tight.

'There's my little girl,' he said as he turned me round so the other people there could see me. They thronged around to say 'hello'; I didn't notice that my parents were leaving until they were almost at the door.

'Mummy!' I shrieked in alarm, but she simply smiled and waved. Daddy blew me a kiss and they were gone.

Alone, with a roomful of strangers, I clung to my grandfather for the security he would surely give me and the glass hovered, waiting to be shattered, although I couldn't see it yet.

2

A little bit of history

My mother was born in the southwest of England in 1929. At the time, my grandfather was a docker and a bookie's runner. Being a bookie's runner was both illegal and lucrative and my granddad never seemed short of cash. He also kept turkeys and chickens in the back yard of their three-storey council house, and these were often slaughtered for the table. Granddad always had a great interest in good food, and he made sure that there was plenty of it about.

My mother had four brothers (two were stepbrothers) and a stepsister. My grandfather's first two wives had died when the three children were quite young. Granddad remarried and had another three children with his next wife, of whom my mother was the eldest.

It was said that Mum was always a very quiet girl, shy at school and a poor achiever. She was always tall for her age and slim. She kept her brown hair fashionably short. It appears that she was no problem to anyone. Other than her height, she never really stood out. She left school at the age of fourteen and went first to work in a chocolate factory, then later in a cigarette factory on the assembly line. One day, when she was sixteen years old, she was riding her bicycle home and attempted to make a right turn. Unfortunately she did not see the bus behind her and turned into its path. She was knocked off her bicycle and was rushed to hospital with a fractured skull; she lay in a coma for six weeks while her broken bones mended.

When she recovered, she had a completely changed personality. She became aggressive and had uncontrollable rages; there seemed to be no boundaries in terms of what she would say or do. My father had already met her at this time and his stories of her accident and changed personality were confirmed by her brothers and sisters. Later on, as an adult, I would wonder if she suffered some brain damage in the accident and whether it, her diagnosis as a manic-depressive schizophrenic, or a combination of the two, was the cause of her aggressive behaviour towards us. I don't know, but I want to believe that it must have contributed. Yet she could behave beautifully when neighbours and business colleagues of my father's were around. Although she was from a working-class background, she (and Dad) worked assiduously to embrace middle-class norms. She would go to the Savoy Hotel in London and behave perfectly respectfully. In fact, my mother could be incredibly charismatic when she wanted to. So how could she do this and be so terrible at home?

Apparently my grandmother, with whom I had little contact, was once a very strict woman. She never showed Mummy any affection and indeed Mummy claimed that Granny did not like her. Even though Mummy was out working, she had to be back in the house by 9.30 p.m. Granny would stand behind the door with a big stick behind her back and if Mum was late coming in she would use it, hitting out wildly. It must have looked pretty funny because Mummy was much taller than her.

Granddad, on the other hand, was always very friendly and affectionate, according to my mother. He also had lots of women friends, which made Granny cry whenever she found out about them. Even when he was well into his seventies, my grandfather was always seen as a man's man, though ladies' man was probably a more apt description.

When my mother met my father, her parents were delighted. For some reason they thought he was perfect for her, so much so that my grandmother refused to allow her to see other young men. Dad was a handsome man who had briefly served some time in the navy during the Second World War. A photograph of this time shows that he had rakish good looks with deep-set eyes that were protected above by thick dark eyebrows. He was lithe and fit looking; according to Mum, Daddy always wanted sex. He would take her behind bus shelters, behind walls, just about anywhere, since they were not allowed to have sex at the house. Daddy always used a form of blackmail to get my mother to respond to his needs, such as, 'If you really love me you'll do it.'

It was not technically rape, but my mother claims that she didn't like it. She didn't feel loved, just used. Soon Mummy became pregnant with me. Daddy didn't want to marry her but his own mother and sisters forced him to. They were married five months before I was born. Mummy then went back to her parents and Daddy, whose work in business management involved a lot of travel, went back to his home in Surrey.

Mummy moved to the top room at my grandparents' house and continued her life as normal. My father was an infrequent visitor, but whenever he visited he wanted sex with Mummy, so she soon became pregnant again and my brother Gordon was born. When she became pregnant a third time, my grandmother went ballistic, according to Mum.

'You are a filthy little whore. Get out and don't come back. Get out. You can't live here.'

Mummy moved to a relative's house and my aunt initially cared for us two children while Mummy went to work. That didn't last long as the problems between them became so severe that Mummy had to move again. Her third child, Philip, arrived. So there we were, three children under three years old, with no father at home, and our young mother thrown out by her parents. In dire financial straits, she had to find someone to provide us with day care while she was out working all day. Her solution was to leave us with one relative or another by simply knocking on the door and not waiting for an answer. We children and a nappy bag would be dumped on the doorstep as she walked away to go to work. Many years later she would say that she herself realised she was beginning to have severe rages. She actually thought that she was having a nervous breakdown, or rather 'going mad', as she called it: hardly surprising as she was under such pressure with no support at all from Daddy.

My father was the youngest of three children and the only boy. He had been born in Scotland; the family had moved to southern England when he was quite young. When his father died, he was just thirteen. Like my mother, he left school at the earliest opportunity and began his working life as a motorcycle courier. According to him, he could have continued his schooling, and wished to do so, but he had to leave to support his mother and two sisters. He said he had won literature awards at school and had wanted to become an opera singer eventually. He remarked constantly on how much he resented the fact that they were poor and that he was the only one to have to suffer, to make sacrifices. However, as he was the youngest child (and stayed in school until he was fourteen), his sisters would already have completed their schooling or been very close to it. Therefore his contribution to their education may actually have been quite small. His two sisters went to teacher-training college and became teachers. One of them had singing lessons as a young woman and it was *she* who became an opera singer with a small company performing in London theatres, not Dad.

It is difficult to know how much of what my father told us is the truth, but it is a fact that he started out doing fairly unskilled jobs, and would have had to look to himself to find opportunities for improvement. He did write short stories in later life and even had a few published. He also told us that he was made to wear his older sisters' dresses as they were too poor to buy him clothes. This I also found hard to believe. If they could afford singing lessons for one sister and for both of them to go to teacher-training college, it beggars belief that they would expect him, the 'man of the house' and 'breadwinner' to run around in dresses. Perhaps he was referring to his babyhood or young childhood, but the way he told it gave me a mental picture of a much older boy being forced to wear ladies' clothing. He also seemed to get on very well with his sisters and mother while they were alive. Later, as an adult, I wondered further about the veracity of these stories as it was usually the *girls* who would leave school and go to work so the *boys* could get an education. Anyway, he was not able to complete his schooling, and was determined to show his ability by being the best worker he could be.

When I was about three and a half years old, we – that is Mummy and us children – moved to a picturesque town near the Scottish border where we lived for more than a year. Daddy had an uncle and aunt there who owned a business selling children's clothing. They had found a bedsit for Mum and the three of us. My memory of the house was that it overlooked a hill that seemed to stretch forever into the distance. I also recalled that Uncle William and Auntie Pauline didn't like Mummy. They were always arguing with her and I realise now that they thought it was Mummy's fault that Daddy didn't live with us.

Then one day, when I was nearly five, my younger brother, Gordon, was about three and a half years old and baby Philip was about two years old, it all changed. Daddy arrived in his car and with a large van. We moved into a newly built semi-detached three-bedroomed house in Surrey. It was amazing and had so much room that I ran around excitedly. There were even two toilets, and for a youngster who was used to living in one room, this was luxury indeed. Outside was a good-sized garden for us to play in. Mum ran around excitedly too. She kept saying what a nice area it was and how good it was to be living there.

Dad was pleased as well. At that time, he was working his way up the ranks on his way to becoming the regional manager of a large British company. So he was ambitious and hardworking, traits I would normally find admirable. However, as I got to know this man who was my father, I soon found there was little in him to admire.

3

The guests and the washtub

Back on my balcony, remembering, Jenny continues to fret inside me and I begin to feel very edgy. Still I ignore her. She starts to cry and, feeling guilty, I try to soothe her as best I can; but my own anxiety levels have shot up so much that all I manage is to reduce her crying to an annoying grizzling. I try to focus on her, intending to comfort her, but that very action throws me back into the past . . . to the day we first met.

I was back in the front room of my grandfather's house. My grandmother was nowhere to be seen, and was probably in the back room, as she normally was. I tried to look towards the door through which my parents had disappeared, but my grandfather distracted me and turned so that I was facing the group of people there.

'There is your Auntie Alicia,' he said as he pointed at one of the women. 'And here is Uncle Jimmy. You remember Uncle Jimmy, don't you?'

I shook my head slowly, not knowing or really caring who these people were. I wanted Mummy and Daddy. Why had they left me? Where had they gone?

I stared at the man who was my grandfather, taking in his familiar features. I could smell his cologne.

I remember that Granddad almost always wore baggy dark suit trousers with a matching waistcoat. He also often wore this with a collarless white shirt. He had dark hair that had a small peak in the middle of his forehead. He always kept it short at the back and sides, but let it get longer in the front. He would then have it swept back in what might have been the fashion in those days. His light-blue eyes peered out of orbits that were hooded above and fleshy below. Lines at the side of them suggested that he laughed a lot, despite the frown lines etched downwards on his forehead above his nose. The dimple at the end of his nose continued down his top lip and there was an echo of it in his chin.

As I gazed at him, fascinated by the bushiness of his eyebrows, he continued the introductions I had no interest in.

'And this is Auntie Rosalind, Uncle Bryan, Uncle Johnny . . .'

I struggled in his arms again to look towards the door. Maybe Mummy and Daddy would be back soon. Granddad brought my attention back to the uncles and aunts in the room. Some were really relatives, I would learn as I grew older, but most were just given the honorary titles the young were expected to give to the old in those days. Even then, I couldn't help but notice that there were not many 'aunties' but an awful lot of 'uncles', and although I didn't understand why, their staring eyes scared me.

'Run!' The child's panicked voice startled me, but as my eyes searched among them, I could see that there were no other children here.

I looked away from the eyes and noticed for the first time that the top of a sideboard was crammed full of food. My grandparents always ate well. A large roast turkey, with a big fork stuck in it, stood beside a plate of cheeses. There were other foods too, and lots of bottles of the golden-brown liquid Granddad liked to drink. He was having some one day when I'd visited, or perhaps it was before that, when Mum, Gordon and I lived with him, and he'd allowed me a sip, but it was disgusting and I cried as I spat it out.

As I squirmed and struggled, Granddad turned away from the throng and I noticed a tin bath on the table on top of a white covering for the polished wood. This was not unusual. I'd had baths there before, though I never liked them. It always puzzled me that we never used the tin bath upstairs, but Mummy said when it was full it was too heavy to carry upstairs, and anyway, we got the hot water from the kitchen one floor below. The house didn't have much in the way of indoor plumbing. There was no bathroom, just an outside toilet. The only running water was in the kitchen. Even as I struggled to get out of his arms, I knew that if that bath was for me, Granddad would be there as usual, to see that I was getting a proper wash.

'Time for your bath,' Granddad said in a jolly voice.

'But Mummy's not here to bathe me,' I reasoned. In all the previous visits, it was always my mother who had bathed me.

'That's all right,' he replied. 'I can do it.'

'No,' I began to cry, 'Mummy will bathe me.'

'Run!' I jumped at the sound of that voice again and I looked around fearfully.

'You're scaring her, Tommy. She's used to a woman. Here, let me try.'

One of the women began to undress me while Granddad filled the bath from a large, covered pitcher beside it. I continued to struggle and squirm and eventually began to cry. My grandfather tried to soothe me, but it was not until my body was in the warm water that I stopped crying.

'There, there. That's not so bad now, is it?' Auntie Alicia said as she unwrapped a new block of Pear's soap and started to bath me. 'Aren't you a good, pretty girl?'

At this time of my life, I was fair-haired and slim, having lost my baby fat. I knew what a good girl was and I quietly agreed with her. I didn't know what pretty meant and didn't feel inclined to ask her. I had a habit of wrinkling my nose, especially when I laughed, but I didn't feel like laughing now.

Instead I scowled at her, and was beginning to cry again, when my grandfather told me sharply to stop it. So I stopped and sat quietly as the bath progressed. I didn't like it. It didn't seem right. I was afraid and I didn't know why and I dared not cry again.

'Run!' There it was – that voice again.

Who's shouting 'run' and where's Mummy and Daddy? The questions were like a refrain constantly repeating in my brain.

'I want my mummy and daddy,' I suddenly spoke up.

'They'll be back soon,' my grandfather said soothingly. 'Don't be scared, pretty girl. Don't be scared, my Ruthie. Granddad's here.'

'But I want Mummy and Daddy,' I persisted.

'Don't you love Granddad? That makes me feel very sad.'

'Don't feel sad, Granddad. I love you.'

It wasn't true. I was scared of him but I was old enough to know that if I said I didn't love him I would get into trouble with Mummy when she heard.

'. . . but I still want Mummy and Daddy.'

'I tell you what we'll do, my lover,' my grandfather replied using a West Country phrase he often used, 'I'll give you some chocolate and later we'll play some games until your mummy and daddy come back. How's that?'

Slowly I nodded, but deep down I hadn't been reassured. The 'uncles' and 'aunties' had not said a word during this exchange and, as Auntie Alicia took her time giving me a thorough bath, they all stood around. The feeling of unease, indeed of fear, never left me.

'Come on. Come on. Look . . . look at them. They gonna hurt us. Run!'

I felt strange. Why were they watching me? Who was gonna hurt me? Who was the other child they were going to hurt? Who was telling me to run?

I began to have a sense of weightlessness, although at the time I didn't know that word. It was as though I was somehow no longer grounded, no longer in that place, yet I was conscious and aware of the people around me.

There must have been something in my face as I looked from one watcher to the next, because suddenly, as though there had been some kind of signal, they began to speak.

'Aren't you a pretty little thing?' Uncle Somebody remarked.

'Yes! You're just gorgeous!' another said.

'You're a very special little girl, you know,' one of the women offered.

'I just wish you were my little girl,' another 'uncle' said. 'You're just beautiful.'

'Now, now, now,' my grandfather said, and they all laughed.

I should have been feeling more relaxed, because everyone was being nice to me, but I still felt that unease that bordered fear and that sense of lack of self. Finally Auntie Alicia said, 'The water's cooling.' And, putting her face just in front of mine, she added, 'We don't want you catching your death now, do we?' Then she rubbed her nose against mine. I recoiled and wiped my nose.

My grandfather held a large towel open for me to be wrapped in and, as he dried me, Auntie Alicia took the tin bath away and another of the 'aunts' followed her with the pitcher.

They returned with some other clothing and I realised that I couldn't see the things that I had arrived in. As Granddad dried me, they all moved closer while I stood naked on the table. Granddad made me lie down and he poured some talcum powder all over me, rubbing it in everywhere, even in places I didn't want him to touch. When he was done, Auntie Alicia dressed me.

Everything was new. First the frilly underwear went on, then the pretty blue, patterned dress, edged with what I now believe was lace. Little white socks with a frill round the top and black shoes with little holes making a pattern on the front completed the ensemble.

'Whoa! That's pretty! Very, very pretty,' Uncle Someone said.

There were murmurs of assent and appreciation all round and Auntie Alicia made me turn slowly around for what seemed like a long time so everyone could see me and add their compliments.

Granddad took me in his arms and lifted me off the table. He looked at me in a proud kind of way and my fears very briefly fled. I hugged him as hard as I could and kissed his nose. Everyone laughed in delight and I laughed too.

Granddad put me down on the floor and for a few minutes more I had to show off my new clothes. Various 'uncles' and 'aunts' stroked my cheeks or hair and cooed their compliments again.

Then Granddad took hold of my hand and said, 'Come on. We are going upstairs. I have something to show you.' And everyone laughed.

Some of the 'uncles' called after us making remarks I didn't understand. As I looked back at them, something in the way they were standing, in the way they were looking, in their very demeanour, made me afraid again.

'Run . . . please.' The voice was low, pleading, scared. 'Please, please, run. I don't want us to get hurt.'

I wanted to run, but Granddad was holding my hand really tightly. I wanted to cry out for my mummy and daddy, but something stopped me. We headed towards the stairs and, as we did so, Granddad talked to me. His tone was soothing, yet it triggered some alarm I did not understand.

I struggled to get up the stairs which seemed never-ending and were very steep. Granddad walked next to the banister on the right and I felt the strain as my right hand was pulled high to meet his. I touched the tall white wall on my left to steady myself as we went higher. Each step had to be negotiated in the way children my size go up stairs. First the left foot, then the right on the same step. I stopped briefly after each stair, partly to get my balance, partly to look at the next stair I had to negotiate and partly to catch my breath.

It was a long journey, right up to the very top of the house. We walked past Granddad's bedroom at the top of the first flight of stairs and I was relieved at this. I can't recall how I knew, but I remembered his room was full of dark furniture and there was a big, high bed. I didn't like it.

We rounded the stairs to go to the next storey and I remembered that my old room was up there. I had lived there with Mum and my brother, Gordon. We had just occupied the one room, then we'd had to leave when Granny and Granddad threw us out because Mummy was going to have my other little brother.

I remembered being glad when we moved out, but not really

why I'd felt like that. Now here I was again and something about Granddad and me on these stairs was worrying me.

As I struggled to walk upstairs, occasionally Granddad had to lift me bodily by my arm so I could safely negotiate another stair. I stepped up and I saw one of my new shoes. It was black and shiny and had holes in it like a flower. The silver buckle shone brightly and I thought it was very pretty. My new white socks gleamed and I focused on the little frill round them.

Finally, we were at the top of the house. There was a room with a big white door, which was closed.

'Run!'

Granddad opened the door slowly, all the while talking to me softly, raising silent alarms to add to the one shrieking through my head. The only time anyone ever spoke to me like that was when I was in trouble, or when there was some other kind of danger. I have tried to be a good girl and not show Granddad I am afraid, so why does he try to soothe me so? And why do I have this urge to run?

I was tired after climbing all those stairs and Granddad picked me up. He placed his cheeks against mine. They were prickly and I saw the fine black dots that were all over his jaw. Then his face was directly in front of mine and he kissed my forehead. Suddenly his mouth was on mine and he was putting his tongue in my mouth. I didn't like this but he was pushing me up against the wall and I couldn't struggle away from him. He put his hand in my knickers and I could feel him moving it round and I began to hear my heart thumping in my ears. He lowered me to the floor and put something in my mouth that smelled pretty bad. I struggled to get away from it but he shushed me and held my head firm. I felt sick and began to gag. He lifted me again and pulled off my knickers, all the while calling me, 'My lovely . . . my pretty'.

'Help me! Help me!' my inner voice shrieked, but Granddad had taken my other voice away with his tongue. 'Help me please.'

Now I wanted the 'uncles' and 'aunts' to help me. I was no longer afraid of them, and where were Mummy and Daddy? They should be back by now. I wanted to scream but he had his tongue in my mouth again and I could hardly breathe.

Still holding me in his arms, he moved on to the bed. It was enormous and I felt us sort of bounce on it. I also felt sick and I was scared. I struggled as hard as I could, but Granddad held me so I could not move.

'Shhh! You are a beautiful baby, my beautiful little girl. Lie still now. Lie still for your granddad.'

He held me firm with one hand while the other snaked its way up my legs. Why is he touching me there? Not again. Didn't he touch me enough when he was rubbing that talcum powder all over me?

'Don't. Please don't,' I managed to squeak.

Suddenly the pain came, I heard myself gurgling as I tried to scream. It was hurting so much and we were bouncing on the bed.

There was a brief moment of something. I was not sure what it was. There was no flashing light, no buzzing noise, but clearly something happened because I was free of him. I had no more pain. I felt cold and far, far away. And something strange was happening.

I had a strange curiosity about how I got out from under him, because there I was, standing beside the bed, looking at him bounce around on it. His bottom was moving in an odd way and, as I stared at it, I noticed the tiny white sock with the frill on it, the small leg attached. Surprised but fascinated, my eyes detached themselves from his lower end and I saw a small fist, curling and uncurling itself under his chest. As my gaze moved upwards, I saw . . . me. I looked down at myself and saw . . . me, at least, I saw the clothes I arrived in and knew I was never in the bath downstairs, never stared at, never dressed in the pretty clothes, never led up the stairs. Never, never, never.

I am standing here at the bedside, yet I am still under him in the fancy new clothes. I can see what Granddad is doing to me . . . no . . . to . . . to someone who is Ruthie . . . yet not . . . and I can't feel anything now. I turn and walk through the closed bedroom door. Even so, I can still see what's happening in the room.

Ruth

'Oh, it hurts. It hurts so much! Please stop. Please stop!' The child shrieked and screamed whenever the man raised himself enough so she got some air. He was no longer trying to silence her. He was too intent on his own pleasure, and perhaps her pain added to it.

'No! No!' The child first moaned, then shrieked again.

Her panic was such that she felt the pain ripping through her tiny body time and time again, as though she was on fire but, even as she suffered, she knew that she and I both had a chance to be safe.

'. . . Well, as safe as I can make us, which is not going to help Ruth's poor abused body much, but provided I do my job well, we'll survive,' I suddenly heard her gasp in my head. Then she continued tearfully, 'But I'm only three and a half and this is a big job. I wanted to run myself, find a safe place to hide, but somehow I knew I couldn't leave you . . . me.'

Years later I wondered, 'If she had not come to that room, would I – and she – have died? Would my . . . our body not have recovered?'

I believe that this might have been the case. In any case, she stayed with me, because the man was no longer hurting me and, as the main one of us, it was important to protect me.

The child under him . . . the body under him needed her to save our mind, our soul, our everything. That was her job. She would stay with me and protect me. She had to. If I died, she died. But it hurt her so much. It hurt her so very much and it trapped her firmly in the time period.

I am sure of how old I was when this happened, as my brother Philip had just learnt to sit up. He was born in March and I was three that May. As babies sit up between six to nine months old, I had to have been about three and a half years old. In any event, Jenny never grew older and is forever a very small child . . . forever trapped in the past.

Jenny

The creature rests, and even through the pain that I can still feel, I wonder about me. Who am I? And, just as I think that, I have an idea about that. My name is Jenny and although I am only three and a half years old, I am here for Ruthie. Am I her guardian angel? I don't think so. Am I her twin, perhaps? I don't think so.

All I know is that I cannot live without her, nor she without me. I feel instinctively that we are bonded in a way that few are bonded, or at least of which few are aware. If I could get out from under him, I would snatch up the penknife on the bedside table and cut this creature's throat and let him die. I hate him, I hate him so much! I know he would die because the person Ruthie calls 'Mum' is always saying that she would cut our throats and that if she did we would die and the devil or the bogeyman would come and get us. I hate him so much that I want the devil and the bogeyman to have him, for he has no more right to the title of father or grandfather than that newspaper on the table. But I am not a twin or a guardian, even though I have to try to act as such. I have to, for there is no one else here for me . . . or Ruthie . . . except perhaps the two others I see who are even younger than I am – a baby and another just about able to walk.

Who are they? Why are they here? As they move out of my line of vision, I focus on the man who has moved a little to the side as he rests, but still has me trapped by an arm and a leg across me.

This is a hard job for me because I am really only three and a half years old, but sometimes I can be almost grown up because I have to protect Ruthie from this kind of abuse. I am especially small when I remember what I have to do, because all of the pain comes rushing back and it hurts. And that is my real job. I hold all the memories of Ruthie's sexual abuse from this day on until I am seen to be in need of relief. I am Ruthie's pain absorber. What a big job for a little kid.

Ruth

I sat curled up with my back to the bedroom door and, as I waited for her, I vaguely saw two smaller children nearby. Even as I wondered about them, the sense of the one under Granddad became all-pervasive. She felt very weak, very disoriented and, although I didn't really understand the concept and she had only an idea of it, we soon knew what it felt like to want to die. She (and I) believed that Granddad – she has always refused to call him Granddad; she calls him 'that creature' – had been assaulting her/us for what seemed like ages, but it was probably not very long. It was weird how I knew all this, but somehow she speaks to me in my head and, although she never told me her name, I knew exactly who she was.

He rested for a while, and Jenny (I shall call her that), poor little girl, was in such shock that she lay there, unmoving. I felt very guilty, for it should have been me lying there. It was the initial shock and pain that seemed to merge with my feeling of unreality to set her free to protect me, which was a good thing. Good for me, that is. It surely was not so good for Jenny. She was and is a cushion for my damaged spirit. She took the pain from me and would do so again and again. She was there to protect me, but I did not realise any of this for a while yet. All I knew was what I saw and that disturbed me deeply. How was this possible?

I walked back through the door to stand by the bed again, for I was curious about this guardian angel who had come to save me.

Jenny

She is standing over there by the bed, as reluctant to leave me as I was to leave her earlier, and I don't understand too much of it because, although I was just born, and should be some kind of a genius for understanding so much so quickly, I am still just a little girl. Even so, I understand many things Ruthie cannot perceive. I have been waiting in the wings because I knew this day would come. I should have been a whole year younger, but the grandmother threw her daughter and Ruthie out. When we lived in Scotland, we were safe, and I grew older as I hovered. I listened, like Ruthie; as her parents fought and squabbled I learnt many words. They openly talked about the thing they call sex, and it was not difficult for me – or Ruthie – to associate what they were doing to each other with the word. More often than not they called it something else, what I call the horrid word. It sounded harsher and more frightening and it scared me because they also said it every time they were angry and arguing. Every two words had the horrid word in between, and when the woman Ruthie called Mummy used it, she was often hitting out.

I understand more clearly than she does exactly what is happening to her/us, what happened earlier with the bathing session downstairs. Oh yes, I was there too, watching them watching us, and giving Ruthie the fright of her life. She didn't understand why she was so frightened, but that was my fault. I knew what was happening. I knew what she was being prepared for and it was my fear she felt. It was me! Why? I knew what I've always known. I volunteered for this job, and I knew that meant I was being 'born' for a life of pain, and pain makes me so scared, but I have to do it. I have to! Or neither of us, indeed none of the others – those that were here before and those who would come after – would survive; and we want to live!

Normally she should have loved this creature who was always hanging around her bringing her toys and chocolates and such. She should have been able to trust him, but she couldn't – and especially today. I was trying to warn her. I kept shouting 'Run!' but she didn't hear me, or at least I don't think she did. Why else didn't she run?

The creature plays with bits of our body until, excited once more, he does it to her/me/us again. He examines us, poking and prodding, before mounting us once again. And still it hurts me.

My disgust grows and I want to throw up. The pain is great and I am frightened more than I can explain. Ruthie is truthfully the strongest of us. She has to be – she is the one that was really born to the mother. We were born from Ruth. She is our leader but I feel her apathy and beg her to be strong. If she dies, I sense that I die, and I have not long been 'born'.

I take my bruised and battered self and enter her briefly, taking of her strength . . . to sustain me for as long as this lasts. I dare not stay too long in case it weakens her too much. I dare not return to her when he is active as the pain of such torture on her/our small body would be more than she could bear.

He has stopped now and, taking a small wedge of chocolate, he puts it in Ruthie's mouth. It is sustaining her even as her attacker cleans her up and re-dresses her. I have done what I could to take her pain and keep us alive. Now I must do what I can to further sustain her, but I am just a little alter and I am so scared.

The disgusting monster puts another piece of chocolate in Ruthie's mouth. He dresses himself, checks that all of his buttons are done up and walks downstairs.

After a few moments, I take Ruthie's hand as she is not moving, I give her a little push so she walks down the stairs very carefully. We walk to the partially closed doors and peek through the crack between the door and the frame into the front room, where he announces to all gathered there that Ruthie would 'rest' a while before returning home with her parents. He takes his congratulations for 'breaking her in' as his rightful due, and, after a few more drinks, the guests having eaten all the food laid on for them, leave. He then sits alone in his 'front' room, drinking brandy and smoking a cigar, munching on a few bits and pieces from the sideboard . . . waiting for the daughter he once considered gorgeous until she became too old for him, and for his son-in-law, to come and collect their damaged child. Exhausted, but satisfied that he would not be returning upstairs, I flee, pulling Ruthie, who is still not doing much, behind me, and we slowly clambered back up the stairs and sit on one of them, near the door to the 'bad' room.

I want to feel some kind of energy and life coming from Ruthie, but she is listless and unresponsive. This is the first time the monster put what he keeps in his trousers inside her and she just closed down, which was exactly as it should be. But I am scared because I don't know how to waken her. Suddenly all the events of the day overwhelm me and I cling to them all, even the baby and the toddler, who preceded me when the monster did other things to Ruthie when she was younger. I don't know what he did because they never speak, but I can see them and I sense that they came for a reason. I weep for my intensifying pain, for our battered body, for our lost innocence, for our broken leader.

Ruth

I was sitting once more on the floor outside the bedroom. It was dark and I felt sick. I was frightened. I imagined I heard my mummy and daddy saying, 'Ruthie? Are you all right? You look so scared baby. What's the matter?' Then they would give me a cuddle . . . make the bad thing go away. They would somehow make it better. But that was just a dream. They were not there and, anyway, Mummy never really

cuddled me. Daddy did when he came to visit us, and I wanted
him, but he was not here.

I looked around in a daze? How did I get outside the
bedroom? Where was Granddad? Where was everyone else?
The last thing I remembered was Granddad climbing over me
and giving me a nasty hurt in my pants. No . . . first he took
my pants off, then he gave me the nasty hurt.

I was becoming breathless. There was someone else there
too, another Ruthie . . . no, Jenny. She was still here . . .
somewhere. I heard her crying and wanted to hug her, but I
couldn't see her. I felt so small. Something bad had happened
to me . . . to Jenny. I didn't like it. It was really bad. I was
bad. Where was everyone? I began to panic, wanting to run, to
scream, then suddenly I sat down and forgot everything.

'Ruthie! Ruth!' Daddy's voice was loud, almost scared.

I felt the tears begin to come to my eyes, but just then I
heard Granddad's voice and — scared stiff — forgot to cry.

'Why are you sitting on the stairs, Ruthie? Come into the
warm sitting room.' He reached over and picked me up. I
turned to my father, stretching out to him, longing for him to
take me, but he just laughed and walked away towards the
front room.

My mother was nearby, and changing direction, I reached
for her, but she too laughed and turned away. Anyway, she
was already holding baby Philip. My other brother, Gordon,
was toddling round the room. Mummy followed Daddy into
the front room, and Gordon walked unsteadily after her.
Granddad and I brought up the rear; I was leaning as far away
from him as I could.

In the room, the adults collected some food and something
to drink and they all sat around chatting about this and that.
No one asked me about the day I had spent with Granddad,

other than Mummy saying, 'What a pretty outfit. Did Grand-dad give that to you? Aren't you a lucky girl? Did you thank him? Did you give him a big kiss?'

Granddad had put me on his knee; when I struggled to get off and go to them, I was told off.

'Now stop that! You're a big girl now and your granddad got you some lovely things, so sit there and be thankful.'

I felt the tears come close and would have cried, except suddenly I felt someone giving me a sweet cuddle and I thought I heard a child saying, 'Shhh. Be still. If you cry you might get hurt some more.'

So I quietened under the caress I was feeling and made no more fuss, even as I wondered how this child could do this even though in her great pain she was still crying. I could hear her in my head. She was still hurting so much. Poor, poor Jenny.

I am not sure how long I sat in that house listening to my parents and grandfather chat as they ate and drank, but eventually Daddy stood up. 'Well, I guess we'd better be going. Thanks for everything,' he said as he picked Gordon up. Mummy was still holding Philip who was asleep.

As we made our way to the car, Granddad carrying me there, he put his hand in his pocket and pulled out several coins.

He jingled them in his hand, trying to attract my attention, but I felt so unhappy and felt such discomfort that I ignored him. The feeling down there told me that he had hurt me in a nasty way. I didn't know then that I should be feeling intense pain, or about my special 'pain absorber'. All I knew was that there was a small girl and two extra babies with me that everyone else was ignoring. As I was getting into the car, Granddad put the coins in my hands.

'You are very special and very pretty, my little Ruthie, and I will see you again soon. We'll have lots of fun and lots of food, and I'll give you some coins again, my little lover.' With that he kissed my forehead and shut the car door.

As Daddy drove off, I let the coins trickle from my hands onto the floor. Mummy turned round to me and said, 'Ooh Ruthie, what did you have to *do* for that then?' She threw her head back and began to laugh. She laughed so hard that she woke the baby who started to cry.

'She knows.' With a shock, I realised that she knew what had happened.

'That's why she left you there,' the child told me, and I began to understand something I could not imagine. Why did they leave me alone with Granddad? Why would they do that?

As Mummy shushed Philip, Daddy's eyes looked at me through the car mirror. I glanced at him and saw him smile and shrug his shoulders. I looked again at the eyes in the mirror as he said, 'It doesn't matter as long as you enjoyed it.' And he giggled.

Mummy started to laugh again, 'Oh Tony! You are funny!' she said, and Daddy joined in the laughter.

'They both know and they think it is funny. How could they think you enjoyed being squashed like a spider by that smelly old creature who hurt you that badly?'

Despite the voice in my head, I had a sense of a small hand caressing my cheek. I wanted to cry, like Jenny was doing. I wanted Mummy and Daddy to love me, to cuddle me, to tell me it wasn't my fault. Then that need fled and all I could think of was, 'I know it was a bad thing but my mum and dad think it was funny.'

Jenny is my angel and I feel an outpouring of love for her. For the moment, that is all I can do to make her feel better. She is still crying, though not so much now, and I must try harder to soothe her. She and I look at each other and, despite the circumstances, we feel a sense of belonging.

Our peace is shattered by Mummy's voice.

'Oh Ruthie? Next weekend you'll be staying with Grand-dad for the whole weekend. Won't that be lovely?'

4

Bedtime horrors

After that day, my parents often took me to visit Granddad and left me there with him. If Grandma knew what was happening, she never stirred herself from her chair in the back room. Everyone acted as though nothing was happening and, after a while, I did too.

After we moved to the Surrey house, just before my fifth birthday, we were over a hundred miles away from Granddad's and my 'visits' to him became much less frequent. Even so, my life was still full of fear. As I grew older, I realised that what I'd learnt on that chilling car ride back from Granddad's was absolutely right: my mother was never going to love and protect me. In fact, she was going to make my life hell.

Going to bed had become a problem for me. Every time I looked at my bed I could sense Jenny's panic, which always quickly infected me.

'Don't be so silly,' Mummy said, 'you have to go to bed. This isn't like Granddad's house or all the other houses where we all lived in one room. You have your own room now, so be grateful for that.'

'But . . .' I began to protest, but Mummy looked at me in the way that she did when she was close to exploding and something within me shut me up. So I said nothing more.

After a final glare at me, Mummy left the room.

I could hear Jenny crying and at first I looked round the room for her, before I remembered that I didn't always see her.

'Shhh. Don't cry,' I said, hoping to console her, but either she hadn't heard me or she didn't want to, because she continued to cry.

'He'll come up the stairs. I'm scared. He'll hurt us. He'll hurt me.'

I looked nervously towards the door. It was almost dusk and the door yawned large and dark. I ran over to the lamp by my bed and switched it on, but beyond the doorway seemed much darker. Even so, I left the lamp on so I could see him if he came into the room.

'Shut the door! Shut the door!' Jenny shrieked, and as I did just that she urged, 'Lock it. Lock it!'

There was no way I could lock it as Mummy had taken the key, so I backed away from the door carefully until I reached my bed, which I sat on.

'You have to lock it!' Suddenly Jenny was in front of me, imploring.

'I can't lock it. There's no key,' I responded, not aware that I had spoken aloud.

The door opened and my mother said, 'Gordon?'

She looked around the room and realised I was alone. 'Didn't I just hear you speak?'

I stared at her, open-mouthed with fear, but luckily she seemed to think that I was surprised at her question. I *was* surprised too, because she completely ignored Jenny, who was standing beside me looking as scared as I felt.

Mummy shook her head as though to clear it and said, 'Time for your bath. Then it's bed for you.'

A half-hour later, I clambered into my bed and settled down under the covers. My mother came in to check that I was where I was supposed to be and she bent over to switch off the light.

'Please leave the light on,' I said timidly.

My mother paused, looked at me and said, 'No, you can lie there in the dark,' and with that she switched the light off.

As she left the room, I tried again, 'Mummy, please shut the door.'

'Why? So you can put the light on again? Are you afraid that the bogeyman is going to come and get you? Or maybe it's the devil, with his big horns and red eyes, and fire coming out of his mouth!'

Mum took a great deal of pleasure frightening us at bedtimes. We always had to be in bed by six in the evening, summer or winter. Sometimes, as we trudged reluctantly upstairs while it was still light outside, she would begin to laugh. 'Can you see him? Look, look, look. There he is. He's waiting for you and he's hungry. He's going to get you, you little monsters, and you deserve it. You deserve to be eaten! He's going to eat you up bit by bit.' Or she would hide at the top of the stairs in winter when it was dark, and jump out at us, yelling like a banshee.

Once we were in bed, we were expected to fall asleep immediately. Whether we did or not, we could not get out of bed at all. Then the house became silent. There was never a sound from downstairs, all of which added to the monsters in my mind. Some nights, after I had fallen into an exhausted and fearful sleep, I would be woken up by Mum running upstairs screaming and shouting abuse in the middle of the night. Sometimes she would come into my room and drag me out of bed, telling me I was a bitch and calling me other names, before telling me to go back to sleep – as if I could after that. Other nights she would go to the boys' room and do the same to them. Therefore I, and no doubt the others too, spent many hours lying in bed, anticipating the worst.

It was many years later, before we discovered what she was really doing, that – far from waiting silently to launch an attack on us – our mother was working at a local hotel as a waitress who could also be paid to have sex with the clients, an arrangement that appears to have been made with my father's knowledge and approval. She had to go out to work because at the time, although Dad was earning a good salary, he gave her virtually none of it.

After a night of this 'work' she would return home and take her rage out on us. It was also the reason why we had to be in bed so early and why we were not to leave our beds. She probably did not want us to be running around in case we made a mess.

But there I was in my room, staring through the gloom at her, noticing the strange pleasure she seemed to gain from my being scared and wanting my bedroom door shut, and I found myself truly hating her.

She laughed and went to my brothers' bedroom next door. I stayed where I was. I knew what would happen if I got out of bed.

I heard a sharp noise. Philip cried out and my mother said, 'Use it now! You *cannot* go to the toilet during the night or that huge, hairy monster of a spider will come up the toilet and bite you on your whatnot and *that* is going to hurt more than anything!'

A few seconds later she shouted in exasperation,

'Sit on that potty! And stay there until you use it, because I will strangle you if your bed is wet in the morning.'

I realised that Philip had struggled to get up, and could almost see her forcing him down again. I'd also heard those words many times before and knew exactly what my little brother was feeling. Then I found myself wishing desperately that the baby wouldn't cry. If he did, something bad would happen. I didn't know how I knew that. I just knew.

I tried to spend as much time with my little brothers as I could because I knew how sad and frightened they were. I loved them and loved to cuddle them. They needed the cuddles too and we managed to comfort each other somewhat until Mummy caught us. We were sitting together on the floor, cuddled tight together like three homeless baby monkeys, and I was stroking their cheeks when my mother walked into the room. Just the very sight of us threw her into a rage and, screaming incoherently, she grabbed the baby and put him in his cot, ignoring his screams as she descended on Gordon and me. We had by then parted and were running like scared chickens wherever we could to avoid her.

She smacked Gordon so hard that he fell over, and I felt her wrath in the form of her hands on my throat. Strangling was one of her favourite punishments. She had honed her technique carefully, and would apply pressure until we passed out but stop short of completely asphyxiating us. The switch in her mood from calm to fury and back to calm was swift and terrifying. After that, although we tended to gravitate to the same room, we always kept our distance from each other, if she was anywhere in the house. Even if she was in the garden, the most we would do was touch each others' hands quickly and surreptitiously, then move away again.

Mum was a big woman in a time when a woman's average height was about 5 foot 3 inches. She was at least 5 foot 11 inches tall and well built. When she clenched her teeth and ground them together, I knew she was beginning to get angry, and to a small child she was a terrifying figure. She also swore like a trooper, and when she threatened to do us serious damage, her eyes always seemed to bulge slightly.

Each morning she would come into our rooms screaming, 'Get up! Get up! Are you going to lie in bed all day?'

Although I should have been used to this, I always woke with a start, feeling a shiver of horror descend upon me. Why was Mummy always angry? What had I done? Is she going to hit me? Can I hurry out of bed without getting too close to her hands? At the very thought of her hands, my throat would close.

Sometimes she would give me a whack about the head, but most days she simply hurried out of my room to shout at the others.

'Come on, get up! Go and get washed!' I would hear this from the bathroom to which I had already hurried. The next thing I remember of our routine is literally being pushed out of the house with the others.

'You're getting under my feet. Get outside and play!'

I couldn't imagine how we got under her feet, as that would require a proximity that none of us wished to have. Instead it was always with a sense of relief and freedom that we ran out of the house. But we had to be careful, or before long a door or window would open, Mum would put her head out and scream, 'Shut up! Shut up! You're making too much noise!' before slamming the window or door shut again.

We'd play outside no matter the season or whether it was raining. As long as we didn't track dirt into the house later, we were safe.

Later, when I began school, I'd be pushed out the front door instead, with the admonishment, 'And come straight back from school, you hear me? If you are even a minute late, I'll rip your hair out.' She never did pull my hair out, but she was creative with her threats, and my imagination of what she was capable of was even more terrifying.

Later in the day she would simply call us inside, where we ate and bathed, before being ordered to bed before the bogeyman got us. She showed us no affection, gave us no hugs, smiles or goodnight kisses. She was completely empty, devoid of any friendliness or animation. She never played with us or read us stories. She never walked us to school and, if we happened to be going somewhere on foot, it was always I, rather than she, who pushed the baby's pram. As far as I was concerned, she simply didn't like us. When there wasn't anger or menace, there was just nothing coming from her. Once I realised that this was all she could give, I found that I simply didn't care. If she was hurting me, or my siblings, I hated her. If she left us alone, I refused to let her exist in my emotions, and in this way she was training me to be as empty about her as she was about us.

On the other hand, Dad was more friendly. If he was home at bedtimes, he would wish us a goodnight, and waggle a friendly hand at us as we left the room, but I didn't like him any more than I liked her.

I, like any other child, wanted a loving, caring mother. I didn't know if she could ever get to like us, but we didn't have another mother and, although we now lived with Daddy, he wasn't around very often. Even at my young age I could see that she was unhappy because she was always so angry and violent, and I longed for things to be better for her and for us.

I had by then heard about her own mother's coldness and cruelty to her. Sometimes she would speak of it herself. Other times my father would throw it in her face during some argument. As they argued a lot, we children heard this and other 'home truths' at an age when it should have been none of our business.

'You're so bloody mad even your mother couldn't stand you. Don't think the whole street didn't know she used to beat you with a stick. When I got married to you, I did you a favour, and don't you forget it.'

According to Mum, her father was nicer to her, and he seemed affectionate enough to both my parents whenever they were together. However, apparently Granddad had always been kissing Mummy, calling her 'my little pretty, my darling, my lover'. He would take her to his bed every afternoon, even as she grew well into her teens, where he would undress her and rub cream all over her body. He would then blow talcum powder all over her before rubbing it in. He told her it was so that her skin and indeed her complexion would be kept looking lovely.

Mum spoke openly of this to Dad and clearly never saw this as abuse. She simply accepted it as a sign of her father's love for her. She obviously wanted to believe that. She says that nothing more went on but, given my own experiences with him, I find that very hard to believe.

My own father only seemed to use Mum for sex. He didn't seem to love her at all. He belittled her so much, constantly telling her she was stupid and idiotic, and her face would either fall with the knowledge of what he was saying, or she would fly into a rage. Sometimes, when he was being kinder he would say, 'You're so damned stupid you make a sheep look clever. Never mind, I suppose you can't help it. When that bus hit you, it addled your brains good and proper.'

So in these open 'discussions' between my parents, I learnt

of the accident, which changed her personality and made her more volatile and aggressive. Even as a young child, I understood that my mother never knew proper affection in her entire life.

Now that we lived with my father, I had childish hopes that he would protect us from Mum. I somehow imagined too that, now he was here, we would have lots of fun, driving here and there in his car. Soon I would be starting school, so there would be journeys there too, I thought. There would indeed be trips in his car, as he would take me here and there to various houses, but it would be no fun for me.

For a while I had contradictory feelings. I was allowing myself to feel hopeful about the future, that perhaps the worst was over. It was a nice feeling, being settled, even though the constant fear of Granddad coming to visit was always in my mind. Although I had wanted to ask my parents why it happened, something always stopped me, and it became a taboo I imposed on myself. Then one day Jenny arrived as I lay on my bed and stared into the black void that was my door. She was not crying, but something about her tension made me nervous. I could almost hear her whispering 'run', but I wasn't sure. I couldn't help but think that Granddad would come walking up those stairs anytime now and I too began to feel agitated. Finally, sleep claimed me as tiredness set in.

And so it went on, the next night and the night after that, listening to my frightened alter warn me of a danger I braced myself for, but which never came. I couldn't understand why she was always with me, but I'd learnt that often excessive activity by her was a warning of horrors to come.

After a day of whatever fate befell me, whether sexual abuse or severe punishment, I would have my bath and go to bed. Daddy's work took him away for days at a time and he was only at home at the weekends so, even if he'd wanted to be, he wouldn't be there to save me.

On the third night since Jenny's agitation had begun, she was again there, and instead of my fear gradually diminishing as it had on the previous two nights, it increased dramatically. The memory of what Granddad did to us was as fresh as though the last assault had happened only a few days earlier, when in fact it was several weeks since we had last seen him and suffered the inevitable abuse. Jenny often moaned loudly with the pain that for her was never-ending, and it was always the pain of the first time. With Daddy being away and Mummy not being someone I could talk to, I watched my brothers. I longed to cuddle them and be cuddled in return. That might help control Jenny's screams, which were rising by the minute. Then I could hear my mother laughing downstairs, and a deep laugh joined in.

Granddad! Granddad was here!

Even as I thought that, I heard Jenny scream piercingly, 'Run!'

Before I knew it, I was trying to get into the wardrobe to hide, but I couldn't open it. Then I remembered that Mummy had locked it because Gordon had got into it earlier in the day and done a poo on the floor. He had been kicked and strangled a few days earlier for doing the same thing in his own wardrobe, and perhaps hoped Mummy wouldn't find it if he did it in mine. Unluckily for him, but luckily for me, she saw him leaving my room and, when she found it, guessed what had happened.

I looked around. There was no other place to hide. There

was no room under the bed, and the small desk I had was open underneath. I jumped into bed, pulled the covers as far up as I could and cowered under them. All the while Jenny was screaming and crying and my heart was beating so hard and fast that I could hear it clearly thumping away.

My mother called up, 'Ruth!'

I didn't answer, and heard her clearly say, 'She's in bed – all bathed and ready. She has been for the past couple of nights but you didn't come home, did you? Were you off with your girlfriends? Were you?

Heavy footsteps came up the stairs, and, even as I squeezed my eyes tightly shut, I could see the dark doorway looming. Jenny was whimpering, 'Please, please, please. Don't hurt us,' and the footsteps grew louder.

Finally they stopped just at the door, and I trembled as I imagined him standing there, just outside. Except that he wasn't. He had walked so quietly over the carpet that I never heard a thing. Suddenly the bedclothes were pulled down. I kept my eyes closed tight and willed him to go away.

'Ruthie,' he said.

'My eyes flew open. 'Daddy! Daddy!' I yelled and I threw myself into his arms. Jenny gave the most awful shriek, as though I had betrayed her, and my head hurt with the sound of it.

My father pulled my head back so I could look into his eyes. He smiled at me, his eyes twinkling.

'How's my baby girl? Did you miss me?' he asked.

I nodded, speechless with the relief that it was him and not Granddad. He was still smiling as his mouth descended on mine.

Jenny

I told her to run, to hide but there was no place to go. Then, when she saw him, she trusted him. Now every night he's here he goes to her, or calls her to him. Her heart is breaking because her 'Daddy' as she calls him, is doing this to her too, but I can't help her with that. I can only take the hurt of her body away. And it hurts so much. IT HURTS!

When he enters me I feel like my legs are going to break off under his weight. Sometimes I notice that pain even more than I notice the pain in the other, private place. Even my heart is breaking. The father has now completely destroyed any remaining trust she had in adults. She couldn't trust her grandmother, who sat and did nothing, even though she probably knew what was happening. She couldn't trust her mother who was so violent and unpredictable. She couldn't trust the grandfather who introduced her to this life that no child should have to experience. All she had was the father, and despite his amusement in the car when the grandfather gave her those coins, she still had some belief that he loved her and would not hurt her. Now this! My legs are breaking! And he breaks them whenever he is here and has the need.

The mother, and I can no more use the word 'Mummy', as I would say 'Daddy' or 'Granddad', is so aggressive, so hurtful, to all of us, her own children, that it breaks my heart even more. Who can we turn to other than ourselves? How can we deal with this terror, other than to put it into little cupboards in our consciousness, then lock the doors firmly so that the terror does not contaminate the rest of us? This damage to Ruthie's sense of self is so great that she developed the alter-egos that will help her. Where this talent for self-protection comes from, I don't know. I only know that she has been doing it since babyhood, as I can see by the baby and the toddler who wander in and out of our consciousness . . . and of course, you know why *I* am here.

Ruth

'I'm sorry, Mummy. I'm sorry.'

'How many times must I tell you when you use the washbasin to dry it thoroughly! Look at these water stains. And here! There are some on the floor.'

She was shaking me with one hand as I begged for forgiveness. I do try to do things she asks me to but I always get it wrong. I saw the other hand snaking towards my throat and began to scream in terror. I don't like it when her hand—

I felt light-headed and Mummy was slapping me. 'Wake up! Wake up, I say!'

I opened my eyes. She pulled me to my feet and shouted, 'Now go to your room and stay there!'

Obediently I began to stagger to my room, feeling like someone had made my throat scratchy. I tried to speak, to say 'Mummy', but only a frog spoke, and my mother was already halfway down the stairs. Jenny was screaming, 'It hurts! It hurts!' but although my throat was froggy, it didn't really hurt me.

By now I understood that Jenny was taking all my pain from me, and I wondered if she was crying because our throat hurt or because we hurt in other places. I don't really know because I don't feel any pain.

I don't know how long I've been abused, though I know it's been a regular thing as sometimes Granddad, Daddy (mostly now) and occasionally a couple of uncles and friends of my father have abused me sexually, either in my home or in theirs. The abuse is carried out calmly and I have learnt what to expect. I guess I am used to it.

But all the time Jenny is screaming and screaming, while I sit beside the bed, watching.

One Sunday morning I woke in a panic. Jenny was hysterical and I was breathing so fast that I thought my heart might stop beating. Just as I remembered that Daddy had come home the day before, he walked into my room.

'Come!' he said as he backed out the door.

I got up and obediently followed. I knew what was going to happen. It had happened often before, though not when Mummy was in the bed. Sexual abuse was by then common-place for me and, strange as it may seem, of all the abuses I suffered it was always the thing that worried me least. It was never rough, not with any of them. All of them were gentle, but there was generally oral sex first which I hated because of the smell. Then sometimes full intercourse would follow. I didn't like it and it made me feel physically sick, but it was predictable and Jenny made it painless so I could cope, whereas my mother's moods and her violence were neither predictable nor something I could deal with.

Whenever Daddy put me in the car to take me to strange houses to be abused, what I remember most was having to walk upstairs. It was always that walk that I, Ruthie, found disturbing. I hate going upstairs. If ever I was in a building I had never visited before and had to go upstairs I would become afraid, and feel dizzy or sick, and I would get that sense of floating that told me Jenny was taking over. From that point on, I would generally have no memory of walking up the stairs or what I had been doing until I was on my way down the stairs. Even much later as an adult, going upstairs in an unfamiliar building would cause me much uneasiness.

So here I was, in my parents' bedroom, and having to be in bed with my mother was simply terrifying. Jenny was anxious about the sex, but I was scared stiff of *her*! And my heart thundered away.

'Get into the bed beside your mother!' my father ordered, and when I hesitated, he picked me up and put me between them. My mother laughed that dreadful laugh she had when nasty things were about to happen or were happening. She tended to grit her teeth together and throw her head back. She does that even now, in 2008, and I realise as my 2008 self writes this that her laughter is forced. There is no joy in it. There never has been.

My father then encouraged my mother, 'Go on. Touch her. She's beautiful. Have some fun with your daughter.'

She was naked, as were Daddy and I, as I slept naked. She didn't touch me as he'd asked, but instead just put my hands on her.

Even as she did so, I sensed her reluctance, her repugnance. She didn't like what she was doing at all. Suddenly, she got out of the bed and left the room, leaving me alone with Daddy, who laughed. Then he did what he usually did. I was never in bed with Mummy again and she never made me touch her in a sexually explicit way again, although she did nothing to stop Daddy when he took me into their bed.

Dad finished what he was doing and let me get out of the bed.

'I have to get my things ready for work tomorrow,' he said. 'Now remember, not a word of this to anyone. If you tell a single soul, that will make you a very bad girl. I would have to take you to the big house that's full of bad girls like you, and I will leave you there for all the men, and the women too, to do this to you all day, every day. Do you understand?'

'Yes, Daddy.'

'Do you want me to leave you there?'

'No, Daddy.'

'You'll be a good girl then and keep your mouth shut?'

'Yes, Daddy.'

'Good. Now give me a hug then run along.'

I did as I was told.

There were other times when Dad would come to my room and take me into his bed. Mum would go downstairs with that look on her face. Sometimes she would smirk. Other times she would laugh hysterically. I virtually never remembered getting back into my own bed because, as soon as he began to touch me, I switched to one of my alters. It was never a conscious thing. I just felt strange and seemed to float to my right, occasionally seeing myself in the bed for a brief few seconds and then nothing. So I have no knowledge of getting back into my bed, yet I always woke up there the next morning.

Occasionally, Dad got me out of my bed and took me into his where a strange man would be waiting and I was left with him – and at his touch I would drift away.

It was while we lived in this house that I began my schooling. I remember clearly the first day of school as I was driven there by my father in his black car. I believed that I was just going to one of his friends for sex, and was terrified when I saw the huge building. The big house! But why! I was a good girl. I went to Mr Price again and never complained. Why am I here? My heart was beating crazily and I thought I would die. There were a large number of children milling about and several adults. One of them whacked a child across the head and I was sure that this was the place of hell that my father had so often threatened to bring me to.

A great big shaggy man who I decided was the devil was wandering about amongst the children as a woman, surely his servant, stepped forwards to greet us. I screamed and screamed in terror, grabbing hold of my father's leg with a strength I didn't know I had.

'Come now. Come now. Hush,' the woman said as she tried to prise me away from my father. 'Come on now. School is not so bad.'

My father laughed and said, 'She's not used to strangers, you know. It comes from having such a protected life.'

'Well, she certainly loves you to bits,' observed the woman, who I later learnt was Mrs Birch, the headmistress of the school. Then she turned to me and tried to coax me away from Daddy's leg again.

Eventually they succeeded, and I howled in anguish, reaching out to my father as he got into the car and drove away. A great surge of anger built up in me and I felt as though I was going to explode. Then suddenly another alter, Liz, was there shouting, 'Stop it. Stay calm. This is neither the time nor place for us to break up!' A still calm descended over me. I could only hear – not see – her, and she was yet to make her first major intervention, but for now it was enough that she was working her magic, and I allowed the woman to lead me into the building.

I soon settled in when the devil hadn't made an appearance and I learnt that all children went to school. One day I was taking part in a 'silent' reading class. After a few moments, the teacher told me to stop talking, but as far as I was aware I wasn't. I protested my innocence and continued with silent reading. A few moments later the teacher clouted me over the head for speaking in class, but I knew I hadn't been. A powerful surge of anger flowed through me and this experience led me to believe that no one liked me. Of course now I know that it was probably my alters having a conversation, because Liz and the others had been joined by one of those I think of as the 'frightened ones'. Her name was Jessica.

I was also afraid of other children. I felt as though they could see inside me, and see what had happened to me at home. Mum was always telling me that no one would like me, that I was ugly. I felt they could all see this. As I couldn't remember everything I had been doing, maybe I was doing bad things and they would see me, they would know. I was desperately lonely but too afraid to make friends. Neither did I want to let them into my world. I could see other people around me that I knew they couldn't see. I couldn't explain that, but they gave me comfort and I didn't want to share them. They were so familiar and helped me when things got really bad; they somehow kept me safe.

My parents insisted that we attended Sunday school as well as ordinary school. Both Mum and Dad felt that it created a particular image with the neighbours, though they weren't at all religious. Dad's mother and sister went to church but, as far as I knew, none of Mum's relatives did. Sunday school also had the additional bonus of giving us more time away from Mum. It was held at my regular school, which was a fair walk away. When I first attended, I was alarmed, as there was so much talk of my Mum's favourite threat, the devil, but when I realised that he was not scheduled to put in an appearance, I relaxed and quite enjoyed the lessons about Jesus and how he loved the little children. I began to believe in God and His goodness and Jesus sounded like someone I'd have been happy to meet.

Mrs Wyatt, the Sunday school teacher, was a very nice woman who often said that her 'chicks had flown the nest'. This always seemed pretty stupid to me because I didn't think chickens flew that much, but I didn't tell her that as I liked her. She was sitting at the front of the classroom and had a smiley, round face which was always very friendly. I was watching her cheeks wobble as she spoke, without really listening to what she was saying. Then one of the other children answered some unheard question . . . unheard by me, that is.

'March the twenty-second, Mrs Wyatt.'

It was clear that the next child along was supposed to speak, but Susan Jordan was one of those who didn't like speaking.

'Come on, Susie. When is your birthday?' Mrs Wyatt leaned forward in her chair, put her hands together as though she was praying, with the tips of her fingers under her chins, and tried to coax Susan with a smile.

Susan replied so softly that I couldn't hear what she said, but suddenly I could feel cold, feathery fingers running up and down my skin. It just so happened that day was my birthday. As the fear rolled over me and subsided, embarrassment set in.

'Ruthie? What about your birthday?' Mrs Wyatt's voice reached me. My face began to burn.

'It's on June the seventeenth, Mrs Wyatt,' I whispered croakily.

'Speak up dear. I can't hear you. I'm getting too old for whispering, you know.' She laughed softly at her own joke and her cheeks and bosom jigged in unison. Despite my flushed embarrassment, the sight brought a smile to my face.

'My birthday is on June the seventeenth.' I spoke more loudly and at her look of surprise felt the embarrassment rushing back. There was a long silence and I could hear the clock tick, tock, tick. It felt like ages but was just seconds long.

'Why, that's today!' She gasped.

'Super!' That was Johnny Devine. 'Are you having a party?'

'Did you get lots of presents?'

'What did your mum and dad get you?'

'Will you have a cake and candles?'

'How many cards did you get?'

'Is anyone coming round for tea?'

I stared at the sea of faces looking at me and fought hard not to cry. However, something must have shown on my face because Mrs Wyatt said, 'Come, come, children. This is a special occasion and we'll let the birthday girl choose today's hymn. Everyone together. Let us all wish Ruth a happy birthday.'

There was a solemn chorus of *Happy Birthday Ruth*, then Mrs Wyatt said, 'Come over here, Ruth.'

I walked over to her with my hymn book as a hush came over the room. Mrs Wyatt put her arm around my waist, gave me a little squeeze, which felt good, and asked me to find a hymn I liked. Trying not to lean into her, but desperate to do so because it felt so good, I flicked slowly through the pages until I found the hymn that would become my favourite. I showed it to her.

'Oh! That's a lovely hymn. Now stand here by me while we sing it.' She turned to the class and continued. 'Ruth has chosen "All things bright and beautiful". It's on page fifty-two. We'll sing on the count of three. One, two . . .'

She kept her arm round me as we sang and it was the most wonderful thing that had happened to me for a long time, not just on that day. That morning had begun as usual with Mum coming in and shouting at me to get out of bed. Neither of my parents had acknowledged my birthday in any way. There were no birthday wishes, no cards, no presents, no special tea, no cake and certainly no party.

As the realisation of the difference between Mrs Wyatt, the other children and my own parents hit me, I felt an over-whelming sadness. I looked at Mrs Wyatt, who was giving me an assessing stare, thanked her and returned to my seat. In my head, I heard my own voice say, *Happy Birthday Ruthie*.

My mother always seemed to pick really late at night to have one of her rages. Even as I think of these episodes, I can see her so clearly.

'I'm going to kill you. It will be slow and horrible and when you're dead, the devil will come up through the floor and drag you away. He'll take you to a place where it is so hot your skin will slowly cook and blister off, like a joint in the oven.'

Other times she would say, 'I'm going to get you. I'll break your skinny arms!' This threat worried me so much that I tried to learn to write with my feet. One day she saw me and laughed.

'What are you doing?'

I delayed answering for a while but she began to shout and that funny 'look' of hers began to show on her face so I answered her. She laughed again and replied, 'Don't be so silly. After I break your arms, I'll go to work on your legs. What will you do then?'

I stared at her aghast and she laughed uproariously as she walked out of my room. I quickly got up and shut the door quietly then, returning to my desk, I put my pencil in my mouth. After that, if I couldn't sleep, then I would get out of bed and get my pencil and book and practise writing with my feet or my mouth. I had to be so quiet but I knew that writing was important if I was to get a good job when I grew up, which is what I would need to have so that I could leave home. I was so afraid that I wouldn't be able to write that my fear of getting out of bed was the lesser of the two evils. In those days, it never occurred to me that a broken arm or leg would mend. In my child's mind, it was going to be a permanent disability because I believed everything was for ever.

She never broke any of our bones, but the threat was enough, particularly as she had carried through so many of her other threats – like strangling us. Often for me, it was worse than an actual punishment. I would sit there and anticipate what it would be like to be killed, to be roasted by the devil and his henchman. Even worse, I began to think of other horrible things, never threatened, but possibilities, that she might dream up to punish us. She was so unpredictable, one moment being the proud mother in public looking as though she might be a contender for 'mother of the year award', the next blowing her top at home and throwing knives or dishes at us, and then, when she calmed down, making us something good to eat or pretty to wear. It was the combination of this unpredictability, my imagination of fearsome things and the waiting – oh, the waiting was something else – that was so intolerable.

It was in September that we had some exciting news that made our life unpredictable in a fun way for a change. Mummy was going to have a baby, she said. She had a very big tummy and said that the baby was inside. How it got there, I didn't know and I didn't ask, but just before baby Mary arrived, the men came and made the house bigger so we could all fit in. The men kept going into the ceiling and they made a room there that became the boys' bedroom. When they moved up to it, Mary got their old bedroom, but we were all excited because with all the mess that was being made by the men, Mummy was too busy cleaning up to bother with us children, and Daddy was driving to lots of different places. He was doing a lot of overtime to pay for all the work, so he wasn't home too much, not even at the weekends. This was the happiest time I ever remember. If only it had lasted – but of course we didn't know then of the 'calm' before storms.

5

In the cupboard

It was one of those afternoons when it was so wet that even Mum wouldn't let us go out to play for fear of us trekking mud into the house, though the reality was that we took our shoes off in the small porch and carried them carefully to our special place in the kitchen, where we were allowed to put newspapers down to clean them. Usually on days like that we would be banished to our rooms, and so it was today. I was working on a drawing when I saw Gordon go past my door, heading downstairs. I finished my artwork and used the toilet, carefully flushing it. Having washed my hands and wiped the basin dry, I ran down into the living room and began to play with my brother. Gordon was sitting in front of the television, staring at it, even though it was not switched on. I began to tickle him, but suddenly felt myself being hauled up roughly by my arm by my mother.

'Did you just use the toilet?' she demanded. 'Did you?' Her questions were peppered with expletives.

She was shaking me so savagely that my head was nodding involuntarily.

'Speak when I talk to you! Did you just use the toilet?'

'Y-yes, Mummy,' I responded, my voice rising with fear.

'Well it stinks now, you dirty little bitch. Who do you think will want to use it now? I hate you, you smelly bastard, and so does everyone else.'

As she spoke, she dragged me out of the living room and into the corridor leading to the front door. She moved to a small door in the side of the stairway and forced me to the floor by pulling my arm down. Pushed into a squatting position in front of the door, I watched as she fumbled with the latch, a small black 'T' bar. It was hooked over a piece of metal on the frame.

She pulled the door open, screaming, 'You will never go to the toilet again. Never!' Then she pushed me inside and shut the door.

My panic knew no bounds. The space I was in was pitch black. There wasn't even a chink of light to show me where the door was, but I scrabbled around trying to find where I thought it was. There was no catch or lock on the inside. No way to open the door – nothing at all. I felt my fear mounting. I sensed something terrible was happening. I was going to die. My heart was thumping and I was breathing fast.

Somehow, I managed to catch some breath, and I screamed, a high-pitched wail that frightened me even more than I could imagine. I saw the monsters I had always been warned about. I knew that the bogeyman and the devil were not far behind and I scrambled up to run, I know not where. I cracked my head against what must have been the bottom of one of the stairs and yelled with the pain of it. The cupboard was much too small to move about in.

As I shrieked in fear, I reached out, and my hand brushed something furry: thinking that I had touched a demon, I felt my terror lift me out of myself. The next thing I knew I was sitting outside on one of the stairs, listening to myself scream below. I sensed that Mummy was in the doorway of the next room, listening to my petrified cries. She was certainly nearby, as I could hear her voice when she spoke and I could imagine the strange smile she always had on her face when she knew she had successfully terrified us. Every now and again, she shouted angrily at Gordon, who was screaming with horror in the living room.

In my mind's eye I continued to imagine her reacting as I had seen her in the past when she was attacking the boys. She would look at the cupboard prison again, as though she could see through the wood, and she probably licked her lips before arching her body backwards, smiling. Of course I couldn't *know* exactly what she was doing, but I had seen her react in this way to our fear often enough to believe that that would be what she'd do.

Even as I listened to Mum yelling, I was startled to see a girl, slightly older than I was, about six years old. She came and sat beside me. She put her arm around me and said, 'Shhh. Easy now. Easy. We mustn't panic. Already our heart is beating too fast.'

As she spoke, I realised that I had heard her before. She was the one who had calmed me on my first day at school. I had never seen her before, only heard her or sensed her presence. Now here she was sitting beside me. She pulled me close and laid her head on mine, and the screaming lessened to a whimper. Jenny was nowhere to be seen, but the two babies joined us briefly before going away again.

When our heart had calmed somewhat, the girl held me at arm's length and looked at me gravely. She looked so sad that I felt the tears come to my eyes and saw them run down her cheeks. Then I heard the small sob and understood that below in the cupboard we were all crying. My mother shrugged and moved away. For her, the show was over.

The girl wiped her tears away slowly, and I felt the caress as mine were wiped away too.

'My name is Liz,' she said. 'And, like Jenny and the babies, I am here for you.'

'Why . . . ? Who . . . ?' I heard my voice as though it came from in the cupboard. Liz seemed to understand and replied, 'You. I am you. Just like Jenny and the others. We are all you, and we come when you need us the most. Jenny is here for the hard times you have with men. I am here to help you, to stop you being so frightened and keep you calm when you need me.'

She paused so I asked her, 'And the little babies? Why are they here? What can they do? They are so little.'

'I don't know exactly when or why they came. I understand only that when you need us, we come. I tried to communicate with them but they are so small, they do not speak. I sensed only that they are like me. They help to look after you in a small way . . . and, as they are already here, I think perhaps when you were their ages, they came to be with you.'

Liz

I am beside myself. I am looking at myself . . . at Ruthie, again. I am Liz. We are in the cupboard listening to her mother screaming at her brother who is also screaming in fear, but we are somewhere else too, somewhere safe. I have been hovering for weeks, trying to burst out of the confines she held me in so that I could reach her consciousness. Finally this event allowed me to break through. She can now see me at last. I stroke her cheek and she knows I am here for her. She has already met Jenny and eventually became aware of the toddler and the baby who emerged when she was the same age as they were – for her mind's protection – but whom she couldn't see until Jenny pointed them out. Unknown to her, there are others waiting in the wings, as I was, for the time when extreme experiences allow them to break through. Time enough for her to meet all of them later. She knows not to be afraid. I encourage her feeling that I am a friend, a guardian angel, for she is too young to understand – she won't until much later – that she, I, Jenny and all the others are bound together in a most unusual way. She is also very strong-willed, which is why I found it so hard to emerge.

I sat with her until the woman released her some time later. I tried to communicate enough to let her understand that she should not be afraid of us, and that while she is under considerable stress, a window of opportunity opens and we can allow her to see us, as and when the time is right. However, even though we are always with her, and some of us will prod and poke at her in disturbing ways, she will generally not remember that we are with her. That is partly my job too, to help her remain in control; for as long as she can do that, she will survive, and in order for her to be in control, she must not be too aware of us.

In a way, being here distresses me and makes me quite depressed. I can be there for her in many instances when she needs my soothing touch, but I know that I am not strong enough, will never be strong enough, to protect her from, first the disorienting and disruptive, then later the potentially destructive forces waiting in the wings. For now all I can do is my job: to keep her as calm as we can, help her to forget and, with Jenny and the babies, to keep her alive and relatively sane.

* * *

It was very bright when Mummy let me out of the cupboard, and it made my eyes hurt. I tried to remember what it was like in there and could only think of the dark smallness of it. I had a sense that someone was with me, caressing me and keeping the demons away, but I am a bad, smelly girl and I don't know if they will eventually hate me too, like everybody else does. Maybe next time they won't come to help me, and the devil or the bogeyman will get me.

As I walked up the stairs to go to my room where Mummy had sent me, I pondered on the bogeyman. I knew what the devil looked like because Mummy had shown me pictures of him that she had painted – she liked to paint, and always her subjects terrified me. But I had never seen a bogeyman and tried to imagine what he looked like. I stood still, closed my eyes and tried to picture my father and paint him red like the devil. Then I did so with the uncle who was a regular abuser and with some of Daddy's friends. Mentally painting them red didn't seem to make them any better or worse, and I was just deciding that I wouldn't be scared of the bogeyman any more when I heard my mother's voice, menacingly close in my ear. She had crept up the carpeted stairs to the one near the top, where I stood with my eyes fast shut.

'Are you meditating, you little smelly creature?' she asked in a nasty voice.

My eyes flashed open and I almost wet myself. 'N-no, M-Mummy,' I managed to stammer.

'Did you learn to meditate in the cupboard?' she continued with the horrid smile on her face.

I stared at her, unable to answer.

'Perhaps you would like to go back there?' she suggested.

Despite my throat seeming to close up, I managed to say, 'N-no, Mummy. No more . . . not again . . . please.'

'Then get up those stairs to your room, and if I as much as see you stick your nose out the door, you'll spend the entire night in the cupboard!'

I fled.

'Are you ready?' my father asked, putting his head round the door of my bedroom where I was skulking, hoping that he would forget me. He was going to drop me off at Mr Price's house and I didn't want to go. Mr Price was a very large man who didn't wash very often. He had never married and lived in a house with his old mother who spent all her time lying in her bed, sleeping. I met her once and she terrified me because she was very wrinkled and had a pointy chin with a big mole or wart on it. She also had no teeth and I had a picture of a witch who looked pretty much like her. Unfortunately in those days we never had 'good' witches. Even though she did nothing more than give me a gummy smile, I was scared of her.

After the introduction was over, her son took me into his bedroom and Jenny shrieked more of her most horrendous screams, which terrified me even as the man's smell threatened to overpower me, and his weight threatened to crush me.

'What the hell are you doing?' my father asked. 'Come on!'

'Daddy, I don't want to go to Mr Price. He smells like something bad and he's so heavy that I can hardly breathe.'

'How can you smell him if you can hardly breathe? Come on, you stupid little cow. You're always complaining about something. You're going to be just like your mother.'

'But Daddy, he'll crush me.'

'I'll tell him to mind that. Anything else, your majesty? And don't bother mentioning the smell. I'm not going to tell him to take a bath. He's a good business associate and I won't insult him because you don't like his smell. Anyway, doesn't he give you presents? Doesn't he give you money when he's done? So stop your yabbering.'

'But Daddy—'

'Stop "but Daddy"-ing me. You are going to him. Full stop, and if I have any more of this from you I am going to take you to the big house. If you are a bad girl like you, the first day you go to the big house, the devil himself will take you into a dark cellar down below. He doesn't need light see? He can see in the dark. And that thing he has in his trousers? It's huge and it's made of fire. When he puts it inside you, you will burn. You hear me? Burn! From the inside out, and he fixes it so that the fire never goes out, so you burn forever. So now, madam. Which do you prefer? The big house or smelly Mr Price?'

Those days were amongst the hardest I can recall of my childhood. The abuse puzzled me for a long while, then I stopped trying to understand it. Although punishments could include rape, I somehow never felt that they were the worst things to happen to me. I knew that it was wrong, that it disgusted me, but I suppose that it didn't seem too bad because my father, uncle, the visitors and the men my father left me with were never cruel. I guess I got used to it. I didn't always remember that Jenny hated it, that she even existed. So what was more terrifying for me were my mother's rages, the throttling until we passed out, the other ways she punished me and my siblings – and that cupboard.

Often I would be alone in my room – possibly after some punishment or other, as I was often banished there afterwards since my mother didn't wish to see me – and truthfully, I began to find solace in being alone there, because it meant I was out of her way. Even so, I could hear the punishments being meted out to my brothers, first when they were in the bedroom next door to mine, then later when they were moved to their attic bedroom and my new baby sister was given their room.

For quite a long time, strangling the boys was Mummy's favourite nightly activity. She would send us to bed and then later she would go up the ladder to the boys' bedroom, screaming her head off the whole time she was up there. She would strangle Philip first as he was nearest the door; Gordon would be screaming in terror as he knew he would be next. It was the anticipation that was always the most frightening thing. Someone else was being hurt and you could feel it happening to them as if it was yourself, and you knew your turn was coming. It was almost better to be first in the queue.

I could hear her screaming abuse at them, occasionally hearing a smack as she hit them. I would sometimes hear the familiar gurgling both boys made as they struggled to catch the breath she was squeezing out of them. I honestly do not know how she managed not to kill any of us. I could see myself watching them. I knew, for example, how Mummy knelt over Gordon or Philip as she throttled them when they were in the attic and I was supposed to be in my bedroom downstairs. Watching them suffer so much felt like the abuse was happening to me all over again. I felt so responsible for them. I was the eldest. Why couldn't I do something to protect them? These feelings assailed me every time my mother attacked them. I had failed to protect them. Like the others, however, when one of us was being abused, we all had to pretend . . . act like there was nothing happening. It was getting harder to ignore, though, because our mother's abusive behaviour was getting more and more inventive. Before long she had thought of a new way to torment us. We always ate our evening meal at 4.30 p.m. sharp, and Mummy would throw our meals out if we were late. She was a good cook who made delicious meals, so we tended not to miss any. This particular day, although I cannot remember exactly what we were eating, I do recall the wonderful smells. It might have been that Mum had a pie or two in the oven, which she would keep in the larder for us to have later.

We all ate with relish, something that seemed especially pleasing to Mum. I had noticed her watching us with her peculiar smile on her face and, although that should have warned me that something was amiss, it didn't. We had just finished eating when Mummy began to laugh.

'Isn't it wonderful? You are all going to die. I've poisoned your food and you will all die very slowly and in horrible pain. I can't wait for the bogeyman to come and take you away. I can't wait for the devil to come along and roast you on his fire. I can just smell you roasting. I can hear your skin crackling and popping. Pop, pop, pop.'

I gasped and ran upstairs to the toilet where I stuck my fingers down my throat, trying to bring the food up again. Even as I did so, Gordon's head, then Philip's, competed for space beside mine. Mary wasn't there. Either she was too young to understand the implications of what Mummy had just said, or she didn't care. The three of us managed to make ourselves sick and Mummy, who appeared in the doorway laughing, paused momentarily to remind us to clean up when we were done.

This happened a couple more times, but then we noticed that Mary hadn't actually suffered any adverse reactions, so we stopped trying to bring the food back up, and we too were okay. Mum decided to try another tack. One weekend, when Daddy was home and we were all at the dining table, he was having a big steak while we had meatballs and mashed potatoes. He had sliced into his steak and was lifting the fork to his mouth when she said, 'I hear you've been f**king Diane Owen. You'll not f**k her again. I've poisoned your f**king food.'

It was a stupid time to tell him, because Daddy hadn't eaten any of it yet. He looked round the table, then thrust the fork in Philip's face.

'Eat it,' he ordered. Philip hesitated but the look on Dad's face was such that he took the meat off the fork and stared at it, horror etched into his face.

'Eat it!' Dad's voice was louder. Mum laughed.

Philip slowly put the meat in his mouth and began to chew. Dad sliced off another piece of steak and offered it to Gordon. His eyes spoke his order. Gordon put the meat in his mouth.

Dad cut two more slices, one for me and another for Mary, and we all ate, terrified. As I ate, I felt my throat constrict and I began to develop a problem that would be lifelong.

When we had swallowed, Dad joined Mum in laughing uproariously and polished off the rest of his meal without further ado.

These sudden changes of mood in my parents confused me terribly. Just a moment ago Mum had been shouting furiously at Dad. But the thing that could always unite them was a shared joy in bullying and abusing their children.

'We're going to the Indian restaurant tomorrow for dinner,' Dad announced. He loved Indian food and there was a very good restaurant in our high street. I too enjoyed the food, but now I was developing food phobias, and these occasional treats became a torture to me.

In the restaurant, Mum managed to find fault with everything, muttering to us under her breath as we were in public.

'For heaven's sake,' my father hissed at her. 'Give it a rest.'

'Give it a rest? Give it a rest? Look at our children. They're
shovelling the food in their mouths like they haven't eaten for
a year. What will people think when they see such bad
manners?'

We all looked at her, puzzled, because we were not eating
quickly and had done nothing to attract her ire. Daddy looked
at her too.

'No they're not and, even if they were, people will only
think it's because they're kids, nothing more!'

'No they won't! They'll think I starve them. That I am not a
good mother – and why are you all staring at me like that?'

When no one answered, she carried on, 'Oh well. I won't be
embarrassed for much longer. When you thought I was in the
loo, I actually went to the kitchen to talk with the cook. When
he wasn't looking, I put some poison in your food. Very
strong poison. You can't taste it in a curry now, can you?' And
she began to laugh.

I felt my throat closing up and I ate more and more slowly.
Gordon decided that the idea of the 'poisoning' was not worth
thinking about and he polished off his own meal and half of
mine. It was too much for him really but he enjoyed it.

Back in the car, Mum really let rip. She and Dad shouted at
each other all the way home, and Gordon, no doubt affected
by the shouting, his overeating and perhaps some carsickness,
begged for them to pull over. Dad stopped just in time for him
to get out and be sick at the kerbside.

That seemed to ingrain in me the idea that eating food
could be dangerous and even today I'm known as a slow eater.
Most people I know accept this and let me eat at my own pace.

What they don't know is that whenever I have to eat anything I have not prepared and watched over myself, my throat constricts so much that it is a struggle to swallow. I know that there is nothing wrong with the food. I know it! But my throat lets me down all the same.

Daddy had changed his car for a more upmarket one and there were days when he took us for trips to various places, either to shop or perhaps visit relatives. We didn't really go anywhere for fun. The trips themselves were supposed to be enough, but Dad was partial to mental arithmetic and general knowledge and often gave us quizzes to do in the car whenever we went on longish journeys. It was a good idea – or at least it should have been – as it would keep us quietly engaged for long periods of time. However, he made it another form of torture for us. He demanded answers quickly, and whenever we got the answers wrong he and Mum would burst out into prolonged laughter, after which we would be criticised, mocked and generally made to feel thoroughly ashamed.

'A train travels at a constant rate of a hundred feet per second. How many miles does it travel in five minutes?'

'Er . . .'

'Come on. Come on. Quickly now!' Needless to say, we could never work it out fast enough, and he would often switch to something else before we could manage an answer.

'How was Joan of Arc killed?'

One of the boys jumped in quickly, trying to save us some face. 'She was burnt as a snake?'

The criticism and ribald remarks that followed that slip of the tongue lasted most of the journey.

Despite their quarrels and apparent intolerance of each other, Mum became pregnant again. I was thirteen when my youngest brother George came along. At first he shared my parents' room, but he was always crying, and this seemed to drive Mum insane. Often she would walk out into the garden or find some place where she couldn't hear him. She always says that the sound of his crying distressed her greatly, and that even today she can't bear to hear a baby cry. George was unlucky in that he was born with a part of his skull missing. He was always sickly and that is probably why he cried so much. At first his head looked a bit lopsided but fortunately, as he grew older, the lopsidedness became less pronounced, and he hasn't had any apparent complications as a result.

One day, baby George was in his pram and Mum was working on some dresses she was making for us. I was in my bedroom, equally employed with a drawing, which I was totally absorbed in. Mum put her head round my door.

'George is crying,' she told me. 'He needs feeding. Prepare his bottle and give it to him.'

Normally I would have been delighted to feed the baby. It meant cuddles for both of us, but on this day something blew.

'I'm working on something. I don't have time to feed him,' I replied, completely out of character.

'*What?*' My mother advanced and I ran. Rather than follow me round the room, she stalked to the window and threw it open, then she looked round at me and smiled. At least, I think the distorted grimace on her face was supposed to be a smile. She moved over to my small desk and looked at what I was busy with, then she picked it up, scrunched the paper together and threw it out of the window. Everything else on the desk — books, paper, pencils and so on — followed. She turned to look at my horrified face. Smiling again, she walked to my bed, gathered everything on it and tossed it all out, and in this fashion slowly went round my room, picking up everything that she could, until she had thrown all my belongings out of my bedroom window which was at the front of the house. When everything had gone, she turned to look at me; as she advanced, I fled, not knowing whether I would be pitched out through the window next.

I ran out of the house into the front garden and saw that some of our neighbours had gathered outside their houses to watch the spectacle unfold. Others were standing at their windows, not even hiding behind the curtains as I'd seen a couple of them do before. Mortified, I dashed out of the garden and ran off down the road. None of them commented or asked me how I was. In any case, I was so horrified and frightened that I simply couldn't have spoken to anyone. I don't know how long it was before I returned to the house. I think I must have switched into another alter because I wasn't aware of the time passing at all. Losing time was something that would come to plague me all my life but for now, I had more immediate problems coping with the nightmarish world that was our home.

The boys were too afraid to get out of bed at night, or at least to come down the loft ladder, so they used the corner of the attic bedroom as a toilet. Gordon sometimes did a poo in the drawer in his room or he would throw it out of the window. In addition, Philip was a chronic bed-wetter. He wet the bed every night without fail. Although he had alarm sheets from the doctor's, these never worked. The buzzer from the alarm sheet would go off, waking me in the room below, but Philip never seemed to wake up. Mum would run up the ladder to him and drag him out of bed, but the deed would already have been done and the bed would be wet.

After a while they stopped using the alarm sheets, even though he continued to wet the bed. This, of course, caused chaos the next morning. Mum would yell at Philip when he got downstairs and would then lay into him physically. Usually she had her face close to his while she called him thick, stupid, filthy and so on, all with swearwords attached. Then, often she would drag him into the front room, sit on him with one knee on either side of his shoulders, and strangle him until he fainted. He never screamed or spoke a word while this was going on, and his silence was both fear- and awe-inspiring.

One morning I was walking down the garden path on my way to school when I heard the commotion. I ran back and peered in the front window and there was Mummy sitting on Philip, choking him with one hand and waving the wet sheet about with the other. I was so scared she would kill him that I rapped and banged on the window. She responded by rubbing the wet sheet in his face before getting off him. She then ran at me, screaming abuse, and I hustled for the garden gate. I ran towards the bus stop and she continued yelling after me but didn't follow. I was terrified, but at least she had stopped what she was doing to Philip. He had to go to school stinking of urine because she hadn't allowed him to bathe.

I found it as hard to watch her doing these things to my siblings as to suffer the abuse myself. I simply didn't recognise any difference. I would sometimes switch to an alter who was there to protect me from *their* abuse and would know nothing for a while.

There was often screaming in the night – children having nightmares. Occasionally I managed to pluck up the nerve to go to them and talk quietly or hold their hands until they went back to sleep. My alter Liz often helped me take care of Gordon and Philip when they wet their bed or did other messes, and when Mummy hit them or put her hands round their throats until they fell asleep, like she sometimes did with me. My brothers used to come to me soon after Mummy's abuse for me to make them feel better until my mother stopped it. I wouldn't have known what to do without Liz helping me.

After Liz's arrival, bedtimes eventually became reasonably comfortable for me, for that was when my alters tended to come for a chat and to assure me that everything was fine and we could sleep feeling relatively safe. This was our time for caring communication, the time when I was aware of them in a 'calm' setting. Of course they emerged all the time when I needed them, the difference being that I didn't always know they were there. I didn't realise then that whenever I was feeling very stressed, one or other of them would take over my body and thoughts and act in what they felt was the most appropriate way. But bedtimes when it was peaceful were the best. It was like having a sleepover with a bunch of friends who loved me.

I am not sure how old I was when my uncle Dickie, my mother's brother, first sexually abused me. He often visited the house and, although Daddy generally made me available to any of his friends who visited, I don't think he was one of them, though he might have been. What I do know for certain is that when I was about eight and a half years old, he had come to stay, for some reason. I now know that his rather obese wife was a 'working woman' and that he lived off her earnings. It is possible that he had to get out of the way for a while. Anyway, he turned up at our house.

I had to move into Mary's room with her and he slept in my bedroom. One night, Mary had a nosebleed that Mum couldn't stop. Our doctor was called out but he couldn't stop it either, so Mum and Dad had to take Mary to the hospital.

Worried about my little sister, I was tossing and turning in bed when the door opened and my uncle got into bed with me. Like all the other men who used me, he was gentle and kept saying nice things to me. I have always thought they did this to keep me calm so I wouldn't fight and cause a fuss. He liked oral sex and to this day I hate slimy substances in my mouth. If I get catarrh I heave very easily and feel scared.

Mary was kept in hospital, where the doctors apparently told Mum and Dad that she had chickenpox and that one pustule in her nose had ruptured causing the nosebleed. She remained there for a few days and every night my uncle used me with impunity.

When other people were brought to the house by my father, he let them abuse me too. It seemed as if they came to the house especially to do this, but it is possible they simply came to visit and my father offered me to them.

There was one night – when I was around eleven years old – that I was summoned to my father's bed. I cannot remember exactly who was in bed with me, whether it was Dad or one of his cronies. As usual an alter had taken my place. The next thing I remember was sitting on the landing, bent double, screaming in pain. My stomach and lower body were on fire. I thought I was dying. Mum came and had a look at me. Dad did, too, but he glanced at me only briefly before he walked away. As I continued to scream, Mum decided to call the doctor, but it was a male doctor who arrived and I wouldn't let him near me. He called an ambulance. I was petrified when I realised that I was being taken to another 'big house'. It was another place for me to be abandoned for goodness knows how long and to what end, and I dearly wished that I'd managed to contain the pain. I was either going to be abused or Mum's prediction of my death was coming true. I was scared witless, but knew that, whatever fate awaited me, I would have to be dragged screaming and fighting there.

When we got to the hospital, other (male) doctors tried to examine me, but I wouldn't let anyone near me. It was bad enough having one stranger make free with my body, but there were several doctors wandering in and out of my screened-off cubicle. I was afraid of being touched but terrified of dying, and although I didn't want to die, somehow I wanted to at the same time. When the doctors tried to do a physical examination, I wrapped my legs together. The nurse approached me but backed away when I bunched my hands into fists. I clearly remember trying to make myself as small as possible.

'If I make myself really small, you can't do much, can you?' I thought.

I was admitted to the ward. In those days your parents were not allowed to stay, so I soon found myself alone. Once Mum had gone I calmed down and stopped screaming. The next doctor who came round was very nice to me but he didn't attempt to touch me.

'Well now. That's good,' he said. 'Are you feeling better?'

I stared at him mutely. How could I tell him that – as I never felt good – I didn't know what 'better' was?

He was with the nurse I'd seen earlier who was giving out sweets to those children already seen by the doctor. As I reached out for my sweet, she looked at me and said, 'So you're not too ill to eat sweets then. Are you?' There was malice in her whole attitude, but the doctor told her to be quiet and give me the sweets.

The doctor continued to see me and he was always very kind. While I was in the hospital, I had two separate X-rays but I don't recall any other treatment. I was made to do various physical exercises for them and, even though there was no apparent internal damage, they kept me in the hospital for almost a week. This was strange, as my pain had disappeared within forty-eight hours. It might have been routine to have been kept in at a time when longer hospital stays were the norm, but I sensed that they suspected that *something* was amiss and were ensuring that they checked all the angles before discharging me from the hospital. Having said that, I do not recall physical examinations or investigations of any sort after the first three days or so. It was simply the doctor's careful attention to everything I said that made me think that he suspected more than he was letting on, and perhaps because I resisted the physical examination.

In hindsight, and in these more enlightened times, it seems incredible that the doctors didn't act on their suspicions. They didn't, as far as I know, question my parents or inform social services. But things were very different then. Anyway, nothing changed for me. There was never a moment at which I felt tempted to tell, either. My father's threats of the 'big house' for girls who told and my general terror of both my parents meant I couldn't risk it. In any case, I couldn't imagine any other life.

With regard to the pain I felt, it would seem that an alter was clearly in control before the abuse started and for some reason she stepped out before it was finished. So for the first time, I, Ruth, experienced the assault as never before. My dutiful mother visited me two or three times, and even bought me a small gift, though I have forgotten what it was. I recall the force of the terror I felt when I saw her approaching for the first visit and, suddenly remembering the watchful doctor, looked round fearfully for him. Fortunately and unfortunately, depending on my points of view, he was not around: the subsequent relief and despair left me in a profound state of confusion.

Finally, though, I was discharged. I don't remember the journey home because I was distressed to be leaving the hospital. I could have happily stayed there permanently. Certainly I got a much needed respite from my parents. My only regret was that my brothers and sister could not have a break too.

As children we seemed not to have the sense of danger that other children did, and if my mother thought we might hurt ourselves, she never did anything to stop us. For example, I loved to ride my bicycle backwards while sitting on the handlebars. If I fell off, I promptly got up and got on again.

Soon after the business of Mum throwing all my belongings out of the window, I and my alters decided that it would be a good game to jump out of the window ourselves. I am not sure whether we had intended harming ourselves, or whether it was a game from the start, but that is what we did. I grabbed my umbrella, stuck it out of the window and opened it. I clambered onto the sill and hurled myself out. Fortunately we landed safely. Soon after that the boys joined me, then Mary too. It became a game for us and we would also jump off a coal bunker. We would get on the swing in the garden, build up momentum until we could sail over the top and, as it came around again we would jump off it, the idea being to see who could jump the furthest. My alters would encourage me.

There was one in particular who I didn't name then and won't name now as he is no longer with me. He was a small, wiry individual with very pale, freckled skin and a rather pointed chin. He had a shock of very dark hair with a cowlick that was always falling into his grey eyes, and an energy that saw him bustling about with great determination. As soon as I became aware of him, I tried as hard as I could to suppress him as I didn't feel comfortable having a male alter. He was probably responsible for me becoming the daredevil tomboy I was in those days. He had no fear of anything and seemed to have a high tolerance for pain. It was always an uncanny experience that, when I did something and hurt myself, the pain went away quickly and completely, so he encouraged the recklessness in me that might otherwise have remained dormant.

'We can do it. Come on. We can jump further.'

As an adult I went back to see the house; to my surprise, the window was much higher than I had remembered before. How we didn't kill ourselves I'll never know, but the memories of jumping out of the window were amongst my more pleasant ones.

Needless to say, we didn't always get off scot-free. One or other of us would miss whatever target we were aiming at and fall heavily. One day, Philip fell and broke his arm as we played one of our high-risk games, and Mum carted him off to the hospital leaving me in charge of the others. Mary fell another time and almost bit her tongue completely in two. Again Mum had to rush her to the hospital to have it sutured. Philip's fall saw him with a rusty nail puncturing his knee, necessitating yet another hospital trip. I remember Mum being anxious on these occasions, which was confusing to me since most of the time she had no compunction about inflicting pain on us herself, so it didn't seem likely that she was concerned about our wellbeing. I think that these run of the mill childhood accidents were totally different in her own mind. They necessitated doing the decent thing in order to keep up appearances and that meant going to hospital.

Appearances were crucially important to both my parents, but especially to my mother. In some ways, she loved to perform. Christmas afforded the perfect opportunity.

'Wakey, wakey. Rise and shine. It's Christmas Day.' Mum's voice clearly showed her excitement as she went from room to room waking us all up. We too were always excited, and always had the forlorn hope that Christmas Day would end as it began, full of promise and thrills.

We would tumble after our mother as she ran downstairs into the lounge where the huge, beautifully decorated Christmas tree would stand protectively over our presents. Dad would also be there, sitting in his favourite armchair reading the papers or, if he had started without us, examining one of his presents. He would watch as Mum scrabbled about the floor finding our presents and handing them over with a flourish after announcing who each gift was for and from whom.

We had already seen the tree the night before with all the presents beneath, as it was a tradition with my parents to invite their friends over for drinks so they could show them how generous they were with us. It was more a 'being superior to' rather than a 'keeping up with' the Joneses exercise. To be sure they were always generous and our gifts were both plentiful and expensive, and it was the only time of year that we got presents.

But the pleasure would not last. Our angst began with the opening of the first presents and culminated with the opening of the last – always those our mother bought and/or made for us. She was always insecure about them and would ask, 'Do you like it?'

'Yes, Mummy,' we'd reply, 'it's lovely.'

'Would you have preferred a different one perhaps?'

Knowing what a rejection of her choice would bring we'd each say something like, 'No, Mummy. This one is truly lovely. Just what I wanted.'

'Are you sure you like it? It cost a lot of money and I could easily take it back and exchange it,' she'd insist.

'Mummy, it is perfect. I love it.'

There was always something that seemed to trigger off Mum's rage, and by evening began an orgy of destruction. Soft toys and dolls were ripped limb from limb. Harder toys were thrown against the wall or out the window. Anything that could be squashed underfoot was squashed, and we children retired to bed bemused and broken-hearted. This became an annual routine. If we played our part well, we'd have our toys to play with at least for a few hours, but sometimes her fury would be set off within an hour of us opening the boxes.

At school, I realised that another of the teachers, Mrs Shaw, had taken a strong dislike to me. I wasn't sure why, but some time later I saw her with her husband whom I recognised as a friend of my father's – another man who had used me. That made me realise that she probably suspected about the abuse and somehow or other held me responsible, because she was always shouting at me. She punished me, it seemed, for nothing at all.

In those days I often suffered urinary infections and needed to use the toilet frequently. One day we were working on a multiple-choice exercise when the urge came upon me suddenly and I raised my hand to get the teacher's attention. Although she saw me immediately, she pursed her lips and looked away. After what seemed like a long time, but was probably just seconds, she looked back at me still frantically waving my hand.

'Yes?'

'Please, Mrs Shaw, may I go to the toilet?'

'No. Get on with your work.'

I glanced at the clock on the wall and saw that we had at least another ten minutes of class. I crossed my legs tightly and tried to concentrate on the task at hand, but I realised that I was beginning to wet myself so I ran out of the room. Needless to say, that did nothing for the student–teacher relationship we should have been developing. Another time she called me 'Rude' and, when I protested, refused to use my correct name. This incident might seem a trivial thing to remember, but to me it was important because my mother never used my name at home unless there was someone there. I was simply called a range of abusive names like ugly (like a fish!), c**t, stupid, thick, bad, horrid, not a nice person, difficult to be with, hateful. At home I almost never heard my name being used in a good context. Yes my father and grandfather used it, but only to get what they wanted. So it hurt when this teacher deliberately mispronounced 'Ruth'. A very small thing, but so important to me. I still enjoy hearing my husband calling me by my name. I don't like even using a pseudonym for this book and, if it weren't for the consideration of my siblings' feelings, I wouldn't. Anyway, whenever I got upset by this, the teacher just laughed as though it was the funniest thing in the world, and as this teacher did not appear to like me, I decided that no adult would.

Another battle with her involved my food phobia, which was still with me. I hated eating mashed potatoes. For some reason they made me heave, and I was always the last to finish my meals. Mrs Shaw made it her particular goal to get me to eat all of my mashed potatoes and would sit beside me watching me eat. I never finished them, and the punishments she could think of were nothing in comparison to what my parents could dish out, so I had no fear of her. I was always depressed anyway and didn't care. If I could survive my mother's so-called poisoned food, I would survive school dinners.

I didn't trust anyone and was afraid of the other children too, even though I never had any major problems with my schoolmates – not at any of the schools I attended. Part of this was because of my mother's repeated name-calling and her insistence that no one would like me. And so I believed; I believed all of those horrid things about myself, and Mrs Shaw was par for the course. And of course Mum did nothing to make school easier for me.

I had been about seven years old when I went home one day and told my mother, as instructed, that the teachers said I needed to have my hair tied back. In those days it was so long I could sit on it. Mummy took me to the hairdresser's and had my head completely shorn so that I looked like a boy. As you can imagine I found that very distressing.

As I grew older, my mental turmoil also grew and it began to manifest itself in occasional violence. I felt my siblings' anguish acutely, and sometimes the anger inside me burst out on their behalf when outsiders were trying to hurt them. On one particular day, we had been playing football in the garden when the ball got kicked out in the street and Philip ran out to retrieve it. I was watching as an older boy picked up the ball.

'Throw it over,' Philip said in a perfectly friendly tone.

'Make me,' the other replied aggressively.

'Please give me my ball.' Philip's tone was uncertain.

The other boy bounced the ball hard off Philip's forehead. It was clear to me that he intended to have some fun at Philip's expense. I simply saw red. I marched out of the garden, up to the boy – who was slightly taller than me – and I punched him hard in the stomach. As he bent double, the ball fell out of his hands, Philip scooped it up, and we returned to the garden. There was no preamble, no asking or discussion, no warning. Just wham! We got our ball back and the would-be bully staggered off. I didn't feel bad about this; I had too many other reasons to feel bad.

The cupboard continued to be a focus for my mental anguish, both for my own sake and increasingly for my siblings. And it was a constant presence. I couldn't understand why a mother would lock her children in a cupboard. All I'd ever wanted from my family was to be loved by them . . . to be held gently and lovingly without the strings of paedophilia attached. All I'd ever wanted was to be a normal child with normal parents.

I couldn't understand how my father, having already secured my silence over his and the others' activities by threatening to send me to the 'big house' could then tell my mother each Monday morning before he left the house for his week's work, 'Make sure she doesn't talk.'

Whereupon Mum would sometimes promptly grab me, even as I stood trying to dress for school, drag me downstairs, and put me in the cupboard screaming at me, 'You'll get more of that if you ever open your mouth.'

One morning, as I sat there cold and virtually naked in the cupboard, I heard Daddy come downstairs and kiss her goodbye, as though they were any loving couple living a normal life.

That cupboard under the stairs, which held so much distress for me, was tiny, no more than two feet high. You had to curl up to sit in it. Because it was in such a central part of the house, I couldn't help but pass it every day, and it was not simply my personal fear of it that caused me problems, but also that of my brothers and later my baby sister. Not one of us, not me or Gordon, Philip, or even our baby sister, Mary, managed to avoid the cupboard when we lived at that house. I learnt to sit quietly with my terrors but their screams were horrific. I would try to will them to stop screaming, but they never did.

One of the first times I recall them suffering the cupboard, I was just returning home from school. Baby Mary was about two years old and, as I walked up the street towards our house, I recognised her and Philip's screams. I slowed down, reluctant to walk up to the front door. Yet I knew I had to. If I was late home, my screams would join theirs. I had also been imprisoned there for being supposedly late home, even when I wasn't.

As I walked up the path, I noticed the curtains at the window of the house next door, the other half of our 'semi' twitch briefly. Although I couldn't see her, I knew our neighbour had heard the screams through our shared wall and seen my reluctance to go indoors. I paused deliberately, hoping that it would encourage her to do something, anything that would help us, but nothing happened except that the screams of the little ones continued.

I opened the front door and saw something that I hadn't

quite recognised before . . . although I had 'seen' something of it when I had sat on the stairs the first time I had been imprisoned there. Mummy was standing outside the cupboard door. She was laughing in that particularly horrid, hysterical way she had, and I knew that she must also have stood outside when I was her prisoner, waiting for me to scream. My alter had sat on the stairs and watched her. After the first time, my mother never stayed there long, and it occurred to me that when Liz had come to me that first time, I had soon stopped screaming. After that, I'd never screamed for long, as Liz would arrive to help me; she always was there when I needed her.

When I saw Mummy listening to Mary and Philip in the cupboard, I realised instinctively that if they stopped screaming she would have had no pleasure in their incarceration and might let them out sooner. I began to recall that her behaviour always became more extreme when we screamed, as it seemed to feed her cruelty. So when the little ones were freed I told them that they shouldn't scream next time. They were not always able to suppress their terror, and I could fully understand why, though I did not always remember why I seemed to cope better than them.

That day, Mummy eventually opened the cupboard door and walked away. They crawled out, scared and breathless. Philip managed to whisper to me, 'We were in the garden playing a game of "catch". Mary was screaming every time I nearly got her and Mummy didn't like it. She ran at us. Mary just froze and I was holding her hand. Before I could run Mummy grabbed us and just dragged us in. Then, when we got to the cupboard, she kicked me so I would get in and then she kicked me some more to make room for Mary. I hate her. I really, really hate her.'

He had taken a real risk to tell me what happened, because normally we just had to get on with things. But Philip and I were close; we often went for walks together. We would wander along the paths onto open, undeveloped fields where all the local children played. There was a pond nearby, and we would sit and watch the ducks. Sometimes Philip would collect tadpoles in a jam jar. In the winter, the frost would scrunch underfoot as we walked and my little brother would tuck his hand inside my elbow as we walked along.

If Mummy had seen us talking about what had happened, all hell would have broken loose, so mostly we just acted as though nothing had happened. And in truth, once the others were let out of the cupboard, life did just go on. Mummy went about doing the housework and we just had to be quiet. If there was any crying she would start again. The situation was hopeless.

Late one winter's afternoon, I and my alters decided that we'd had enough of my mother's screaming, the sexual abuse, the being disliked by everyone. All of us had periods of deep depression and feeling suicidal, but fortunately, in terms of our survival, we didn't all have these feelings at the same time. So we lumped along, the happy alters dragging the suicidal ones on. Now we were all in agreement.

I cannot remember exactly what Mum had done, only that it suddenly seemed as if life was never going to be better, and therefore death was preferable. All the sexual abuse by so many, up to and including Uncle Dickie, who was the last one to join the group of regular abusers, and the knowledge of them, and what they made me do, had culminated in this moment. My alters and I discussed the whys and wherefores as I sat alone in my bedroom. I looked out of the window into what was a gathering gloom above a snow-filled landscape, and we decided that the snow in the fields would be soft to lie on and that, as night fell, the cold would kill quickly. We would simply fall asleep and die, and with childish logic we decided that as our 'deathbed' would be such a cold place, neither the devil nor the bogeyman, both of whom preferred warmth, would be able to get us.

I grabbed my torch, put on my navy mackintosh, and as I slipped out the front door, closing it quickly but quietly behind me, I heard my mother's voice. She had stepped out of the kitchen just at the same moment and I could almost see her looking up the stairs as she shouted my name.

Quickly I made my way to the path and onto the fields. Guided by my alters, I found a quiet spot, then lay down. Eventually, as darkness began to close in and I grew colder, I began to doze. I don't know how long I was there, but I was suddenly being shaken.

'Hey! Wake up! Wake up! Come on.' I was lifted to my feet and I became groggily aware that someone was shaking me. He called to someone, 'She's over here!'

Before long a second policeman (I could see from the light of his torch) was beside me and the first began to pick me up like a baby.

'No! No! Leave me alone,' I screamed and struggled to my feet.

'It's all right. You're safe. We're policemen,' the new arrival said.

'Don't take me back. I don't want to go back.'

'You have to go back. Your mother is very worried about you. Don't you ever do this again. You could die out here. Never run away again,' the first policeman said.

'I don't care. I want to die. I hate her.' I continued to struggle frantically, whereupon both officers picked me up and held me as though I were a log. They carted me off back to the house. This was the first time I'd ever given anyone more than a hint of the way I was feeling. I had been emboldened by despair. But it didn't make any difference. The policemen obviously thought I was being a melodramatic kid.

My mother appeared to be beside herself with worry, and greeted me as though I was the prodigal son returning. She invited the two officers in for a cup of tea, and after making me a warm drink, which I drank sullenly, she made me go to bed. I don't know what she and the police officers spoke of after that, but I'm sure she managed to persuade them that I'd run off after some minor spat.

Gordon and Philip were most amused by the whole adventure, not so much because I had run off, but because of Mum's reactions. They had no idea that I had intended to die, and so could afford to sit back and enjoy the drama. After all, it was what we all wanted to do: to escape and be free. While Mum was still downstairs talking with the police, we were huddled in my bedroom and they told me excitedly what had happened at home.

'Mum saw your footprints in the snow—'

'She followed them as far as the path—'

'But it had all gone mushy because everybody walked all over them—'

'She came back in grumbling and saying what she would do to you when you came back . . .'

'And Philip got scared—'

'Did not—'

'Did—'

'So what happened then?' I asked, knowing this argument could go on for hours.

'She kept looking at the clock.'

' "I'll give her till five o'clock", she said—'

'And when you still didn't come back, she started to run up and down to the gate.'

'She was in a right old panic—'

'So she called the police—'

'And they brought you back—'

'Where did you go?'

'What did you do?'

'Why didn't you hide?'

We had to break off our conversation because the police were leaving and we were terrified that once they'd gone, all hell would break loose. The boys left my room quickly when they heard Mum saying goodnight to the police. I pulled the covers over my head as I often did when I slept; although I heard Mummy at the door, she didn't disturb me, but went downstairs again. I've no idea why she didn't punish me that night. But she was always completely unpredictable: that was a huge part of the terror. Meanwhile the alters came out and snuggled against me. We chatted briefly, then there was a chorus of *goodnight* as we began to fall asleep.

People might ask, 'Why didn't you get help? Why didn't you tell someone who could have helped you?' But they didn't know what I knew. There was no one there. In hindsight people are always wise and brave, but everyone I knew seemed to hate me. That was probably not true, but it was what I believed. It was what I was conditioned to believe. But even if I hadn't believed it, the world is full of stories of children who did try to speak out and the further damage that was done to them when the system failed them. It was a case of using whatever strategies we had to survive.

That is a child's *raison d'être*, to survive to become a parent themself. It is what drives every organism, and what strategies does a child have for surviving? It's the same as anyone else's – to cope within their immediate environment as best they can, and that is precisely what all abused individuals – children or adults – do. That's how I see things now, but back then despair was a constant companion.

By that point in my life I trusted no one but my alters: not my parents, my teachers, my neighbours, or – now I added to the list – the police.

Later that year everything just seemed to build up inside me. I simply couldn't bear my life any more and I needed a release. Not far away from our house, they were building a new library and there were bricks and other building materials lying around on the site. One day I discovered that I could find some relief by smashing bottles and jam jars against the newly erected walls. I was screaming and generally going berserk. Once the bottles were all gone, I began to run. I found myself on the village green and paused in my madness long enough to discover what looked like a papery rugby ball lying under a hedge.

Still feeling an unrelenting rage, I kicked it several times and stamped on it. Enraged wasps emerged from it and attacked me. As is usual for stressful situations, I 'lost' myself and came around later at home. How I got there I do not know, but I'd been severely stung around the head and I thought I was going to die. Mum pulled my cardigan off as it was covered in wasps. Then she put my head under the tap in the bath and washed my hair till all the wasps had gone. She looked at the damage and, clearly amused by my predicament, decided that a doctor wasn't needed. Neighbours who had apparently heard my screams and seen me running down the street with wasps following me, came to see if I was all right. Mum immediately became a caring and concerned mother, but as soon as they had gone she began shouting at me for being so silly.

'You're a stupid idiot, aren't you?' She moved my head backwards and forwards and chuckled as she examined the various stings. 'What made you think you could go around playing with wasps?'

I never bothered to explain that I wasn't playing with the things.

'Well, I don't think you'll need a doctor.' She moved to the refrigerator and took out her usual remedy – a bottle of cold water. She grabbed one of the tea towels, poured the cold water onto it and gave the bundle to me, dismissing me with, 'Put this wherever it hurts.'

Something about her that day made me briefly look at her with a feeling of longing, of wanting her to be different. Even though the neighbours had gone, and her amusement stung, I recognised that her hands were gentle when she touched me, something I generally hated.

'Why don't you love us?' The words were out before I could think about them and my heart began to thump in anticipation.

She looked at me and frowned. Her eyes took on a faraway look for a moment or two, and when she spoke, her voice was low. What she said, plus the strength of the desolation in her voice, almost made me cry.

'I don't know how to love.' She shook her head slightly and, still frowning, she turned and walked out of the room.

I felt an overwhelming sadness. How could she not know

how to love? I thought about those words many times over the next few days. I was in pain from the wasp stings, which took a while to wear off, but I simply couldn't stop thinking about what Mum had said and, after a while, understanding finally dawned. It was confirmed a few weeks later when she and Dad had another row.

I was in my room doing my homework when I heard them coming up the stairs. There was clearly a problem between them as I could hear my father speaking in a low, aggressive-sounding growl. As they reached my door my father said, 'You are such a stupid bitch. Why did you do it?'

My mother's response was so low, so subdued, that I didn't hear what she said and I never found out what it was she'd said. However, the fact that her response was so quiet made me look up.

'You're a f**king mad woman and they'll take you away one of these good days. Mark my words!' Dad was leaning towards her, his face close to hers. Even so, he was accentuating every word by making a prodding motion towards her face with his index finger.

I saw Mum flinch at his words and, as she raised her eyes slowly up to meet his gaze, she looked scared. At that moment I saw her not as a cruel mother, but rather as one of my frightened, bullied siblings. I couldn't help what I did next.

'Shut up! shut up!' I cried out. 'Can't you see you're hurting her?'

My father stopped and stared at me in surprise. He didn't say anything but walked away into their room, leaving my mother standing in the doorway. She glanced at me briefly before turning and walking back downstairs.

I couldn't understand my reaction. Why had I spoken up? It

seemed illogical because I didn't love her yet I felt a need to protect her. Why? If I'd needed a sign that I was truly going nuts that was it! I sat with my elbows on my desk and my face in my hands as I rubbed my forehead. I tended to do that whenever I was agitated and I could feel the alters stirring. I tried to concentrate and calm everyone down, because if they got started I didn't know whether I would cope. I don't know how long I'd been sitting like that when I heard a noise by my door. I looked up to see my mother walking slowly into my room. In her hand she had a choc ice, which she held out to me. I reached out and took it hesitantly, while the questions swirled around in my head. Why is she giving me a choc ice? What does she want?

It was strange watching her. She still seemed somehow subdued. Although she was looking in my direction, her eyes were not focused on my face. I got a sense that she was almost ashamed of herself. For what seemed like a long moment, we stood there, then she lifted her eyes to meet mine. It was only a fleeting look, but as our eyes locked I noticed a vulnerability. A brief hint of a smile touched her lips, then she turned and walked out of the room.

I was now full of compassion for her. I had suffered so much unkindness at her hands, yet her plight had moved me. It was the beginning of a new understanding of this woman who bore me. I didn't love her, was beyond even wanting to try, yet she was my mother and she was hurting. My poor mother was ill and I figured I must owe her something for that.

On the other hand, I owed my father nothing. If Mum did not always know what she was doing, he was in total control of his actions. After all, he was sane, wasn't he? And in my mind, his abuse was a million times worse than hers. His cruel treatment of Mum and my growing awareness and maturity allowed me to see him as a twisted, vain man, intent only on his own pleasures. This in turn allowed me to vow to only speak to him when I absolutely had to. It was a vow I had absolutely no trouble keeping.

6

Mother and her demons

Philip is in the cupboard again. He'd been afraid of the hairy monster of a spider that might come up from the bowels of the bowl and eat him as he sat on it and so he didn't use the toilet before he went to bed. I had learnt quickly to use the loo just before bedtime, and I have tried to get him to do this too, but he has been threatened so often with that spider and other creatures, not to mention the devil and his bogeyman friend, that now he raises the toilet seat carefully, peering into it all the while as he does so. Sometimes just this action causes his stress levels to fly so high that he wets his pants before he can lift the lid high enough to use the toilet. Other times there will be a resounding crash as he drops the lid and flees up the loft ladder to the safety of his room without relief. I have tried to help him, really I have, and I don't always understand the boys' inability to control this part of their lives.

So Philip is in the cupboard again, because he slipped out of bed in the night and did a poo in the wardrobe. I knew he sometimes overcame his fear and managed to get to the bathroom across the hall, even though it meant coming down the creaking loft ladder, but one time when he did it, he didn't flush for fear of waking her, and we all got strangled for it the next day, because none of us would own up to doing it.

Having considered his options – the spider in the loo waiting
to eat his genitals, a severe hiding combined with a strangling
from our mother, even death as she had often threatened – he
had chosen to do a poo in the wardrobe as he was just too
scared to get out of his room.

Later that night, I had been in bed and could hear my
mother screaming.

'I will kill you, you bastards. I will choke you to death . . .
squeeze every last breath out of you.'

She was in the loft and I thought she was strangling Philip,
for I could hear Gordon saying, 'No more, please Mummy.'

He was rewarded by a string of foul-mouthed abuse, but at
least she'd moved away from Philip and I heard Gordon
running round the room to escape her, screaming all the while
as he did, 'No, Mummy. Please, no! Please, not again.'

As I listened to his distressed screams, I felt the anger
building in me. It was a strange emotion, because I am more
likely to feel only fear. Now this anger was building,
building, and I began to float. I remembered Jenny, Liz,
the little ones, and the surge I felt at the school, but never
this feeling, never anything this powerful. The emotion
frothed and bubbled before bursting out, and I wanted to
run to my brother, to attack the monster who puts us
through this miserable life. Even as I had this thought, I
heard Jessica's voice saying, 'And about time too!' Jessica
and Susan are frightened alters, but Jess is bolshy enough to
show flashes of anger. Although I didn't act on my anger
that time, I knew I had a new ally in my fight in the shape of
this dark-haired, brown-eyed child.

I had begun to develop other obsessions. These had started
when I began to practise writing first with my feet, then with
my teeth. Now I began to count, I think in part so that when

we were in the car and Dad gave us one of his arithmetic quizzes, I would be proficient, but it was mostly because if I was busy figuring something out, I wouldn't have to listen to Jenny or any of my other alters crying about what was still happening to them. I wouldn't have to focus on the fear they constantly felt, no matter what the situation was. Whenever Jenny saw a man, she'd begin to shriek. Jessie and Susan would begin moaning and crying whenever any of my distressed siblings were nearby. These two alters sat exactly how I did when I was incarcerated in the under-stairs cupboard. However, as they tended to be around when my siblings were locked in the cupboard, I imagine they'd arrived to help me with the enormous distress I felt when I heard my brothers or sister screaming. Their mirrored sitting position made me suppose that, as they seemed to be there for them, that was how the others sat too. Liz would be trying to shush them all while trying to hide the image of the blackness inside the cupboard from me, but I sensed her doing it anyway, and the tiny babies would just cry, cry, cry. It was simply an interminable cacophony inside my head and I had to concentrate on something so it could be pushed into the background. So I began to count.

I counted windows in the buildings I went past, flowers on a bush, lines in a curtain, lamp standards as we drove by – anything and everything. Then I increased the difficulty and had to find objects or things or groups of people, numbers, which were divisible by five . . . or twelve. It was difficult to stop and very frightening at times. I developed a problem with the number nine. In my mind it was the number of death, as in the emergency telephone number, 999. Therefore, if I was left with the number nine, or the numbers I'd reached could add up to nine, I had to find at least one more of whatever. There were days when I verged on sheer panic because I couldn't find that next one.

Another thing that began to happen was that things pulsated. Colours would fluctuate – red, green, red, green. Objects, including my own hands and feet, would get bigger, smaller, bigger, smaller. Even my own body began to change as I moved from alter to alter: as they were different ages, they were also different sizes – baby, toddler, child; big, small, big, small. Sometimes I would be big and small at the same time!

Even when Mum was being nice, she had this amazing ability to demolish her own goodness. She was an excellent dressmaker and made most of our clothes, which were often very pretty. She made dresses for both of us girls – each dress was made of the same white material that had yellow and white embroidered daisies all over it. One evening, when I had been sent to bed at six as usual, she suddenly burst in and dragged me from under the covers.

'What are you doing f**king sleeping? I've been f**king slaving over this dress but you are too f**king ugly to look nice in it. I hate you. I really do and I don't know why I bother to try and make you look f**king nice. Now get up and put it on. Put it ON!'

I got out of bed and put the dress on and she said, 'Come on then. Come on!'

We slipped out of the house and walked to a neighbour's house across the road to show her how lovely I looked and – of course – for the neighbour to see how clever Mum was.

The next day, she bought us girls white socks, gloves and hats and we were taken out for walks in these clothes for all to see what a lovely middle-class family we were.

Mum liked dressing well too, and often made her clothes in the latest fashions. Even so she was always very critical of her appearance. She seemed to like herself even less than she liked us.

'Just look at me. I look ridiculous. I'm too fat.' Another time she'd be too thin. Her bust was too flat, her arse too big. To me she was just ordinary – tall but ordinary, and I couldn't understand why she was always extreme when she spoke about herself.

When I was thirteen years old, Dad got a new job as the international manager for a large company, and it was clear we would have to move again. Our new home would still be in Surrey, about forty miles south of the old one and, as befitted Dad's increasing status, we would be living in another brand-new building. Our other home was put on the market and was quickly sold but, as the new house was not yet ready, we moved to Essex for a few months.

Finally the house was almost ready and we moved into it at the end of the year. This one had five bedrooms to accommodate the five of us and our parents, and it was completely detached. There were little jobs left to be done – the wooden floor downstairs was not finished, for instance – but the house was a dream. That was the only thing that was perfect, though.

The house backed on to fields to which I often escaped when the stress became too much to bear. It had an open-plan living-cum-dining room with wooden floors, big windows and underfloor heating, and there was a French door on to the patio. In the dining room was a huge glass table with metal chairs, and occasionally we made marks on the table for which we would be severely punished. It was the same if we got marks on any of the tiled floors. The stairs, landing and bedrooms had a white carpet that we were not allowed to get dirty: an almost impossible feat for five children. The bathroom was white with black tiles, and since any watermarks on those tiles tended to make them look grubby and the whole house had to look highly polished, we would be punished for leaving watermarks on these tiles. As a result we children tried to ensure that the sink, bath and anything else that got water droplets on it were dried properly, so that there would be no water stains for her to find. Again, in this new house, I had my own room, which was next door to Mummy's and Daddy's bedroom.

Perhaps it was the stress of moving house and Mum's need for order but from the first day we moved in, her temper was especially dreadful. Her rages were constant and uncontrollable and seemed different. Although she had frightened all of us before, at least we'd been able to find our feet and run to escape her. Now her aggression made us almost catatonic with fear. She was – to put it simply – completely volcanic, sitting quietly one second and then without any warning erupting with rage. She'd scream invective at us, throwing things like plates, knives, toys and food around the rooms and then at us. Now it needed nothing at all to provoke her – now she simply vented her fury. Then, having thrown food around, she'd act even crazier because the house was dirty.

Other times it was a gradual build-up, but even this was different from anything we'd seen before. She would start to twitch, her eyes would screw up, she would constantly clench then open her fists and her face would contort. She would sometimes start muttering under her breath before the eruption would come. I felt more in control with this gradual build-up as I thought I could keep myself and my siblings out of her way as much as possible. We would also be ready for the explosion, but I was getting more worried because I didn't know where all this was leading. Would she lose it so much that she could do one or other of us serious harm? Would it get worse as she got older? How soon could we leave home?

I lived in constant dread of her. I was always waiting for something terrible to happen. Sometimes I would talk to my alters about it – telling them it was okay, that nothing was going to happen and generally preparing them for the rage to come. I suppose I was really just trying to prepare and convince myself.

The rages became more and more frequent – it seemed there was never a break from it all. Her obsessions about the house and cleanliness knew no bounds. Nothing could be out of place. No fluff was allowed anywhere, not even on the carpets. We could never keep it tidy enough for her so more violence followed. She would punch us at random, it seemed, as we had done nothing to incur her wrath.

Of course when we were out of the house, Mum would control her monsters, put on her posh voice and tell all who would listen that we were lovely children and really clever. It seemed important for us to be clever.

Despite her apparent ability to disguise her behaviour in public, it was becoming clear even to me that Mum needed help. One day, after a particularly violent altercation with Dad that ended with him having to restrain her after she began to pound him with her fists, he said, 'Bloody hell! You're f**king strong, aren't you? You'll do yourself damage one of these days. I'm taking you down to the doctor's.'

'No you're not, you bastard. I'll kill you first! I'll rip your ****s off.'

He laughed but managed to look worried at the same time and he twisted himself away from her. It took a few more days of nagging her, before Mum calmly announced that she thought she should see a doctor. After that she seemed to calm down a little. She and Dad talked about medication and schizophrenia and I understood that she was sick and needed to take her medicine to help her stay in control. In some ways this was a relief. Having an explanation made her anger seem less monstrous. But it didn't take away the fact that we still had no way to predict her moods or to control them.

It still seems baffling to me that the doctor did nothing to protect us children, beyond prescribing medication for my mother. He was supposed to be responsible for our physical health, yet somehow did not fulfil that role. He was our family doctor for nine years. He saw our bruises and scars and he treated my mother for her depressions and her mental health problems. We must often have looked sad and frightened. Why didn't he put two and two together? In such a small neighbourhood, he must also have heard rumours about our home life.

It was while we lived here that we saw another major shift in my mother's behaviour, which both puzzled and relieved us – at least us older children, as the younger ones still had various of their crosses to bear. Part of the behavioural change was caused by the physical design of the house, which had no under-stairs cupboard, or indeed any other cupboards that were large enough to accommodate a child or two but small enough to terrify them. Imprisonment in cupboards therefore vanished from our lives.

Less explicable was the fact that my mother stopped strangling the three older children. Why? Had we become too big for this type of punishment? I was the eldest and the two following me were boys who were growing quickly. Was her medicine really helping her? I thought not because she wasn't much different with the little ones. Or perhaps there was some other reason why she'd eased up on us.

We were also being allowed to use the toilet after bedtime had passed and, even though Philip was still not dry at night, she reacted with much less aggression than before. This might have been because our new home came with all the mod cons, and Philip always cleaned up after himself, washing the soiled sheets in our new washing machine. It wasn't until years later when we heard of our mother's previous night job at the hotel that we understood how our new 'toilet freedom' at night had come about for, in these days, in this new town, she didn't have work outside the home and could therefore 'keep an eye on our activities'.

Also, to my astonishment, when George cried at night, I was allowed to go and comfort him. However, this apparent compassion for the baby did not lull me into a sense of thinking that Mummy was really becoming a kinder soul. There were too many other indications to the contrary.

Our new home amazed me with its modernity, but the pressure to deal with mother's obsession with cleanliness grew exponentially and drove us to distraction. She hated us walking on the carpets, though the upstairs of the house was carpeted throughout, as were some of the rooms downstairs.

'Can't you be lighter on your feet, you clumsy idiot? You're digging your heels in. Look at the dents you're leaving in the carpet.'

I looked down, but whatever indentation was there could only be seen by her eagle eyes. Even sitting was problematic.

'Get your arms off the armrest,' she ordered one day as I sat in an armchair. 'You're making a mess of it. And for heaven's sake, sit up straight. There is absolutely no need for your back to touch the back of the chair.'

I sat up ramrod straight, and kept my arms in my lap. It was an uncomfortable posture, as I had crossed my legs when I sat down and was fearful of moving my feet and attracting her attention to them. However, she was already proceeding.

'Are you stupid or something? Uncross your legs! Can't you see that the extra weight on the one leg is putting dents in my new carpet? Uncross them now, or I'll thump you.'

I hastily uncrossed my legs as she advanced upon me and shoved a clenched fist into my face. I involuntarily closed my eyes and waited for the blow that never came. Seconds later I was watching her back away from me with a sly look on her face.

The lessening of her actual physical abuse could be undone by any kind of repetitive noise. Clicking your fingers or making tapping noises tended to drive her over the edge, and it was a ploy my father used whenever he was home. He frequently visited the pub before coming home after a week's work and, from what he'd say, it was clear that he hated the atmosphere at home. Soon after he'd arrive, he would start tapping or something to annoy and stimulate an explosion from her. Whereupon he would begin a refrain that was to become a feature of our lives.

'You're mad! You're as mad as a hatter. What's the point of coming home to a mad woman. You're evil, mad and stupid!'

'I'm not so stupid that I don't know of the other women you have in your life!'

'Of course there are other women. Why not when you are so bloody mad?'

Occasionally he would spot me observing their exchanges and retort, 'And you're mad too. As mad as your mother! You'll turn out just like her. Mark my words!'

Despite his antagonism towards her, I became aware of my mother's hold over my father and realised that, whatever she wanted, he provided. This was a complete reversal of our early days living with him and eventually led to her virtually holding the purse strings. An uncle who had often spent time in my body one day confidentially explained to me that Mummy was blackmailing Daddy.

There were other changes in my life too. I was being required less often to satisfy the lusts of my father, other relatives and Daddy's friends; indeed I had not been taken to any other houses for a long time. I remember the last time it happened. A friend of my father's who used to wear a dark suit came to the house to have sex with me. He was a podgy man who had brown hair, which had been plastered down on his head, and he had a parting somewhere between the middle and the side of his head. By the time of this assault I was so used to it that it really didn't matter to me. It was just sex. I had been so brutalised by years of horror that I had long ago given up on the idea of there being any other way to live. It wasn't that I didn't hate what was happening to me, but my alters allowed me a way to cope with the pain and the fear and it had become totally normal. I couldn't know it then, but that was the last time it happened. My periods began soon after that, when I was around thirteen and a half years old, and I wondered if the abuse stopped because of that. Either they had fears of impregnating me or I had become too old for their perverted tastes. Incredibly, life moved on, and if there was chaos in the order, no outsiders could see it. When schools closed for the Christmas break that year, I resigned myself to two weeks of longing for school to restart so that I did not have to endure my parents all day. I would find any excuse I could to escape and I would go down to the high streets and local markets to watch people hurrying and scurrying about with the excitement of preparing for the approaching Christmas. I would find a place to sit and plan how I would celebrate Christmas if I had a choice. I chose presents for my siblings, and one for myself too. I could see in my mind's eye what foods I would buy: rosy red apples, plump pears and grapes by the bucketful. There would be nuts, and chocolate, a golden roasted turkey with the stuffing pouring out of it, roast potatoes, sprouts, peas – and for afters a wonderful trifle, as well as fizzy drinks by the gallon! I could see it so clearly as I daydreamed and smelt the wonderful scents coming out of the butcher's. Then I would return home to a completely different scene.

It was a surprising Christmas Day, as we gazed at the large boxes round the Christmas tree. After a year in which they had demonstrated an extraordinary dearth of human kindness, they had bought a television for each of us. They were first displayed, as usual, to the friends who visited, for my parents did everything they could to emphasise their middle-class status. It seemed so important to them to be seen as better than the rest. As the eldest I got my box first and we all cried out in amazement when, as I opened it, we saw the television. Each child's room would have a television, something unheard of in those days, but we were not complaining, as our parents' one-upmanship always resulted in us receiving outrageously expensive gifts at Christmas.

Sadly it was also no surprise that by the end of the day, each TV had been smashed. I could never understand why my father allowed Mum to spend so much money and then stand by while she smashed everything up.

I don't even recall what set her off, only that our televisions were broken before we'd even had the chance to use them for the first time. She liked to throw knives, food – anything that she could get her hands on; and then she'd go berserk because the floor was a mess. She would threaten me with her fist in my face saying, 'I will bloody kill you', but she never followed through. It might have been because I was growing up fast, even though I was still a pushover for her, and it's possible that she thought that one day I might snap and react. It is highly likely that she was still taking her medication at this time and was more able to control any violent physical reactions, although her verbal attacks had not improved at all. Mum didn't seem to like taking her medicines, or perhaps sometimes she simply forgot to do so: we always knew when she'd lapsed because her rages became more frequent. Then another quarrel between my parents alerted me to another possibility.

Mum had been very strange that day. She was grumbling and moaning under her breath for hours. If she'd been a baby I would have described it as 'grizzling'. When Dad came home and found that she hadn't prepared his evening meal, he ordered her into the kitchen. Instead she continued to make the strange noise. Dad walked over to where she usually kept the drugs in the kitchen cabinet and looked at them.

'Are you taking this stuff?' he shouted at her as he checked pills and held dark bottles of syrupy liquid up to the light to check their levels. 'This one is empty. You need more.'

Mum grizzled some more.

Dad checked more bottles. 'You know what I think? I think this rubbish isn't doing you any good. You need stronger stuff, because you're getting stranger every day!' With that he stalked out of the house, no doubt to get himself something to eat somewhere.

My father was right. Even I could see that something was changing in the intensity and oddness of Mummy's behaviour. She *was* becoming madder, and this necessitated many visits to the doctor's, with varying results.

Things continued to deteriorate in our home as Mummy's behaviour became more bizarre over the next several months. That summer she took to nudity, spending all her time wandering around the house naked. She particularly liked walking past, or standing in front of the big picture window that overlooked the street. After a few days of this, someone called the police, who came round to the house and told her that her behaviour was offending the neighbours.

She responded by saying, 'I can bloody do what I like in my own home.'

She was cautioned and the police went away.

Soon after that she began to sunbathe, again naked, in the back garden. Her favourite days for this activity was on refuse collection days, and when the dustmen appeared round the back for the bins, she would strut around suggestively for their benefit, while laughing seductively. Occasionally I would walk into the house from school to hear her screaming at the baby, 'Everyone! Everyone wants my body. Except the bastard that's your father. He gave me five children, now he doesn't want me any more. But look at me. Just look at me. I have a firm, beautiful, youthful body. Everybody wants it!'

Beyond their concern about my mother's increasingly strange behaviour, I was sure the neighbours must know that we were being abused, but I believe they said nothing for several reasons. Fear. Fear of getting involved, of what might happen to them, and what they might have to do. They were probably also a little afraid of my mother – having seen first-hand her eccentricities – as well. Perhaps another reason for their inaction had to do with where we lived. The neighbourhood was middle class. The houses backed onto open countryside and a golf course was within walking distance. The houses were new buildings and were quite large and most of the occupants were about the same age as my parents and had children. It was almost as though there was a collective thought process: *Our neighbours can't be involved in scandal because these things only happen in working-class areas, don't they? If abuse is going on in our neighbourhood, what does that say about us and about where we are living? How can we tell the police or anyone else? What will people then say about us? And what might the other neighbours think of us for not 'minding our own business'?*

I should have enjoyed gaining respite from the madness at school. Yet, generally speaking, I do not always remember my schooldays fondly. I was at secondary school one day, playing hockey when I got hit in the face with a hockey stick. I saw stars and my nose bled profusely. What frightened me most was the feeling of dizziness and I thought I would faint. I hated this feeling. I felt the same as when terrible things were happening to me at home, or when I was being sexually abused. I just panicked and started running off the hockey pitch. The teacher in charge was furious with me.

'Hey you! Dee! Stop that caterwauling right now! Stop it I say! And you have no right to be galloping around like this and making a fuss over nothing. Here, let me see that!'

She grabbed my head in a manner that reminded me of my mother as she inspected the damage. There was lots of blood, and one boy who had run up to see the spectacle, fainted.

'Oh for heaven's sake!' she said when she saw him collapse. Her annoyance with him and me was clear.

'And you,' she turned back to me, 'go away and wash up and stop making such a fuss. You're not a baby you know!'

I went to the changing rooms to wash and stop the nosebleed. No one was allowed to come with me and she didn't check on me. Eventually the bleeding stopped and I went back outside to join the lesson. She didn't ask how I was. So again I thought she must see something bad in me which meant she didn't have to be kind to me. I just deserved it.

I quickly learnt not to trust the teachers. I had noticed that when a child turned up to school with a visible bruise, one of them would ask, 'Oh dear, what on earth did you do to yourself?' They would be full of sympathy and kindness. However, when a teacher noticed a crop of bruises on me, she simply turned me around to check them. She might turn my head to inspect Mum's finger marks around my neck. She might open the buttons of my shirt to see the bruises on my chest, or to peer at those on my back. She would lift my skirt slightly. I fidgeted too much if she tried to lift it any higher, so she didn't, but she would inspect those on my legs. All the while her lips would be squeezed together tighter than a miser's purse strings, and I sensed that if I had any bruises in my pants, she knew they were there. When I found out that Gordon had had the same experience with his teachers, I knew that some of them knew we were being physically abused at least, and they didn't care. We weren't always nice children, and I, especially, could be a very bad girl.

There was only ever one teacher, Mr Moody, who seemed to realise that I had problems at home. He was my form teacher and stopped me once on my way out of school.

'Ruth! A word with you!' he called as I headed for the door. He then asked me if everything was okay at home and whether I got on with my mum and dad. I was trembling in my coat as I answered but he didn't seem to notice.

'No sir. Everything's fine' I said.

I appreciated that he asked me but I couldn't speak of what was happening at home.

However school wasn't all bad. To my great surprise their was one other nice teacher. Mr Davidson was a very kind man who spoke gently to me. He always told me things like 'I was a quiet girl who worked well' and so I did for him. Other times I would be over-excitable but he took it all in his stride. Because of his attention I found that I was clever and always got top marks in his subject, mathematics. I never feared that he would harm me. Sometimes I simply couldn't do the work but he never got cross with me and was always encouraging.

Sometimes he would say, 'You did this yesterday and you were fine', but I couldn't remember doing it.

'I don't understand why you're saying that. I can't do it.' Then a few days later I would be fine and work well. He never got cross with me. He just said, 'Get on and do it.'

As you can imagine, I found it all very confusing in those days.

Other days were complete blanks. I would remember leaving for school and returning to the house but not what happened in between. I soon got a reputation for being erratic. I was bright and then not bright. I was alert and then not alert. Although I never had any problems with my schoolmates, this did not endear me to them, especially when I was clever. I therefore tried not to be too clever.

Life went on. I took ballet classes, went horse riding, had elocution lessons and deportment classes to keep up the appearances my parents wished us to show to the outside world. I really enjoyed these activities and threw myself into them, becoming so good that I got several medals and rosettes, which I still have as a reminder of those few happy times.

One of the best things that happened to me was a friendship I made at a new secondary school I had now started. As usual I was nervous about going to unfamiliar places and it may have shown when I peered hesitantly round the door of the classroom I had been sent to. As I inched into the room, which was full of children but as yet had no teacher, several girls looked up. One of them smiled and I instinctively smiled back. She beckoned to me and I walked over to find a place next to her.

'Hi,' she said, 'I'm Heather. Are you new?'

Heather had shining, dark hair and deep brown eyes that seemed so merry that they twinkled at me. As she smiled, I noticed the white even teeth and instinctively thought that when I got home I must check mine out. She tended to reach out and touch as she spoke and I was entirely captivated by this.

Her friendliness and cheery smile were so attractive to me that I just knew she would be a friend for life . . . and she is. I found her to be a delightful chatty person and I opened up to her, but only up to a point. By the end of the day we were best friends.

'You must come round to our house,' she invited.

I accepted her invitation with alacrity, knowing that no one would be bothered about where I was. In these days of changes in our household, we older ones were granted many more freedoms regarding being out of the house. As long as we were back by bedtime, we could do as we wished.

Heather's mum and dad were wonderful to me when I visited. I found out that they were Salvation Army people and, although they were strict, there was also an easiness about them that I had never experienced in family life. It seems to me that I remember much more of the walks and bus trips I often went on with Heather, and how much pleasure I derived from being with someone who didn't scream, either in terror or in anger, than I recall of my time at the school.

Heather and I began to spend a lot of time together, though I tried to limit the times she visited my home, something that wasn't hard after her first visit introduced her to language from my mother that she had surely never heard in her own home. Despite that we remained firm friends. She and I would also spend break-time together. We generally met on the way to school. She lived at the other end of the village from me and we would both walk to the main street and meet in the middle.

Heather always had some pocket money and she would buy loads of sweets for us to share. We sat next to each other in class and spent a lot of our time giggling. She made me laugh. Whenever she was around, I was always laughing. I forgot the horrors of my life for a while and basked in her friendship and warmth.

Her sympathetic friendship contrasted starkly with that of another girl I had got friendly with. One day she came home with me after school and we arrived at the house to find Mum in 'fine form'. She was so abusive that Pauline understandably left and never had much to do with me again . . . not even at school.

So, the memories of my school years are very mixed, but on the whole I felt left out, disliked – mainly because I refused to believe that anyone could really *like* me – and odd.

7

The crash

My younger sister Mary was now aged seven and my mother's attention seemed to be turning more and more frequently towards her. Mary was her favourite target. Perhaps it was because she was still so small; I was nearly fourteen years old. She had got used to Mum telling her, 'F**k off you bitch' whenever she was around and simply shrugged it off. Then, one morning at school, she handed in her homework, and soon after the teacher opened it she gasped, 'Mary Dee, come here at once!'

Mary got up and gingerly walked to the teacher's desk, knowing that she was in some kind of trouble. When she reached her, the teacher showed her the pages. Mary was appalled to see scribbles all over her homework. My mother had scribbled notes such as, 'F**k off you bitch'. Then she found that her textbooks were similarly covered. There were also pages torn out of many of her books. Can you imagine little Mary trying to explain that to her teachers?

It was around this time that my mother's behaviour became so obvious that most if not all of the neighbours could not help but notice, and the gossips had more field days than I could count.

To my great consternation, she then began to cry a lot. For no apparent reason at all, she would cry piteously and begin to scream and rage. I didn't know what to do at all. She was not nearly so violent towards me at this stage. Sometimes I would arrive home to find her crying. One day I found her sitting at the top of the stairs, weeping as though her heart was breaking; despite my dislike and fear of her, I could not help but feel concerned.

'Is everything all right, Mummy?' I asked timidly.

'If it was, do you think I'd be sitting here crying?' She sounded so lost that I involuntarily reached out to touch her, which was a big mistake.

'What the hell do you think you're doing? Don't you dare touch me! Do you think that just because we're related that you can touch me like I'm your property? Get away from me before I knock you down the stairs. I'll kill you, you know. I'll kill you!'

Her face contorted with rage, her hands reached out for my throat. I wheeled round and, taking the stairs two at a time, ran out into the garden. I suspected I'd be relatively safe here. At least I hoped I'd be, because she is normally the 'perfect mother' when anyone can see us. It's only in the house that she's a monster . . . but she was so different, so strange, and I didn't think that the rules for public display were still the same.

Moments later, she did something that embarrassed me and made me feel ashamed for years. Afterwards, I couldn't even look the people who lived in our street in the face. Even today when I think of it, my body gets hot and red and I feel as if everyone is watching me, knowing full well why I am blushing.

It wasn't a particularly warm day, even though it was reasonably sunny. I could see her in the front room from the garden and my heart fell when she took all her clothes off.

Even though I'd become used to seeing her this way, I sighed, wondering whether she was going to parade in front of the window again and have the police visit. Instead, to my great horror, she flung open the front door and ran out into the street, ignoring the people who stared open-mouthed.

I could hear her shouting something as she ran up the street, then did a U-turn, running back. As she got closer I could hear her screaming, 'Rape me! Rape me! Come on you f**kers, RAPE me! Go on then, RAPE ME!'

Aghast, I stared as she wheeled round again, running up and down the street, inviting all-comers as she did. I wanted to run out to her with a blanket to cover her up and bring her back to the house, but I knew what would happen if I went near her, and I was terrified. I wanted neither her hands round my throat, nor for her to include me in her amazing offer.

I wanted to phone someone, but I could only think of Daddy, who was away working and wouldn't thank me for bothering him, even if I had a telephone number for him. I tried to think of someone else I could call, but balked at the idea of inviting my grandfather or any of the uncles, real or otherwise, to come to the house.

As I dithered, trying to make a decision one way or another, I became aware that I was alternately turning to the street, as though to run out and protect my mother and back to the house to get to the phone. In any event, no other action from me was needed, as she came quietly back to the house and carried on as though nothing had happened. When Dad got home the next day I told him what had happened and he took her to the doctor who prescribed some more medication for her. Unfortunately it didn't stop the crying or the outbursts, and life continued to be as chaotic as ever.

One day I returned home from school to find my father at home but not my mother. This was unusual as it was not the weekend. As I walked through the front door, he hurried out of the kitchen towards me.

'Your mother's been taken to the hospital. The doctor's still here. Mad as a hatter, she is. The neighbours said she was in the garden screaming her head off and called the police. They got an ambulance and called me to order me back here. I suppose they think I have to look after you lot! So where's the rest of you?'

'Gordon and Philip were making their own way home and I'd thought Mummy had collected Mary.' I wasn't sure where baby George was.

'Well she hasn't, so go and get them now. When you get back, get the dinner on. As soon as I've got rid of the doctor, I'm down to the pub for a while.'

I was surprised at how uncaring he seemed to be because, even though they were constantly fighting, I somehow thought that he would be concerned if the authorities stepped in. After all, who knows what she might have disclosed. With hindsight it's clear to me why he wasn't worried, for who would believe a woman who was known to be mad after her earlier escapades? If challenged, Dad could easily have convinced them that he was just a normal, caring husband, baffled as to how to cope with his sick wife.

Dad and I returned to the kitchen, where the doctor was scribbling something down on a piece of paper. A cup of tea was at his elbow. He wore very narrow glasses and peered over the top of them at us.

'She'll be taken good care of. She's a manic-depressive schizophrenic, as you know, and the section means that she'll have to stay in the psychiatric hospital for one month.' The doctor was focused on his writing again. All I could see was his brown suit and his thick silvery hair.

'A month! I reckon she needs more treatment than that. She's been going bonkers for years!' Dad leaned against some cupboards and crossed his legs at the ankles. He stared at the doctor.

The doctor's eyes moved up to look over his glasses. I could see that his mouth had turned down. 'If she needs further treatment, she can be re-sectioned, for as long as a year.'

'With my bloody luck, she'll be back in a month.'

In fact, she would spend over a year away, living first in a psychiatric hospital, then in another one run by nuns after she suffered a severe slipped disc and had to be put into traction.

I experienced such a mixture of emotions at learning of Mum's hospitalisation that my head spun with them. I was in complete shock at this turn of events. It had all happened so suddenly. I knew she was not right, but I never thought they would take her away.

When the initial shock wore off, it was replaced by pity. Whatever she was, she was also my mother, and she seemed so helpless with everyone controlling her. It really brought home to me that she had an illness and probably couldn't help being what she was. Pity was quickly replaced by intense relief that she was going to be kept away from us for a while. Perhaps now the physical and verbal abuse would stop. It would certainly be seriously reduced because Dad was out working so much.

Thinking of Dad made me frightened. I had seen Mum's progression from being slightly mad to being incarcerated, and Dad had predicted her descent to madness. He'd also predicted mine. What lay ahead for me? How soon would it come? Would I be able to cope? Would I become horrible like

Mum and then be taken away? Why was this happening to me? What did I do to deserve this? It would be better if I died before I had children to be horrid to. Perhaps I should die soon. Hot on the heels of that thought came the memory of my siblings. I couldn't die. They needed me.

Panic found room next among my emotions. How am I going to cope with four young children? I was not yet fourteen years old. What on earth was I going to do?

A day or two after my mother's admittance to the mental institution, my father took me with him to visit her. I honestly cannot remember whether any arrangements had been made for the other children to be cared for, or whether they were simply left alone at home. What stands out clearly in my memory of that particular day was my experience of the psychiatric hospital. We were admitted to the ward by a male nurse who opened the door for us. The room was huge, and had a line of beds along each of the two walls. Mummy lay on a strange-looking metal bed, clearly completely doped up to the eyeballs, even to my inexperienced eyes.

Although I visited her several times with my father, none of the younger ones ever did. I was never sure who, if anyone, took care of them whenever I was away at the hospital, and I never felt confident enough to ask my father what was happening to them.

One day we walked into the ward to see nurses suddenly running in through a door at the far end. There were two people on the floor and it took me only one second to realise that Mum was straddling someone with her back to us, screaming her head off. Shocked, I looked over to see my father taking the scene in, his mouth and his eyes wide open.

'You f**ker! I'll throttle you! I'll send you to the devil, your maker!' my mother screamed repeatedly.

Several nurses were trying to pull her off the man under her who was gurgling and writhing about. I caught a brief look at his face as he twisted and turned. His face was a deep shade of red, and purple veins snaked prominently above my mother's hands on his neck. A nurse managed to prise her hands away and the man took several loud, shuddering breaths.

Mum continued to shout and soon sent the nurse, who was trying to bend her arm behind her, flying. More nurses arrived; this time they were burly men and I felt a moment's panic that they would seriously harm Mum. It took six male staff to pull her off the rather scrawny-looking man, and I could see that some strands of his long stringy hair lay on the floor. Just then one of the female nurses plunged a syringe into my mother's backside, straight through the trousers she was wearing, and after a time, she grew quiet.

'I'm sorry, you can't visit now.' I hadn't even seen the nurse approach. As I looked at her I felt the tears prick my eyes.

'But she's hurt,' I began.

'No, she's fine. The injection she got will calm her down and she is probably half asleep already. You mustn't worry.'

Those were easy words for her to say, but I would not have wanted to see an animal in such distress, let alone my own mother. As the sadness swamped me, I heard my father ask, 'What was that all about anyway?'

'The man she attacked thinks he is Jesus. Your wife is sure he's the devil. It was just a little difference of opinion. All in a day's work.'

I heard my father's soft laugh as he laid his hand on my shoulder and turned for us to leave.

A little difference of opinion indeed . . . and what is it that makes Mum see the devil in everything and everyone? Will I grow to see him too? Why did Dad think this was funny? Mum needed to be helped, not manhandled and sedated. He is supposed to care for her. She is his wife. Why is he such a mean person? At that moment I truly hated him, more than anyone in this world. I renewed my vow never to speak with him unless I absolutely had to, and this began a firm and unbroken estrangement between us.

Sometime after this incident, they gave Mum a long course of electro-convulsive therapy (ECT), which left her completely unaware of anyone or anything. ECT caused irreparable harm to many people in the early 1960s. In those days they gave the treatment without anaesthetic and the electrodes were of course fitted to both sides of the head. Now the procedure is carried out under anaesthetic and on only one side; it still continues to horrify many people, but is seen by some psychiatrists to be effective for some people. It didn't work for Mum, who just sat and stared. After that, I hated going to the ward even more.

Despite my mother's hospitalisation, Daddy made no effort to find a carer for us. He was doing well at his firm and often travelled abroad for days at a time. He left me to look after four children – the oldest of whom was twelve, the youngest not quite one year old.

I found the strain of looking after them all very difficult but in many ways it was of course better that he wasn't there much himself. Whenever he *was* there, Dad was verbally aggressive to all of us, making remarks such as, 'You're as thick as two short planks' or 'You're mad, just like your mother.' I tried to be a real mother to my siblings and often cuddled them. I was as nice to them as I could be because that's what I had needed from my mother.

In school, except for my friendship with Heather, life was no better. I had a new maths teacher but for some reason I did not do as well as I did in my old school. The teachers seemed to have too many expectations of me and they often said that I was quite intelligent and could do well if only I would try harder. I hated their comments because they placed more pressures on me at a time when I had too many responsibilities. It seemed yet again that no matter what I did it wasn't enough.

However, I was never able to get away from their refrain. *Should do better at maths. Should be doing more. Should run faster at sports. Should. Should. Should.* Sometimes I would be overcome by anger and give them a rude response. They responded by reporting to my father that I was running wild and was disobedient. *He* would always respond to them politely and agreed that I should be punished, but other than call me a few choice names, he did nothing. He had more important matters to deal with.

Because I had full responsibility for caring for my young family, I was constantly late at school. I would be punished for this as well as for any other transgressions I committed. Whenever I was troublesome in school, I would be given a detention, but I often left without serving it as I had to get home. The teacher knew of my household responsibilities but couldn't care less, so when I needed to go I simply walked out. In those days, there was little that social services would do to help. The department did not exist or work in the same way as it does today and it became clear that I would have to cope as best I could. We would have been seen as a middle-class family with plenty of money anyway, so they showed no interest in our plight. So in addition to becoming a little mother of four at one fell swoop, I also had to deal with my education and the confusion that was growing ever greater in my head.

Early each morning, I would take George over to a neighbour so that she could look after him while I was away. Then I would take Mary and Philip to their schools before going on to my own school, which Gordon also attended.

Back home from school, I would cook, clean and do all that was necessary to make a home for us. I had learnt to bake little cakes and so on at school, and as Mum made excellent roasts and I often observed her when she wasn't looking, I found that I too could prepare roast dinners for the family. With the meat and potatoes cooked in this way, it didn't matter if the other vegetables were less than perfect. For the baby, I would mince up everything we had in the blender, or sometimes I would feed him baby food I'd bought. Breakfast for all of us, including the baby, was porridge made with evaporated milk, just as Mum made it. It was hard having to get everyone up for school and to get up early enough to see them all fed before we left home. I also got little help from my brothers, who saw it all as girls' work. They seemed determined to enjoy the freedom they were having now that Mum's yoke was removed. It was particularly difficult with Gordon, but sometimes Philip would feed baby George for me, as Mary was still young enough to need help with her preparation for school, though he drew the line at nappy changing.

More problematic was getting enough money from Dad for all our needs, for in addition to the household purchases, I had to have enough to give the younger ones for their school dinners. It seemed that I was constantly having to beg, but one day his excuses wore thin.

'Dad, please . . .'

'I said "no!" What do you think I am? Made of money?'

'But Dad, we haven't enough food for—'

'Look at me! Now tell me. Are my pockets a bottomless pit? No! No! No!'

'You f**king bastard!' I heard the words as though my mother was back in the house, but as I separated myself from the scene, I knew it was an alter. Her language was amazing and she had clearly been eavesdropping when Mum was in full flow.

I watched my enraged self as I told him a thing or two. I watched him as his mouth fell open and eventually closed, his eyes opening wide and his eyebrows lifting higher and higher. To my surprise, he put his hand in one of his bottomless pits and pulled out a sheaf of notes, which he extended to me. I took them and he turned and walked out without another word.

I slipped back into myself and stared at the notes, amazed. It was a lot of money and, as I was always careful, it lasted a long time. There would be more arguments with him about money, but they would be minor; after that incident, he always seemed to reach a point where he would seem to recognise something in me and simply hand it over.

It was strange, but after all the restrictions we'd suffered when Mum was at home, you'd think we'd run completely wild where cleanliness was concerned, but I found myself doing everything I could to keep the house spotless. It was almost as though I had taken on Mum's obsession and I wanted somehow to do at least this for her. I vacuumed, wiped down all surfaces including the walls, and found myself looking for the smallest marks to clean away . . . just like Mum.

One day, I had just finished cleaning the kitchen floor until it gleamed, and Gordon, who had been standing in the garden watching me, suddenly barged into the kitchen and trampled mud all over the wet floor before tramping out again.

I was aghast and started screaming at him, but he merely shrugged as he looked at me through narrowed eyes. Helpless before his gaze, I decided to ignore him and set about cleaning the floor again. It was spotless once more, looking really nice, when the back door opened and Gordon tramped in again. I rushed at him but he danced around me easily as he left muddy footprints all over before escaping back to the garden. I was almost in tears but I tried not to show it. Instead I locked the door and, knowing he couldn't get back in, I cleaned up again. I resolved not to let him in until the floor was dry.

Satisfied that my floor would be safe from his attention, I left the kitchen and turned my attentions to the lounge. Less than five minutes later, I noticed Gordon in the doorway, staring at me as I hoovered. Surprised, I switched off the machine and he walked away towards the kitchen. I followed him and couldn't believe my eyes. Somehow, he never told me how, he had managed to get into the kitchen. There was no broken glass and as far as I could see the door was still locked, and my floor was filthy!

'I'm not going to let you turn into Mum.' Gordon's eyes seemed to bore into mine, then I noticed his lip begin to tremble. He turned and walked out of the room and I could hear him going upstairs. Alone in the kitchen, the tears came into my eyes. I'd heard what he was saying. I cleaned up once more, knowing that he'd not be down again to make another mess. After that, I kept the house clean, but not with the fanaticism of my mother. My brother simply wanted his sister there, not his mother, and the idea that I was becoming her was completely appalling to me.

Sometimes my siblings would be so disobedient that my perceptions of some of my mother's domestic problems also underwent some adjustment. Instead of justly rebellious children, I simply saw them as wild things. They were used to a kind of discipline I could never employ myself. Mum would have simply regained order by saying, 'Stop that or I'll thump you!'

It was a major learning experience for me, and eventually things settled down. Because I felt that there was never anyone there for me, I wanted to be there for my brothers and sister. I needed to give them the care, the protection that should be a part of every child's life and was never part of ours. I wanted so much for them because I loved them and didn't want them to be as unhappy as I was. I was ashamed of my parents and what they did. I thought people would be able to see what was happening to me just by looking at me, so I hated being noticed, something that was difficult to achieve when some of my alters were angry or lively in school and drew attention to us.

Bedtime terrors also changed in their complexity. When I was younger it had been to do with sexual abuse. Now it was the fear of being alone at home and the burden of persuading my siblings to go to bed now we were no longer forced to our rooms at 6 p.m. The boys could now play outdoors with other children their age, and I would take George for a walk in his pushchair accompanied by Mary, who I decided was too young to play outside unsupervised and so I did not allow it.

We had all been terrified of our parents, and Mother ensured that her awful stories of the devil and the bogeyman stayed with us for many years. She often told us, 'You'll die in your sleep and go straight to hell', and it was just our bad luck that the house we lived in when there were no parents at home to at least give us some sense of security was built on land that previously held a prison with a gallows. All the houses on this bit of land were said to be haunted. This was made worse for us as our garage light had a mind of its own, switching itself on and off whenever it felt like it.

Add to this mix the sense of freedom from tyranny that my brothers and sister felt now that Mum was incarcerated and getting them to go to bed was be no easy task. To give us all a sense of safety, I locked the door between the room we used as a playroom and the living room, as the playroom had two glass walls and no curtains. In the dark it was easy to look out and see the devil and the bogeyman waiting. One night, Philip had been running around the house when he began to scream hysterically. I had been used to him yelling in play, but this was different. I immediately recognised the sound of terror. As one, Gordon and I rushed into the kitchen, where Philip continued to scream hysterically. It took both of us to hold him down and find out what happened. He had seen a man at the back door. As I comforted him, Gordon, who had just crept into his teens, switched on all the lights. Then, taking a torch, he went to the back door, opened it and stepped outside. After a while he returned. He had seen nothing, but since then I made sure that all external doors were kept locked, and the playroom door too.

All secure, the children wanted to stay up and watch TV, finding safety in numbers, I suppose. I soon realised that they also felt safe when they were actually in their beds. The problem was getting them from one safety to the other, and it was a nightly battle. I tried not to be too strict, as I soon found this caused them to dig their heels in – and anyway it was not who I wanted to be. So I learnt to negotiate. They could play for an extra hour if they then went to bed without fuss. After a

while, we learnt to respect each other's roles and problems
and it worked.

Taking care of George was a special challenge for me. He
had a strange habit of holding his breath. The first time he did
it I was terrified. He suddenly gasped, stopped breathing and
fell over. I rushed to him and picked him up. He was very pale
and his lips were beginning to look blue. I was terrified as I
thought he'd died. As I held him, I made a beeline for the
telephone. Just as I reached it, he started to breathe again, and
after a few moments he carried on as though nothing had
happened. He would do this fairly often and I learnt to accept
it as part of his everyday behaviour.

Often at night he wouldn't go to sleep. His cot was in
Mum and Dad's bedroom and I would take him out of it
and carry him to my bed. It occurred to me that it would
have been easier to lie on my parents' bed with him until he
fell asleep but I just couldn't do it. I didn't want to be in that
bed, which held so many awful memories. After he'd fallen
asleep, I would get up and take him back to his cot. If he
woke again, I would again take him to my bed, and these
nights were especially hard when we had to be at school the
next morning.

As time went by, my friend Heather saw something of the
problems I was having getting to school on time and asked her
mum what could be done to help me. Mrs Travis immediately
offered to help and would often take baby George to give the
neighbour a break. One day soon after, Mrs Travis visited and
very quickly picked up what was going on. She asked some of
her friends in the Salvation Army to come and help me with
my housekeeping duties, so I'd have more time for my school-
work, and two older women would come every couple of days
or so. It was all done on a completely voluntary basis and no

money changed hands. Indeed they impressed me greatly as they never asked for anything in return for their work.

I'm not sure whether this caused Dad some embarrassment, but he soon put a stop to it by getting us a live-in housekeeper called Miss Jackson. At first I resented her as I hadn't resented the help Mrs Travis had arranged. It was almost as though Dad was saying that I wasn't good enough to take care of the family. However, I soon discovered that she was a nice woman. She tried to impose her values and routines on us but – as by now we all had our own ideas about what we wanted – she was not very successful.

Part of it had to do with the routines we had negotiated with each other, and I was touched to see that even if I stepped out of the negotiated deal sometimes to keep the peace, they would rather obey me than her. Even Gordon did, and that was for me an indication of the depth of feeling he had for me. It was simple things that seemed so important. For example, she believed that children would be much healthier if they ate nothing sugary so, rather than giving the baby his favourite shop-bought apple compote, she made it fresh and without sugar. George refused it.

'It's because it has no sugar. When I make it for him, I always put a little sugar in it,' I reasoned.

'Sugar is not good for small children,' she insisted, trying George with the spoon again. He refused it.

'Just a little sugar,' I continued, half amused. 'Half a spoonful.'

After a while George began to cry. He was hungry but wasn't about to eat anything he thought didn't taste good. She gave in and he ate.

Another night, Gordon and Mary refused to go to bed. She ordered them to go. They dug their heels in. After a while, I intervened and they went obediently to bed.

'You're very mature for your age, aren't you? Very capable.'

I was nonplussed. No one had ever spoken to me like this before.

'What do you mean?'

'They listen to you. They obey you. They don't obey me and I'm the adult.'

'That's only because they are used to me.' I found myself having to console her when, to be truthful, I didn't think that was my job. I had enough responsibility with my siblings and the youngest of my alters. So I didn't need this, but I did what I could.

The final straw came when one night she had a problem with Mary. I'm not entirely sure why, but Mary hit out, caught her hand in Miss Jackson's necklace and, as she pulled her hand away, the necklace broke. The beads spilled off it, ran down the central heating vents and disappeared. Miss Jackson was distraught and, realising that the necklace meant something special to her, I tried to retrieve the beads out of the vent, but they were gone.

The next morning was a Saturday so there was no school. When I got downstairs, she was sitting at the table having a cup of tea. I saw that she was packed and ready to go. Dad was on his travels but this didn't deter her.

'Are they still asleep?' she asked.

'I think so,' I replied. I hadn't looked in on them but I was usually first up.

She finished her tea, got up and washed the cup, which she put on the drainer. She picked up her bags and made for the door. I followed, not knowing what else to do. Her last words to me were, 'I don't know how you cope with them all.'

*   *   *

Mum began to show signs of recovery just before Christmas and the hospital authorities decided to let her make a short visit home to see how she would get on.

It was complete chaos for me. One part of me feared that she was on her way to coming back for good, and the other wanted to show her that I could keep the house and care for the family at least as well as she could. I was rushing about like a mad thing trying to make sure that everything was perfect.

I had no idea how long she would be home for, since Dad and I rarely spoke. He was hardly ever at the house, anyway, and we never knew when to expect him; sometimes he would appear for just a few hours before heading off again. If he needed something done, he would usually leave a note where I could find it. I generally did not respond to the notes, but rather to the orders in them, and whatever he wanted was done and ready for him whenever he returned. But this day he spoke. All he said was, 'Your mother's coming home on Saturday. Make everything nice for her.'

His manner angered me. First because of the implication that I wasn't keeping the house nicely, and secondly because he volunteered no more, thinking it would force me to respond to him. I did not, and he turned on his heels and strode out of the house. So I stewed in my ignorance of the facts, and simply got on with the business of preparing for her.

'Gordon, Philip and Mary, you have to help me get everything ready for Mum.' I gathered the younger ones around me. Even young George seemed to be listening to me.

'Why?' Gordon asked. 'She's not here!'

'Hip, hip, hooray!' That was Mary, who was probably the most relieved of us that Mum was away as she'd been so much of a target in the days before Mum's collapse.

'She's coming home . . .' Before I could say any more, pandemonium broke out.

'S**t, s**t, and bugger.' Gordon's arms windmilled as he stamped around the room.

'She's c-c-coming home?' Philip developed a momentary stutter.

'F**k, bitch, no.' Mary looked terrified as she said this.

As she was closest to me, I pulled her in my arms and we clung together for a moment. Then, realising my parental responsibilities, I said to her, 'Mary you mustn't use those words.'

'Why not?'

'They're not nice.'

'Why?'

'They make you sound like Mummy.' Gordon and Philip were watching us closely, and Philip spoke up before I could think of an answer for her.

Mary stared with widening eyes, at each of us in turn. Then she said an explosive, 'Oh f**k!' before pushing her way out of my arms and running out of the room. Before any of us could react to this, she ran back in, startling me.

'Is that for real?' she asked.

I felt so sad for her. She needed to get things out of her system and she only knew one way – Mum's way. I smiled sadly and nodded at her.

'Okay,' she said. 'No more bad words. I'm not like Mummy.' And she came back to me for another hug.

'When's she coming back?' Gordon brought us all back to the moment.

'On Saturday,' I replied.

'Sh-sh-she coming for good?' Philip's grammar failed him but none of us said anything. Mum was always a stickler for us making a good impression in everything, and his response would have earned him a clout if she'd been here.

'I don't know.'

'Oh bugger!' Gordon said again, then with a glance to Mary he added, 'Sorry.'

'We have to get the house looking just right . . .'

'And get her some nice food,' Philip added. 'When she has nice food, she's not always so bad.'

I had never noticed this before, and it suddenly hit me that 'the babies', as I often thought of them, were young people capable of making their own astute observations.

'So what have we got to do?'

Grateful for their acceptance that we had to pull together to give our mother a chance to show she had been cured, we planned our chores and timetable for action. George was too young to do anything much but even he toddled around, lugging what he could to tidy away.

On the day of her arrival, everything in the house was spotless. Mum was brought back in an ambulance and two nurses, one a man, escorted her into the house.

'She's had her medication, but if you have any problem, just ring this number. Someone will be here straight away with the necessary and we'll take her back.' The male nurse spoke to Dad.

'The *necessary*? What necessary?' Dad looked alarmed.

'Oh just an injection to calm her down. We don't think she'll be a problem because she got a hefty dose before we left the hospital, but sometimes with a change of environment . . .'

'Righto!' Dad replied, taking the piece of paper with a telephone number on it. 'You'd better sit her down here.' He pointed to her favourite armchair.

After Mum was settled, the female nurse looked at us and gave us a chirpy smile.

'I bet you're glad to see your mum again.'

Dad escorted them back to the front door and waved them off. When he came back into the lounge, he said, 'Have you said "hello" to your mother?'

We dutifully turned to her. She had not said a word. Had not even acknowledged our presence. 'Hello Mummy,' we all chorused.

Her eyes focused and she slowly looked at us one after the other. After what seemed like a long time, she dredged up the energy to say, 'Hello.' Just that one word and the vague look of awareness left her eyes again.

She did not speak again, and we spent the rest of the day tiptoeing round her; after she left, the others showed both their exhaustion and relief by obediently trooping off to bed. As I tucked Mary in, she threw her arms round me and said, 'Mummy didn't hit me today. She didn't even shout.'

I hid my face in her hair, feeling the top of my nose burn with threatened tears. Somehow, I managed to blink those that came to my eyes away and, sniffing quickly, I moved back to face her.

'I guess she's getting better, baby. Wouldn't that be nice?'

'I'm not a baby. *George* is a baby.' She grinned at me cheekily and rolled over into her favourite sleeping position.

As this visit was deemed reasonably successful by the hospital, they took the decision to allow her home for Christmas Day. I found out she was coming back when, two weeks after her first visit, my father spoke to me again. 'Your mother is coming home for Christmas.'

I nodded and got on with what I was doing. I had no idea what her stay meant. Was she here for the whole of Christmas? When did her visit start? Christmas Eve? When did she leave? Boxing Day? Or would she be with us until the New

Year? Christmas was just five days away. Once again I got my siblings to help me, which they did with mixed feelings.

'Why is she coming back? She didn't seem to like her last visit.' Gordon sounded more practical than he probably felt.

'Yeah! She just sat there like a wet lettuce. It was boring. She just slept and we had to be so careful not to wake her up,' Philip added.

'I like her as a wet lettuce,' Mary chipped in. 'She's more quiet.'

'Not like a potato eh?' Gordon ruffled her hair.

'They can be noisy, especially when you fry them . . .'

I left them to their teasing and walked into the kitchen, thinking about what lay ahead. My role as the woman of the house continued and I prepared the rota for all of the household tasks we needed to do in preparation for her visit.

Christmas Eve came and went and the only addition to our household was the huge turkey Dad brought home. As Christmas Day dawned, I got up early to prepare the stuffing for the turkey. I had spent most of the previous evening looking up things like cooking times and so on, to ensure the turkey would be perfectly done. I managed to surpass myself in the kitchen and our traditional Christmas dinner was in its last stages of preparation when Mum arrived home with Dad, who had been allowed to collect her. For some reason, she sat in the car while Dad came into the house. He took me aside and, as he stuck a forefinger in front of my face, he said, 'Now make sure everything goes well today. I don't want any of her f**king tantrums before she goes back this evening.'

He walked off and I saw him gather the other children together and speak with them, but I wasn't interested in whatever instruction he was giving them. She was only here for the day! The relief struck me like a sledgehammer and I almost swooned with the delight of it. She's going back tonight! I would be able to give the little gifts I had managed to buy to my brothers and sister after she'd gone. This would be one Christmas when our things wouldn't be smashed or thrown out of the window. We only had to endure one day!

'Ruth!' Dad shouted at me, and I noticed that he had the others standing like little soldiers by the front door. It was clear that I had to join them. Dad gave me one long, assessing look, opened the door and walked down the path to the car. He took some packages from the back seat, and I watched as he opened Mum's door, helped her out and gallantly held out his free arm to her. Even to us who knew better, this was a picture that seemed impressive: the caring husband bringing his sick wife home for Christmas, complete with her Christmas presents for her 'adored' children.

As she entered the house, Mary, Philip and Gordon gathered round her. George, in Gordon's arms, began to whimper, and Gordon bounced up and down gently to quieten him. He was, however, looking at Mum with an expression on his face that made me think he wanted to snarl at her. Mary and Philip were saying, 'Hello, Mummy,' and would each have taken one of her hands to lead her indoors, except that she folded them on her bosom and looked down at them with a slight frown on her face.

Dad led her to her favourite armchair and put her presents under the Christmas tree, which he and the boys had put up and decorated the night before. When he was near her, he looked as if he was walking on eggshells. Mum sat, looking all the world like the queen of the house, as the children gathered round her feet and paid her attention, as they'd been clearly instructed to do. That is, all except Gordon, who had put George between Mary and Philip, and who looked over at me with an ironic look.

I couldn't believe that she was getting so much attention. I knew that Dad had bullied the others with some threat or other, but still it hurt me. Dad never mentioned all my hard work in getting everything organised . . . and now *she* was here and we all had to act like she was our wonderful mother. I was feeling a mix of both jealousy and anger when Mum looked at me and said, 'The room looks nice.'

I had not said a word to her till then and in spite of my inner turmoil was desperately trying to think of something friendly to say to her. Her words disarmed me completely.

'Thanks, Mum. Happy Christmas,' I said, then something inside me made me ask, 'Are you better?'

'She's here, isn't she?' Dad was back with us. 'Is the food ready? I'm starving.' With an exaggeratedly polite bow, he waved me into the kitchen. It seemed he was trying to be on his best behaviour and, as I left the room, followed closely by Gordon, I heard Dad say, 'Well now, shall we get ready for our Christmas dinner?'

Gordon and I proudly took the food to the table while Dad organised getting everyone washed up for the meal. By the time Gordon and I carried the huge platter with the turkey on it to the table, everyone was sitting there waiting. Even George was sitting in his high chair.

I was happy to see the looks of delight and awe on the younger children's faces, but Mum just looked as if it was only what should be expected. Dad said not a word. He simply sharpened the carving knife against the sharpening steel and began to carve the turkey.

When it was all over and the table was cleared away, we were allowed to open our parcels. It is strange, but on that surreal day, the only gifts I remembered any of us getting were from Mum, probably because of her bizarre behaviour. While she was in the hospital she had knitted various scarves and mittens as part of her occupational therapy, and these were to be our Christmas presents.

'Open them! Open them!' she commanded us with an air of suppressed excitement.

Caught up in her enthusiasm, we did exactly that, ripping the garish paper off as quickly as we could.

They were awful! I stared at my gift, which looked as though it had been knitted in the dark with mismatched needles and various bits of wool. Up till then, Mum had been a great knitter. Normally she excelled in making clothing.

'Do you like them?' she asked us anxiously.

There was a quiet chorus of 'Yes, Mummy.'

I put my gift down and began to clear the table. Mary dutifully came over to help me, as that was one of the jobs she had taken over in Mum's absence. As she was walking carefully out of the room holding a few plates, Mum said, 'Mary! Do you like your present? Is it pretty?'

'Yes, Mummy.' Mary seemed startled but she replied politely. It was a miracle that she hadn't dropped the plates.

By the time the table was cleared, Mum was again saying, 'I knitted you some scarves and mittens. Did you see them? Do you like them?'

Surprised, I looked at her. *Is she being stupid or what*? A voice in my head clearly asked. *Please,* I begged silently. *Go away. I don't need you now. I have too much to do.* I could almost hear someone pout, and the chagrin in the voice when it answered told me that someone was cross with me. *Please yourself then*, and I was suddenly free once more to concentrate on my mother.

At first I wondered if her gifts to us were some sort of joke as they were so below her usual standards; soon, however, I realised that the terrible knitting was just another sign of how ill my mother was. By the end of the day it became clear that she had forgotten giving us her gifts. Her mind wasn't focusing.

'Do you like the scarves? Did I give them to you? Now where did I put them?'

Gordon scowled at her. 'You already gave them to us!' he replied.

Mum turned to him and said eagerly, 'Oh good! Did you like them? Aren't they pretty?'

After we left the dining room, and for the rest of that day, Mum simply sat in her armchair quietly, occasionally asking us if we liked her presents. She had become lethargic and characterless, a pale shadow of herself, as a result of the ECT and the medication she was now on. While it was good that she was not raving, and we all needed her to be calm, this empty shell seemed even more frightening to me. My father's predictions about my sanity haunted me every time I looked at my mother, who was so obviously mentally ill.

Later, when Dad had returned from taking her back to the hospital, Philip sidled over to him.

'When is Mummy coming home for good? Is she going to stay in the hospital forever?' he asked with an expression on his face that gave away his hopes.

Dad looked at him and laughed. 'I bet you'd like her to stay away for good, wouldn't you, sport?'

Philip's head was moving in a strange way, as though he wanted to nod and shake his head at the same time. Instead, he pulled his lips in together and looked worried. Dad laughed again. 'You and me both, sport. You and me both,' he said. At that moment, I suspected that neither he nor perhaps even the hospital authorities knew when Mum would be home for good, but that thought gave me little comfort.

On the first day of the spring term, Mrs Birch, the head teacher from the school, asked to see me in her office. I dutifully went there as requested. I knocked and, at her 'Come in!', put my head round the door.

'Mrs Birch?'

'Oh Miss Dee, come in.'

I entered warily. Something told me that there was some sort of problem and I watched her as she stood with her arms across her bosom. She looked at me critically and began without preamble.

'I have some news for you. You will not be coming back to this school after the end of next week. All of you, except the baby of course, will be attending boarding schools. It will do you all a lot of good. You'll have to mind your manners when you get there, because they will not stand for any contrariness from you.'

'But . . . what boarding schools? Who will go where?'

'The boys will go to one school and you and your sister to other schools. Don't worry. Your school and the boys' school are fairly close to each other, so you'll be able to visit your two brothers occasionally, but your sister will be at a school further away and you will not find visiting her so easy.'

'But—'

She cut me off, saying, 'I really don't know much more than that. Now run along. I've got a lot to organise.'

I walked out of her office in complete shock.

8

Growing good

Mum was apparently reacting quite well to treatment and she was temporarily released from the hospital to take us to the boarding schools with Dad. She immediately took us shopping at a large department store where she bought four of everything: four cases, four toothbrushes, four washbags and so on. I was worried about what would happen to George when we went to school but no one ever told me anything, and even years later Mum .claimed she didn't know where he went. I do recall that by the time I was in the sixth form at the grammar school I attended after boarding school, he was living at home with Mum and Dad.

As Mrs Birch, the head teacher from my last school had said, the boys' and my boarding school were not very far from each other, but I would sorely miss little Mary, whose school was a long way away. She was so small; it seemed dreadful that she should be separated from us. I never knew who chose our schools or why we were sent to different ones. I don't think the authorities were ever involved so it must have been my father, and he certainly didn't care about our feelings on the matter. Money and his own convenience were the only factors on his mind.

The boarding school I went to was a huge but lovely old-fashioned building with high ceilings. It was also cold. When we arrived, we were met by one of the teachers who welcomed us. She introduced me to a prefect who showed me around the common room, dormitories and so on. The dormitories were large and contained metal beds with wire springs and very thin mattresses. The girls' school took only 100 girls; the school the boys attended was about twice as big.

Then I had to be fitted with a school uniform. In the robing room, they told me to take off my blouse and, as I did so, everyone in the room gasped.

'Put your top back on, now!'

Surprised, I did as I was told. The headmistress, Mrs Clarkson, was called and she immediately began to interrogate me. 'Why aren't you wearing a bra?'

'I-I don't have any.'

'What? None?'

'No. I've never had any.'

'Oh dear!' she replied. Mrs Clarkson immediately made arrangements for my mother, who hadn't yet returned home, to take me to the nearest town to buy a bra. I discovered that I was a size 36C and for the first time in my life wore a bra. It either never occurred to Mum that I needed to start wearing a bra, bound up with her own inner demons as she was, or she'd noticed and simply didn't care. For my part, I never looked at myself in the mirror. I was also always ashamed of my body, so I tended to wear baggy clothing and so maybe my development had gone unnoticed. Anyway, my mother then made arrangements for my brassieres to be specially made, as hers were.

The Great Hall of the boarding school contained panels of beautiful dark wood. It had tall, church-like windows and an organ. Our desks had integral seats and each morning we would have assembly accompanied by the most wonderful organ music. The music was a revelation to me; it soothed me. My whole body seemed to be full of it.

Life at boarding school was very regimented and formal, as in most boarding schools in the country. This was fine with me, as I was used to very strict routines. Later on the rules were relaxed a bit and we would be allowed to meet up for social occasions at the boys' school, at special times in the schools' calendars. Sometimes we would even dine in a mixed environment and if one was careful, there would be some talking in class and in the dorms at night.

Before all this happened, though, I was caught talking one night and my bed was moved into the corridor. Although I was in my mid-teens, all my childhood fears of the dark came rushing back and, as I stared down the corridor, I could swear the devil was on his way to get me. I ducked under my cover and lay there, cowering and whimpering, until the light of dawn crept into the corridor.

During those first scary nights at school I got help from an unexpected quarter, though. A teenage alter came briefly to help me cope with the stress of having to sleep in a strange place and the worry I felt at being separated from my brothers and sister. Our home life had been horrendous, but at least it was familiar. The uncertainty of our new surroundings upset the younger alters, who wailed disconsolately, and this stimulated her arrival. But the fact that there was such a strict routine in place at the school made it easier for us all to get used to the situation, and the teenager's visit didn't last long.

Our day began when matron woke us up using a whistle and a bell. We were allowed some time to wash and get dressed, then at one minute before eight, the prefect on duty would blow the whistle, which meant that we had to be downstairs for inspection. We lined up and our uniforms, shoes and so on, would be checked. If everything was not absolutely perfect we'd get a punishment.

Punishments could be meted out for any reason – if your socks were not pulled up or your shoes were not cleaned. There were also washing-up punishments, which I was always having to do. One day I squirted washing-up liquid in the teapot so that when the prefects made their tea later it was spoilt. For that I was given more punishments to do, but they and their silly rules didn't matter to me. Usually I just laughed. One day I had to clean the prefects' common room, which I objected to doing. I took a large number of milk-bottle tops, strung them together and hung them up all round the room, laughing my head off as I did so. Although the headmistress punished me, she couldn't help smirking at the scene.

Another punishment would be that we had to get up at 6 a.m. to go for a run for one hour, regardless of the weather. I often had to run in pouring rain and the prefects seemed to enjoy watching us go through this – even though they had been punished in this way when they were younger.

Still, it could have been worse: I heard from my brothers that in the boys' school they used caning and even punching as punishments. Sometimes the female prefects hit us too but not very often. When one tried hitting me over the head, I turned to her with an expression of such rage that she immediately backed off. I never said anything. Just a look was enough. The word got around and none of them ever tried to physically intimidate me again.

The girls asked me about my background but I couldn't say anything. They accepted me, even though initially I must have appeared pretty unfriendly. It always took me a while to settle in somewhere new. At first I missed the friendships I had made at the previous school, and particularly Heather. I also had to go through my usual process of discovering who was trustworthy, which was always a nervous time for me. If I made friends with someone and later she found me a little odd, would she laugh at me? Tell the whole school and have them laugh at me? Might she begin to suspect the truth about what my life was like? It was only after I dealt with all these issues in my own mind that I could relax and truly have some fun. Additionally, there were eighteen girls in my year, and most had been together since they were very young. They were all very close and that increased my feelings of being an intruder, as always.

With regards to sport, I continued getting up early for what I called 'my freedom runs'. As a result, my level of fitness improved dramatically. When I won a race at the school sports day having run the entire 220 yards from in front, the second-placed girl was not very happy. I was especially proud of myself that day as my brothers and the boys from the other boarding school were there to watch. As I received the cup I was awarded, my brothers cheered and whistled their pride in me.

Then one star pupil stopped talking to me because I got higher marks in an exam than she did. My cleverness was not liked as usual; even so my teachers thought I could do better still: I was repeatedly told by them that I was not working to my potential and they gave me extra work to do.

I would spend two hours after tea doing the various preps, watched by one or other of the prefects. I hated it as I couldn't always remember what I was supposed to be doing. I could revise one day but by the next day not remember what I had learnt. Yet on other days I would do a task perfectly, without remembering having done any revision for it. I now know that my alters were helping me. It was fortunate but, if I wasn't 'present' in class, it was because another of me was, and that alter would take part in the lesson. My constituent parts had favourite subjects and would be present at those lessons. However, occasionally one of me would play truant and I would be left to flounder in that class.

There were funny times at school too. Marie and Vanessa were my new best friends and really seemed to like me. I, for my part, thought they were super. I was able to relax with them up to a point and I discovered that I had a sense of humour that they not only appreciated but matched. Having them around was just great, because they made me feel just like one of the others and with them I had a wonderful sense of normalcy. Although I loved Heather, she had met my family, and there was always the underlying fear that one day she would abandon me because of them. There was no such angst with Marie and Vanessa.

I remember the time they went with me into the staff dining room. There were a number of cream cakes on the table, leftovers from their tea, which had not yet been cleared away by kitchens. So we stole the cakes. We were at the bottom of the stairs going up when a prefect called Brenda called out our names.

'Dee, Warner and Harris! Gotcha! You're in for the high jump!'

Marie jumped guiltily and the cakes fell out of her sweater where she had tucked them. We couldn't help it. We all burst out laughing. Having been told we were in for the high jump, there she was, jumping as high as she could, losing our cakes. There was more punishment naturally. For mine, I had to copy a document written in Russian.

Another time, four of us decided we would have a midnight feast. A girl called Janice had joined our group. We were crawling along one of the dormitories in the pitch-black when the overhead lights snapped on and left me blinking as my eyes adjusted to the sudden brightness. Mrs Clarkson had found us.

'What on earth are you girls doing?'

'Um . . .'

'Ah . . .'

'Er . . .'

'I . . .'

Mrs Clarkson went on. 'What do you think you are doing? I've heard about your night-time prowling, stealing from the kitchen. Just look at you lot! What do you have there?'

Guiltily we showed her our haul. Tomatoes, lettuce, a bit of ham, some hard-boiled eggs, a biggish bottle of ready mixed squash, some pastries and a few other bits and pieces.

'Back to the kitchens. March!'

We hurried back to the kitchen and I could hear the sniggering becoming louder. I was struggling not to giggle myself and it was made worse when I looked at my friends and saw that they too were trying hard not to laugh.

'Put those items where they belong.'

Again we did as we were told.

'Now tell me. Do we starve you?'

'No, Mrs Clarkson.'

'Then you are just greedy!'

None of us said anything.

'Repeat after me. I am just greedy!'

A new voice in my head said, *and doesn't she just look it?* As Mrs Clarkson could not – by any standard – be described as sylph-like, the snort of laughter erupted from me, and the giggles were unleashed from Janice, Marie and Vanessa.

Mrs Clarkson looked at me balefully. 'That will be two hours outside my office on Sunday, Dee. Now, all of you, it is wrong to be out of bed after lights-out. So back to the dormitory.'

As we started back, she followed. 'What is the matter with you anyway? Have you worms that you need to eat so much? Perhaps you would all like a good worming to get rid of them.'

The giggling both out of and inside my head continued, even though I was trying to be serious.

'Roaming around at night shows a basic evil in you,' Mrs Clarkson continued. 'Night is the time for vampires and ghouls.' I waited to see if she would mention the devil, and what punishment my pals would get. 'It is also the time for loose women to be wandering about.'

Loose women? Wow! I wonder what a tight woman looks like. The new alter made this observation, and I grinned, despite myself. We had reached our beds and with a terse, 'Get in!', Mrs Clarkson watched us for a moment, then turned and – snapping off the lights as she went – disappeared from view.

'Loose women. That we are,' Marie sang out. 'All we need now is a fast, red car.'

We collapsed with laughter and spent the next hour or so discussing the events of the night so far. It was so much better than the midnight feast we'd planned!

The next night Mrs Clarkson came into the dormitory late. She woke us up and made us go to the girls' library, which was next door to her room. In the library she had laid out a large platter of Jacob's Cream Crackers.

'As you are so fond of eating, I have a treat for you,' she said.

There was no butter and nothing to drink. Our collective punishment for the night before was to eat them. The other three found it problematic, crying as they munched the dried crackers, but I've always liked to eat my crackers dry, and still do today, so it was no punishment for me. I laughed as I ate, infuriating Mrs Clarkson even further and garnering me more hours of punishment.

There was nothing they could do to me that could compare with what I had experienced since I was a baby. I was inured to these small, non-violent punishments. To me they were about as annoying as a dog barking in the distance. I had already noticed that crying increased my mother's abuse, and I suspected that the same would be true here, so I never cried and it really made them more angry. Laughing did, too, but I didn't care! And I soon found out that the new alter in my life, Alexis, was ready to lead me into more mischief than I would have been able to handle, if I had let her.

Sometimes I could hear the girls talking about sex and, with a boys' school so close by, rules would be broken. I never participated in these conversations. I felt ashamed, embarrassed and frightened by these chats. I had grown into an attractive teenager (according to my friends) and my once fair hair had darkened to a deep chestnut. When I gazed at myself in the mirror, eyes that were an unusual mixture of blue and green with brown flecks stared back at me. Very dark eyebrows arched protectively over them, curving to meet a straight nose. As a result, some of the boys showed an interest in me, wolf-whistling as I went by, and before long I had a boyfriend, Craig, who had been at the boys' school since he was seven years old. Craig was a handsome lad and I was immediately attracted to him, not so much because of his good looks, but because of the hurt I saw inside his eyes. His father had died when he was just six years old and his mother couldn't cope with him. To me it seemed that both his parents had abandoned him.

Marie had seen me looking speculatively at him and she said, 'Oh do you like him? 'Cos he fancies you something rotten.'

I laughed. 'How would you know that?'

'Oh, I think everyone at his school knows. Apparently he is always banging on about your "nice legs".'

This time she joined me when I laughed.

Linking arms with me, she sauntered over to him, carrying me along with her, though in fact I was going willingly.

'Hey Craig!' she said when we were close enough for conversation. 'Have you met Ruth? She's my best mate.'

And that's how Craig became my boyfriend. I had never felt any need to care deeply for someone other than my siblings, but I cared a little for Craig. He needed to be loved and nurtured and I was up to the job. He was also hungry for love, and for the brief moments we could snatch away from the teachers' eyes, when we could cuddle and kiss each other. I had a lot of love to give and the more I gave, the more he wanted.

My feelings for Craig were new and interesting for me. I loved being cuddled as much as he did. I was flattered that he fancied me and, as he was always telling me that I was beautiful, or that I had 'amazing' legs, I was also grateful for the boost he was giving my self-esteem.

I was also afraid of this relationship, though. Even the most innocent of the girls at my school knew what men wanted from women – and that worried me. Much as I loved kissing and cuddling Craig, and I had accepted the occasional exploratory fumbles he made, I had absolutely no interest in sex. Fortunately, he showed no interest in going any further. As long as he got his cuddles, he was happy.

Yet, I needed Craig for other reasons too. He wasn't the only boy who showed an interest in me, but I saw intent in the other boys' eyes that worried me. Having Craig with me meant that I was unavailable and so, unknown to him, he gave me much-needed protection, and for that I was grateful. I liked him a lot, I enjoyed our cuddles, but I did not love him and I loved that he didn't seem to be interested in sex. As with my girl friends, and in fact with everyone I'd ever met, I never told him about the abuse I experienced at home. It simply wasn't an option.

Having Craig around was like putting a plaster over the deep festering wound that was my self-esteem. He flattered me, but even as I felt good I could hear the voices.

He doesn't really know you . . . if he did, he wouldn't like you. You are a bad person. You're ugly. If he could see the bad in you . . . if he could see how ugly you truly are, he'd run a mile.

And . . .

Shhh! Don't ever let him know. If he knows how men use you he'll not want to know you any more. Look at him. He can't even be a man for himself. Do you think he can be a man for you? No way. He'll leave you as soon as he finds out.

My fear and distrust of men simply wasn't going away, despite my relationship with Craig. And, before long, I found more reasons to feel that my fear was justified.

It was the following year, when I was fifteen years old, that the music teacher came into the sports hall to talk with me. As it was one of our sports days I was simply wearing the navy knickers that we wore when we ran.

'Ruth Dee. Over here.'

I looked up at the sound of my name and saw Mrs Close beckoning to me. I trotted over to her.

'I've forgotten the keys to the lockers. They are at home. Would you get them for me please?'

This wasn't as weird as it sounded because her house was just across the road from the school.

I looked down at my bare legs and began to run off in the opposite direction.

'Hey! Where are you going?' she asked, looking puzzled.

'I need to get changed. I can't leave the grounds looking like this. I'll get into trouble.'

'Never you mind that. This is urgent. There's no time for you to change. Anyway, I'm sending you there so it's okay.'

Still I hesitated. Seeing this she added, 'My husband will open the door. Just ring the bell. And while you're over there, you can look in on the baby, after you've picked up the keys.'

I turned away from her, frowning. If it was so urgent that I couldn't even put some clothes on, how could I take time to admire the baby? Feeling somewhat apprehensive, I went over to the house and knocked on the door. Why couldn't she get her own keys? Her husband could let her in just as easily as he could let me in. I was worried because – after having lived the life I had – I tended to sense when someone was being evasive, and when that someone was an adult, it usually meant a close and disturbing encounter of the sexual type was looming.

Just as I thought this I felt the old anxieties well up and flood through me. Just as it threatened to overwhelm me, I heard my alter, Alexis, speak.

Get ready to rock and roll. I almost laughed. Alexis must have been listening to the radio. I felt myself squaring my shoulders as I rang the doorbell, though I couldn't really pinpoint why I was feeling this way; programmed as we were to obey teachers, I felt I had no alternative but to follow Mrs Close's instructions.

Mr Close answered it. He was a harmless-looking man and he oozed urbanity. He was dressed in navy tracksuit bottoms and a white T-shirt. He wore his hair scraped over the bald bits and his heavy black-framed glasses made him look somehow familiar. His nicotine-stained fingers showed that he was a chronic smoker and, when he smiled, he displayed yellowish-brown teeth that failed to hold his bad breath inside his mouth. His odour immediately brought back a vision from the past and Jenny, who was obviously monitoring everything, suddenly shrieked, *Run!*

Watch out! Be ready! Alexis was enjoying herself. She had never been sexually assaulted, but she knew what was about to happen and she wasn't going to take it lying down.

Or standing up . . . or any which way. She was responding to my thoughts.

'Well do come in. Come in.' Mr Close tilted his head and appeared to be looking down the street for his wife, or perhaps he was checking that no one saw me going into his house. 'Forgot her keys, has she? She'd forget her head if it wasn't screwed on.' He added this last at my nod.

'Want to see our new baby?' he asked as he opened the door wide and backed away to let me in.

'Mrs Close said I could,' I responded.

'Come on then. She's upstairs.' He led the way. As soon as I saw the stairs, I found my hands coming up in a combative stance like a boxer's and I had to force myself to drop them to my sides again. Even as the cacophony of my alters began, I obediently followed him up. Once on the first floor he opened a bedroom door for me to go in ahead of him. I thought it was the baby's room, but then saw it was the main bedroom. Quickly he grabbed my arm and pushed me on to a double bed as he pulled his tracksuit bottoms down.

'What are you doing? Who do you think you are?' I managed to scream at him as I fell backwards. He tried to climb on top of me. I was having none of this so I struggled and fought.

'If you don't get off me right now, I'm going to scream.'
Kick him where it hurts most! Go on! Kick him!
Don't let him hurt us!

'Oh come on. Don't be such a prima donna. It's not going to hurt.' Mr Close had stopped pressing forward but he still hadn't moved back.

'How dare you?' I was pushing as hard as I could against his chest.

There was a shift in his manner. He had become unsure, hesitant, as though he hadn't been expecting resistance. I pressed home what I thought of as my advantage.

'And if you don't stop right now, you'd better just kill me because I'll go to the police,' I continued. By now I'd managed to draw my knees up into such a position that he would probably have to break my legs to part them.

'Look. It won't hurt. And since the baby's been born she won't let me near her,' he wheedled.

'I don't care. Now get off me, and if I hear that you've hurt some other kid like you're trying to hurt me now, I'm going straight down to the police.' I was belligerent, bordering on the violently aggressive.

Suddenly he got up, pulled his trousers up and led me to the next room where he showed me the baby. He then gave me the keys and an orange! I couldn't believe it! I threw it at him with a force that only Alex could summon, and I smiled with pleasure when it knocked his glasses off. I tore downstairs and ran out of the house.

I realised that I was lucky. Mr Close was bigger, heavier and stronger than me, but he probably knew that he would have had to do me serious harm to get his way. At fifteen, I had already reached my full adult height and I was pretty strong. He'd clearly bitten off more than he could chew. I was also more bellicose than most young women my age as I had been free of sexual abuse for over two years and I wasn't about to let it start again. My days as a victim were over!

Too damned true! Alex laughed and the sudden ease I felt told me that all the alters had either left me again or they were content to move back into the background for now.

I walked up to the music teacher, whose brows knitted when she saw me.

'Is everything all right?' she asked as she opened her hand for me to drop the keys into it. It seemed to me that she knew what her husband was planning on doing. I didn't respond, but the look I gave her left her in no doubt as to what I thought about her.

I really had no intention of reporting him to anyone. Who would believe me? He was an adult and technically I was still a child, one who didn't trust adults. It was my word against his. Clearly he didn't like the idea of any sort of scandal. Perhaps he had a fear of sticking mud. I also blamed his wife for the incident. How could she set me up like this? What made her choose me? Was there something in my demeanour that attracted these kinds of people to me? There was something in his manner that puzzled me too. He'd expected me to just *accept* his attentions. Had he done this kind of thing before? How many other helpless girls had Mrs Close sent over to her husband? How many families destroy their and other people's children in this way? I hated this world; it was hard to think of it without feeling distressed.

Although I had no need to talk to an adult, I did have a need to talk to someone about this incident. I chose Craig because I thought he might understand somehow.

He had come over for the usual visit when I led him to a quiet corner in the grounds.

Even before I spoke, he seemed to sense that something was wrong.

'Ruth, you're shaking! What's the matter?'

His concern made me open up more quickly than I thought I would.

'Do you know Mrs Close?'

'Yeah. She takes music classes, doesn't she?'

'Yes she does. Well she . . .' I faltered to a stop.

'Go on. Don't keep me hanging.'

'On sports day, she sent me over to her house to pick up some keys.'

'What's so special about that?' Craig pulled a small sprig from a nearby bush and began to chew on it.

'Her husband was there and he tried to rape me . . .' The words came tumbling out and as I used the 'r' word, Craig's mouth fell open, the twig dropped out onto the ground and he simply stared at me for a moment. As I stared back at him, horror mounting in me, he got up and abruptly walked away. He simply stopped talking to me. I felt totally rejected by him.

See, I told you. As soon as you show anyone what a nasty, ugly person you are, they'll drop you like a stone.

Nobody likes you. Not really. How could they?

You don't deserve to be liked!

The voices of these alters were new and represented a hitherto unknown side to me. I had only heard them once before, not too long ago, and they terrified me. I thought of them as the horrid alters. They never showed themselves to me, but I heard them, and in hearing them a darkness and foreboding would fill me. Several hours later, I emerged from wherever I'd been to find myself preparing for bed. However, I was to have no peace. The alters, good and bad, were on the move, and I was switching between them almost constantly. My friends seemed puzzled by my behaviour, and it was soon known that Craig and I had problems. People began to ask what was happening between us and I avoided their questions. I was good at doing this.

Three long weeks later, Craig eventually ran up to me as I sat on the ground watching a football game that my brothers were playing in at their school .

'Hey!'

'Hi,' I replied and I waited to see what he had to say.

'I'm sorry. I couldn't help it. I couldn't believe what Mr Close had done. I couldn't take it in. It was hard. I had difficulty in taking it all in. I didn't know what to say to you. I'm really very sorry.'

'What! *You* found it hard? How do you think I felt about it?' I was furious. Having plucked up courage to tell him, I felt incredibly let down by his response. *My* feelings hardly seemed to come into it.

I saw his eyes open wide and he got up and hurried off. It was several days before I would acknowledge him again, but this was yet another emotionally painful incident that my alters helped me to cope with. Whichever of us had been hurt simply didn't come out any more when he was around. I, Ruth, decided that I had no problem with him. He couldn't handle it and that was just too bad. He couldn't think about my needs at all, just his own, and that was fine by me. I knew for sure now that I didn't *trust* him. He couldn't be there for me, and he, in the midst of all his selfish concerns – well, it never occurred to him that things had changed between us, but he'd learn.

From then on, my alters' constant chattering, crying, or whatever would produce such noise that when I was in class I could barely concentrate most of the time. We had all been more badly affected than I really wanted to admit by the attempted sexual assault, Mrs Close's role and the realisation that we were unlovable, as shown by Craig's reaction to me. For this period in my life I was thinking of suicide almost constantly. Sport was the only thing that seemed to focus my mind on something else.

At night every sound was too much. However, what really made me suffer was if there were loud outside noises as well, for example the pneumatic drill used in roadworks. The school was near a busy railway line and often we would hear the trains thundering past in the quiet of the night. One Sunday, they were doing some maintenance work on the track and the machine they were using intermittently made a low, droning noise. It woke my alters up and I was thrown back to the scenes of my father trying to annoy Mum with repetitive noises. Now they were working on me.

Drone, groan, drone, drone . . . the repetitive monotone was sending me crazy!

The next afternoon, the machine started again. As they never normally worked on the line on a weekday, I wasn't expecting this, and my alters were taken by surprise.

I'm scared!

You're no good.

You're going to die!
He's coming. Run!
Nobody likes you . . . Your boyfriend didn't . . .
Here's an orange. Here's an orange, orange, orange . . .
I swapped anxiety for fear. The horrid alters were back!
Drone, groan, drone, drone . . .

Things were getting unbearable and I could no longer cope with the pressure of maintaining a façade of normality. One day, I snapped.

I never saw Mr Boswell coming.

'Ruth? Hell-ooo. Perhaps you would like to join the class.' I started and looked around. From the looks on everyone's faces, I realised that Mr Boswell had been trying to get my attention for some time. He was also not at the front of the class but was standing beside my desk as he spoke, his face almost in mine. Even as I registered his face, I somehow imagined that he was the devil. I completely freaked and ran out of the class screaming.

Get rid of the badness.
Cut it out of you.
Rip your skin off!
Tear your insides out!

As I ran, the refrain followed me. I ran to escape them. I ran to escape madness. I ran to escape me! And as I ran from me, I could see myself running beside me, matching me step for step. I ran out into the grounds looking for a place to hide but could see nowhere safe.

Ruthie!
Liz, help me!
Rip your face open! As I ran, my hands went up to my face.
Rip your hair out! My hands moved to my hair.
Pull your guts out! My hands fell to my stomach.

Ruth! Come back! Push them out! Fight!
Alex, help me!
I'm trying. Push!
Yes, push!
I tried to push, tripped up and fell over.
Ha, ha, ha, ha, ha. A chorus of laughter broke out.
Leave her alone! That was Liz.
I'll kick you! That was Alexis.

'Go away! Now! I won't say it twice!' I spoke the words out loud, but they were not mine. Another stranger came to help. I felt her arms around me. Liz stroked my cheek, as she always does and, as I was falling into a deep sleep, I heard Alex say, 'Yeah!'

When I was next aware, I was standing in one of the toilet cubicles near the girls' dorm.

'I'm afraid. I'm afraid. I'm afraid.' I was weeping and repeating the words over and over. Yet something was different. I couldn't sense the horrid ones. I opened the toilet door and looked out into the washroom. No one was about and I became more agitated.

She shouldn't be here. Why is she here?
You're right. She should be somewhere else.
Why am I wandering around here?
Why?
Why?
Why?
Where should I be? Where do I have to go?
Somewhere else. I shouldn't be here.
Where's somewhere else? Where should I be?
Not here. Somewhere else is somewhere else.
And so it went on.
Then someone was there, holding my hand.

'Why are you here? What are you doing?'

'I don't know. Why am I here? What should I be doing? Where should I go?'

'You're missing your lessons. Why aren't you in class?'

The teacher took me back to the classroom.

During these days and weeks, I came as close as is possible to disintegrating into complete madness without crossing the line. I do not know how I would have managed if it hadn't been for my alters' caring concern, but I do know that, without them, I would have ended up in a hospital bed like my mother's.

That school year, the same thing happened several more times: I would 'wake up' to find myself feeling distressed and not where I was supposed to be. Teachers and students alike just put it down to my increasing eccentricity and I never really got into any trouble – but that was about to change.

One day I was in the dormitory washing my hair when I realised that there was something odd going on. We were only allowed to wash our hair on Saturdays and this was a weekday. What's more, I suspected that I should be in class. I certainly remembered walking into a class and I had no idea how I'd ended up here.

I was hurriedly drying my hair when Sandra Blowers ran up the stairs and dashed into the dorm.

'What are you doing here? I've been looking all over for you.'

'I—'

'You're in real trouble now. Potato Face is doing her nut!'

'Why?' I was stunned. Potato Face was the physical education teacher.

'You're supposed to be on the field playing hockey, remember?' Sandra sounded exasperated.

'Help!' I exclaimed explosively, knowing what that meant. I was captain of the hockey team, a role I was pleased to accept, and I had intended to lead by example. I had no explanation for anyone – I didn't know what was happening myself – but apparently I had not disappeared until after the last class that day.

I hurried out to the field where Potato Face glared at me and said, 'Well, it's about time. Now get on with it.'

Playing hockey was one of the occasions when I felt that I was me alone, and I quickly got into the swing of the game. I played centre forward and, by half-time, I had scored three goals. As we huddled together sucking bits of orange in the break, Potato Face told us, 'Well done!' Several times. In addition to my exploits, our goalie had been very successful in deflecting the other team's attempts to score. The second half was just as successful for me, and our side won easily.

In the afterglow and the celebration, we all got only praise and, as winning at sport was important to the school, I got my fair share of it. I was the heroine and my tardiness was never mentioned.

So my lateness didn't bother them, but it did bother me. How it bothered me! The hockey incident was particularly inexplicable as I loved the sport and would never deliberately not play. This strange behaviour simply added another entry to the column marked erratic and difficult. Even I began to think of myself as strange, because most of the time I did not remember going from one place to the other. How could I forget the match? All my father's threats came back to haunt me: when were they going to see that I was going mad and cart me off?

On free days I would wander off, sometimes setting off a full-scale search for me. Hours might pass before I got back to the school and I would have no idea what I had been doing during that time. Once I returned, irate teachers would accost me.

'Where were you?'

'What are you playing at?'

'Where have you been?'

'What have you been doing?'

'Why are you being so difficult?'

'What would your parents say?'

What would my parents say? That was a laugh. Of course my parents didn't care about me. On visits home, which amounted to just one afternoon a term, Dad and I almost never even acknowledged each other's presence, and I veered between feeling dislike and pity for Mum. Of course the youngest children were not so lucky, and it would be some time before they would leave home. But I cared about me. I wanted to know the answers to their questions. Why did I leave the school grounds? Where did I go? What did I do? This last question bothered me all my life and bothers me still. I was terrified of these gaps in my memory, in my life. What was happening to me?

I began to be more aware . . . to see even more of me. By now I had several regular alters in my life – Liz, Jenny and the two very young ones, Jill and Sarah, as well as Susan and Jessica and Alexis. Others came briefly and left again, like the horrid ones; often their stay was so brief that I wondered if I had dreamt them. I had grown quite fond of Alexis, even though she scared me sometimes. She was clearly me, except she wasn't me or, if she was, I'd be Dr Jekyll to her Mr Hyde. At first I didn't much like the look of her as she sat quietly, scowling at me every time I peeked at her. I sighed. So many of me sitting and standing all around – all in their own special places. I knew why all the others had come, but not this new one. I wasn't being abused in any way. I was holding my own when people tried to bully me. At this thought, I heard a puff of air coming from the angry one as I was beginning to think of her.

You? Holding your own? Pul-ease! Was that her? Or me thinking again? I peeked at her and this time I saw the sneer that accompanied another puff of air. She was laughing at me! In time, I learnt to laugh with her, as her sense of humour was lively.

Alexis was probably about thirteen years old. I had been ignoring her since she pierced my awareness, but she was insistent, demanding my attention by occasionally laughing at things I did. I never got the feeling that she was being cruel, just that she wanted my acknowledgement, as she wouldn't be going away any time soon. So I tried to focus on her and I took a really good look at her. Alexis is very like me in appearance at that age – tall, slim, athletic and energetic. She has deep chestnut hair and expressive eyes, over which are very dark, arching eyebrows. When she smiles, which is rare, she shows a moderate over-bite of the top two, middle front teeth. She was always finding something to be angry about and could be really bolshy at times. Whenever she was upset, she would throw her arms about, often making chopping movements with her hands to make her point. If anyone tried anything untoward with us, including Mum when she'd returned home from the hospital, she would tell us to get angry, to be difficult, to stand up for ourselves.

If Mum did or said something that annoyed her, she would argue, *She can't do that. Make her stop it.*

Often in school, when I had a problem, she would come to my attention screaming, *Why should we put up with this?*

What can they do to us? or *No, I'm not doing that. They can't speak to me like that!*

In those years, whenever I was bold enough to stand up to someone, it was largely Alexis doing it for me. Whatever fight I had inside me, she would bolster it with gusto. She was the one who egged on my natural rebelliousness. Because of her encouragement, I spent hours standing outside the headmistress's office in 'growing good' punishments, as Mrs Clarkson called them.

I was somewhat afraid of her because of her rages and aggressive reactions, and often I had to overrule her. I shudder to think what might have happened if I had done what she wanted me to do, especially when the person she was angry with was Mum.

I often tried to pretend the stranger alters (stranger in the sense that I didn't know them) were not there when they came. I even tried to ignore my old friends, because I was old enough to fully appreciate the implications of their presence. They weren't really there and this wasn't normal. I wished my friends away. I wished their noise away. I wished I could open a door and encourage them to walk through, and that they would disappear as I ran as fast and as far away as I could from the building. I would leave them there and never return! But of course I couldn't.

I tried to do some investigating, to find out from my schoolmates what was normal for them . . . what their own experiences were.

'Do you ever talk to yourself?'

'Sure. I used to do it all the time when I was younger.'

'Still do.' There was general laughter.

'What kinds of things do . . . did you talk about?'

Several faces turned to stare at me and I shrugged. Investigation over.

Instead I moved away as I began to hear the laughter in my head. It was Alexis again. When Alexis was angry she generally wanted to say the kind of thing that would not have been prudent for us to say. However, she was often right and she would argue that I should be more assertive more often. Even now, in 2008, she is creative and loves art. I also like art and in the past she and I have had battles regarding style, medium, theme, and so on. I was exact and meticulous, favouring historical approaches to my work. Alex was more impulsive, wanting to try new ideas and methods. She also liked arguing with the art teacher. I quickly realised that we would have major problems if we didn't work something out, and we made a compromise where we would take turns to work in peace with our different styles at different times, and that while she would be allowed to participate in the art class, only I would speak. To my great relief, she stuck to our agreement.

She doesn't mind getting dirty, which the rest of us do. Alex was different to all the alters that came before her in that they wanted to be loved by our parents and she didn't. It wasn't that she wasn't bothered whether they loved us or not, she simply didn't want to know them. She holds the resentment and anger over what happened to me. She will say it isn't fair, whereas the rest of us tend to think, *Well, it happened so we'll just have to get on with it.*

Alex doesn't suffer fools gladly, and took no nonsense from anyone, especially those prefects who tended to be a bit bullying. She loved winding one particular prefect up. The prefect, Nora, eventually turned to me and said, 'Sarcasm is the lowest form of wit.'

Quick as a flash, I responded, 'It is the highest form of intelligence.'

Until Nora made the 'sarcasm' comment, I was not even there. I turned up in the middle of their argument and knew immediately that it was Alex because I heard her chuckle before she went back to wherever she stayed when she wasn't in control.

Most of the prefects resented her/me; I was aware that she (and therefore I) was always calm and smiling. I have a sense that Alex didn't come to deal with any pain, neither did she seem to hold any painful memories. She came to fight, and is in part responsible for my developing a reputation as a confident, outgoing, lively person.

Despite the occasional problems with Alexis, and when various stresses would cause the youngsters to scream and cry, I felt at one with my alters, even when anxiety caused me to wish them away. They were my comforts, my defence, my best friends. It was not for me to question why they were there or where they came from. They helped me survive and, as more turned up, I simply had to accept them.

People with MPD commonly refer to the self as 'we' or 'us', and this often got me in more trouble.

'Dee! Where is your homework? Weren't you supposed to bring it in today?'

'No, Miss Bayley. We had to do something for Mrs Clarkson all day yesterday and she gave us permission to submit our work tomorrow.'

Miss Bayley walked to the front of her desk and sat on it. Like all the teachers, she was reasonably professional, but she was one of those who didn't suffer fools gladly, and often made polite but nevertheless scathing remarks when she was displeased. I could see from the way she pursed her lips together, that she was now displeased. I began to feel like fidgeting and, because she didn't like that either, and preferred you to look at her when she spoke, I tried to focus on the wispy, dark moustache she was beginning to develop, as somehow it always seemed to relax me.

Her lips moved out, then back in twice, as though she was about to kiss someone, before she spoke.

'We? Miss Dee? Is this the royal "we"?' She waited for a response, her lips twitching out and in.

I could feel the heat rising to my face as the class turned round to look at me. Ivy Conway, who enjoyed my discomfiture, largely because my end-of-term exam results tended to consign her to second place, smiled widely.

'Come, come. Miss Dee. Are you using the royal "we"? Perhaps as it befits your stature?'

I still didn't respond as the horror of my predicament hit me. How will I get out of this one? They cannot . . . must not learn of the others. Miss Bayley's lips worked double time.

'Miss Dee. You don't seem to understand. I would prefer it to be the case that you are using the royal prerogative, as the alternative is much worse in my opinion.'

She soon realised that I had absolutely nothing to say and continued, 'I suspect that you are working with someone else on your homework project whereas, if you recall, I expressly indicated when I gave it to you that it had to be individual effort. *Individual effort*, Miss Dee. Anything else is cheating. Now I suggest you report to Mrs Clarkson for another session of "something to do all day" next Sunday. I'll set it up with her, and if I do not have your homework first thing in the morning – *individual* work mind, you'll have a date with the headmistress on Saturday as well.'

She heaved herself off the desk and turned away, so, sadly, she didn't see the rude gesture Ivy Conway made. I say sadly, because Miss Bayley always tried to be fair, and if she *had* seen, the following Sunday Ivy would have found herself standing beside me outside Mrs Clarkson's office 'growing good'.

We used to meet our boyfriends under some arches just outside the girls' school grounds, after supper but before bedtime. Craig and I were still seeing each other because, despite the hurt that I felt, or rather one of my alters felt, at the way he had let us down, I still needed to love him and to be loved in return. There was no one else he wanted to see either and I was happy about that. The teachers were usually in the staff room and, if we were quiet, we were safe. This was our opportunity to have a kiss and a cuddle. One evening about eight of us were caught by a teacher from the boys' school and he reported us to Mrs Clarkson. As a result we had to report to her office. For some reason only I received any punishments and I was not allowed to go to the end-of-term dance in addition to having to stand outside the head's office for a full six weeks' 'growing good'.

One day Mrs Clarkson approached me.

'Ruth. You know you have to learn to take responsibility. You are getting older and I think you'd make a good prefect. What do you think?'

'I-I . . .' I opened and closed my mouth, stunned. It was the last thing I'd expected.

'I have been watching you. You have considerable influence over the younger girls. Taking on the additional responsibility would be good for both you and the school. You could be such a good person if only you could control yourself and be less erratic.'

I considered her words, but I felt I had enough on my plate and didn't want the additional responsibility, especially as the school had such strict rules regarding discipline. I'd been disciplined all my life at home and I didn't want to start policing other people. So I refused her offer and I believe that, as a result, I was given extra punishments.

Lines, detentions and people shouting at me had no effect on me, however. I spent virtually all my free time after school outside Mrs Clarkson's office. On a typical Saturday, for example, I would have lessons in the morning, sport in the afternoon and in between I would be standing outside the office. On Sunday there would be church in the morning and evening, which we would go to marching in a crocodile line, and in between the two church sessions I would once more be standing outside the office 'growing good'. All this inevitably served to reinforce the conditioning I'd had at home that I was a bad person.

Despite the school's fairly poor academic standards, I did reasonably well at my 'O' levels. By then Mum was being allowed out of the hospital for short periods of time and had begun to visit on a Sunday afternoon. Her visits were not sanctioned but, as was typical with her, she would do as she pleased, and if she got me into trouble, so much the better. She would telephone the school, and often a prefect would give me the message that she was on the phone. I always dreaded these calls.

'Hello?'

'Ruth! It's me, Mummy. I want to see you. I'm coming down on Sunday. Would you meet me outside the gates?'

'Mummy, we're not allowed to. You can't visit without special permission, unless it's on Visitors' Day.'

'I know that! Why else would I be asking you to meet me outside the gates? It's a stupid rule. You're my child and if I want to see you I will.'

'But I could get into trouble!' I protested. I watched the prefect who was pacing outside the telephone booth and saw her look at her watch. I was being timed.

'I'm sure you could handle trouble. You must be used to it by now. I'll be there at three-thirty sharp. Meet me, or I shall have to find my way in with all the cakes.'

'What cakes?' I asked. I could hear my voice squeak as it rose.

'The cakes I'm bringing, of course, for you and all your little friends.'

'But . . .' The dialling tone sounded in my ear.

That's typical. She must have her own way. She must show everyone that she is different. I could hear it now. *Ruth Dee's mother is a rather odd woman. She likes to break the rules. Yes. Ruth's just the same you know. She's just like her mother.*

No! I'm not!

My biggest fear was that she would come into the school and meet my friends. I had managed to separate home from school up until now, and I was desperate to keep the status quo. I had no option but to sneak out and meet her.

Dad was driving.

'Ruth! Get in,' he said affably. 'How are you? Is school treating you well?'

'Yeah. Okay.'

'Oh, it's lovely to see you.' That was Mum. 'You must tell me all about your classes and your friends.'

There wasn't much to say. I enjoyed my classes but I didn't want to discuss any of my friends with Mum, so I acted like I had none. Mum then went on to talk about what she had been doing, what the others had been doing but, since she didn't visit those at boarding school much, that was a short conversation too. George wasn't in the car. Somebody was babysitting. Before long, the well of conversation had run dry.

'Well, we'd best be off,' Dad said.

'Yeah.'

'Don't forget the cakes. Let me know if everyone enjoys them and I'll bring more next time,' Mum added. Once again my mother was using presents as a means of buying affection. The gifts no longer felt like treats to me; I knew nothing had changed. It was just another way in which she could exert control over me.

I groaned inwardly, picked up the cakes and sneaked back into the grounds. My friends loved the cakes and were full of admiration for my parents.

'Aren't you lucky? My mother would never be so brave.'

'Nor mine. I reckon you're on to a winner with *your* mother.'

After that it was a fairly regular thing and she'd bring cakes and presents of sweets, biscuits and so on for distribution to the other children.

The headmistress found out what was happening and spoke to me about it.

'I want you to tell your mother to stop her gifts and "external" visits.'

'I can't. I've already told her it's not allowed.' I had no intention of pursuing the matter, knowing how Mum would react. 'I think it would be better coming from you, Mrs Clarkson.' I knew it would never happen. Although I never found out why, I realised that the head was afraid of my mother. Eventually Mum stopped the visits herself.

A few weeks later, my mother was discharged from the psychiatric hospital, but because she had developed serious back problems, she was sent to a convent hospital where she lay in traction for several months. To my great astonishment, whenever I visited her at the convent hospital, she was always very friendly, even praising me to anyone who would listen, proclaiming me to be a wonderful daughter.

'Oh, Sister Agnatha. Meet my daughter Ruth! Isn't she just beautiful?'

'Oh, but isn't she just? You must be proud of her.'

'She takes after me, you know. Can you not see the resemblance?'

Was that a smile twitching on the nun's lips? She turned to me and said, 'And you must be such a dear, loving girl to your mother.'

I was most unimpressed by this. I remained cynical about my mother's behaviour, and with good reason.

My boarding school was closing down and, though my parents had wanted me to go to another one, they couldn't find any that were suitable as far as they were concerned, so we had to settle for a good state day school. In a way this worked against me, because at boarding school I would have been away from Mum and Dad. Instead I had to return home to my parents, as I was under the legal age of adulthood. Yet I found I didn't mind. Overall, boarding school hadn't been nice for me. It was regimented and dictatorial. At a new boarding school I would have been living amongst strangers again, whereas I was familiar with the environment at home. And I was a young woman. What could they do to me now? My time away had given me the confidence to deal with them. I felt I was strong enough to reject their authority, and my future was coming . . . I would soon be eighteen and leaving home for college. I only had this one year left to live with them.

However, despite all my rationalising of the situation, in reality my dislike of them deepened enormously. The two older boys and I were no longer in danger of their abuse, but the youngest two children still suffered. George still lived at home and Mary returned home from boarding school during the holidays. I did sometimes step in to help them, by hurrying them away if they were in trouble or claiming that I had done whatever it was they were being punished for, but I was not at home all of the time, and when I heard their piteous stories of what had befallen them on any given day, I felt the anger grow. So, as I suspected, Mum had not really improved. The changes in her that I saw were probably more to do with my growing maturity than with her treatment, though there had been times when she had been clearly over-medicated. I made up my mind then and there that I would survive her and, for this last year I'd be living under their roof, I would be on hand to help George during term-time. My brothers were still at their boarding school.

I had decided that I wanted a professional career of some sort; the sooner I could complete school and move away from home the better. I managed to get admitted to a day grammar school. I had done my first year of sixth form at boarding school and they allowed me straight into the second year of sixth form. There was another bonus: Heather and her boyfriend, Michael, were there too. Michael had a car and used to drive us to school. There was no uniform to wear, lots of freedom, and if there were no classes for us to attend that day, we didn't have to remain in the building.

As there were different textbooks to study for my 'A' levels at this school, it was a struggle. I had a lot to catch up with, and I didn't get the grades I had hoped for. On the plus side, I got on well with everyone, for Heather was very popular and she helped me to settle in, introducing me to her friends and making sure I had invitations to student parties. Whenever there were any small problems, Heather would be there helping me solve them.

It was here that I realised I wanted to teach, and during my 'A' levels I applied for teacher training. I was accepted at the interview, which was a major surprise; I believe I got in because of my boarding school background. The other applicants from the grammar school would have to rely on their grades to get them in.

If any part of me had hoped that my mother's behaviour had fundamentally changed, it wasn't long before I was given ample proof that her old obsessions and attitudes hadn't gone away. One day at school we were asked if we would like to put up a person from Paris. I dutifully reported back to my mother, who was ecstatic. Much to my astonishment, she wanted to have a guest.

'Oh, what a lovely idea,' she exclaimed. 'What do we have to do?'

'There's a parents' meeting on Thursday evening, and if you're interested, you have to attend it,' I replied.

She went to the school with me on the appropriate parents' evening – to my surprise, the visiting students were already in the country. She made a beeline for one of the lads and we ended up with three students, all male, staying in our house. There was plenty of room as, with the exception of George, all the others were at boarding school.

She was so incredibly nice to them, I couldn't believe it. The first night they were there, as she was going to bed, she turned to them. 'Well, I hope you feel right at home here.'

'Thank you Mrs Dee,' the least shy, and oldest of them, replied.

'Good. By the way, if you need relief, it is fine for you to sleep with Ruth. Take turns if you like, or see if you can all squeeze into the bed together. Go right ahead.' She walked into her room and shut the door.

Their mouths had fallen open and, almost as one, they turned to look at me. I was appalled and embarrassed.

'That is a stupid joke. Don't you even think about it,' I said to them, and as soon as I could make my excuses, I too went up to my room.

By now I had stopped sleeping in the nude, and I had just changed for bed when the biggest of the boys opened the door and walked into my room with obvious intentions. Mum must have been listening, because just then she laughed from her room.

'What are you doing here?'

'I have accepted your mother's offer.'

'Then you should go to her room,' I responded as I turned to the chest of drawers and quickly took out a pair of dressmaking scissors. Go back to your own room. I am not going to sleep with you or any of your friends.'

His eyes searched my face, then he made a stiff little nod, turned on his heels and left. I was upset and embarrassed by the whole thing. Mum had ruined things for me yet again. It could have been fun having three students from a different country, but as usual she had soiled the whole experience. I found it difficult to face them after that because I was so embarrassed, but I took a deep breath and tried to get on with things.

The rest of their stay with us was made harder because Mum told him to keep trying because I was just shy. I was appalled at the way she was still prepared to try and manipulate me, and to place me in danger. I felt that she was simply finding new ways to abuse me. For her, everything was potentially sexual; she was more than willing to encourage strangers to force themselves on me. The student did try again, but I had found an assertiveness I didn't know that I had and he soon realised that to continue to make the attempt would get him nowhere. In the end, he never got what he wanted.

Mum constantly prodded me on their behalf.

'What's the matter with you? Look at them. They are young and virile. It will be a real treat. Just look how good-looking they are. It would be great to have sex with them.'

I looked away from her, not knowing what to say. This wasn't a good thing to do either as, when I was a child, not responding to a direct comment had always been asking for trouble. Sure enough, she exploded.

'For God's sake. Answer me when I talk to you. Why won't you sleep with these gorgeous young men?'

'No! I won't do it.' I felt that cold, hard feeling build up inside me.

Memories of Mr Close crowded back, but this time I was under control. I was in my own house. It was familiar and I could deal with this. I moved closer to her and placed my face close to hers, as she'd often done to me when I was a tot.

'You do it!' I said. 'Go on. Give yourself a thrill. You obviously need it.'

I waited for the explosion but, to my great surprise, she simply smiled and turned away from me. She was so calm it was surreal. Of course she was still taking her medication regularly, and soon she would become fed up of that!

I didn't care any more. Her grotesque behaviour had made me feel desolate and worthless, but there was anger there too. I would take her on even if it killed me.

9

Escape

Going off to teachers' training college in London was both exciting and worrying. I was not that nervous because my experiences at boarding school had in some way prepared me for this new venture. Nevertheless, I was worried, because of all the old fears that plagued me whenever I had to go to a new place. I was pulled this way and that, with the angst that my alters and I felt constantly changing to elation because I had escaped from the prison that was my home. My 'cupboard' days might have been in the distant past – except for Liz's presence, a legacy of that time – but my spirit had never been free. Now, going to college made me feel like I had finally brought my spirit away with me.

I felt that nothing more could be done to me, even though I would be returning to my parents during the holidays. Even so, the battling in me between happiness and fear resulted in my usual 'neutral' emotions. Internally, though, I was in turmoil. I was leaving a hated familiar for a possibly frightening unknown. Externally, I couldn't even show the emotion of the average young person embarking on their adult life's adventure, let alone one who had escaped a pressure cooker. If there was any 'high' caused by my leaving home, it was neatly counterbalanced by everything else that was churning around inside me.

The sexual and physical assaults had long stopped, but the mental ones remained. The strains and stresses of living with a schizophrenic mother left me quivering in fear of her, most of the time we were together. Meanwhile I held my secret loathing of my father deep inside me for fear of what might happen if it came out. Although outwardly I had to show a child's respect to him, my hatred was quietly eating away inside me, deeply disturbing Jenny and helping her to destabilise my composure many times.

Now that Mum was back home, she had fallen more or less back into her old ways, still hurting my young siblings when she could. As they were growing fast, though, her torment was increasingly likely to be psychological rather than physical. Dad spent as much time as he could away from home on business, but whenever he was home, the fireworks would fly as usual. One weekend, when I was visiting home from college, I realised with a shock that a strange shift in their relationship had occurred. Dad was now in a very senior position at work, and was apparently highly respected. Yet at home he had become much less dominant than before. At first I thought that perhaps he was finally beginning to mellow, then one of their arguments brought the truth home to me in a flash. I'm not sure how it started, or what triggered this change in her personality, but suddenly I heard my mother shouting, 'You're not a real man. You're a sick, sick, sick pervert!'

I poked my head out of my room to see them standing on the landing near the stairs. They were so intent on each other that they didn't notice me.

'Will you be quiet? You're as mad as a hatter, you are!'

Dad's words brought a twisted smile to her face, and it astonished me. Before, such words would have caused her pain; now they just brought a bitter amusement.

'You're an awful man to live with, you and your other women . . . and your smut . . .' Her voice was so calm, so cold, so eerie that I felt a shiver run down my spine. Dad stared at her, saying nothing, but looking increasingly frail.

She continued, 'You think I'd be afraid to say what I know, but I'm not! In a divorce, I would get the house and you would still have to support me. You should have kept me mad! You mightn't think it, but I am not the mad woman or the fool you think I am. The drugs do help in some ways. Now hand it over.' She smiled a terrible smile as she imperiously held out her hand.

Dad looked as if he wanted to be sick right there on her precious carpet. Instead he put his hand in his pocket and pulled out a roll of money. He extended his hand and slowly, like a cat stretching, she smiled as she took it.

'Is there any more?' she asked, moving her head in an 'I've-got-you' manner.

Dad shook his head mutely and slapped his pockets to show they were empty. Mum gave him a brief speculative stare then, unrolling the pile of notes, she took two out of the wad and returned them to him.

'Pocket money,' she said softly as she turned away. Then she paused, turned back to him and added, 'I remember the days when you never used to give me money, not even to feed your three small children,' and, with a satisfied smile, she returned to her room.

Dad made a groaning sound and slumped to the top step, his head in his hands. If the truth about him became known, everything he'd worked for, everything that gave him prestige

– his job, perhaps even his possessions – would be lost to him. The small terrier he married had become a full-grown pitbull.

I tried, but could summon no pity for him. And in the months and years to follow until his death, my father found himself stuck between the devil and the deep blue sea.

He even learnt to praise her, speaking of her kindly despite the fact that she wasn't around to hear him. She once threw him out of the car after some argument and he had to walk home but, as he said with a laugh later, 'I took it all in my stride.' I wasn't privy to all of their relationship changes since I went home as little as possible, but it was clear that Mum had the upper hand and that she had gained it by threatening him with his past activities.

As for Mum, she kept up the appearances she'd culti-vated when we were small children, as did he. Listening to the pair of them interact, as though they were a 'normal' couple and loving parents, all the while knowing what they had done – what they were still doing – caused a bitterness to build inside me; but I strove mightily to get rid of it through caring interactions with those I met. Those child-hood assaults imprisoned my spirit and threatened to shatter my soul. But now I was away from home, I could at least believe I was safe.

At the college, there were mixed halls of residence and a free-and-easy atmosphere. I met people from all over the country and made new friends. By now Craig and I were beginning to part company. I cared for him even though I doubted that he loved me. However, it wasn't our insecurities that caused the split, but his mother, who for some reason didn't at all care for me and did everything she could to discourage our friendship. She didn't know me. She just didn't like me. After Craig left school, he went off to work in a university near his home, and under his mother's urging we slowly drifted apart.

He wrote to me. *I am feeling very down. I have no friends except you, and Mum is trying so hard to stop me contacting you.* His letters to me showed me an increasing depression. He had not maintained contact with anyone from his boarding school. Although we met a few times during my first year at college, I could see his mother's apron strings getting more firmly tied, and it was no surprise when we eventually drifted apart, though we remained friends.

At college, somehow I exuded an air of confidence and competency, although it startled me to learn this from one of the students.

'Hi. I'm Margaret. You can call me Meg. Everyone does.' She spoke with the air of an excited child and seemed to bounce on her toes a bit.

'I'm Ruth,' I replied, amused.

'You look big, strong and competent,' she added, somewhat to my consternation. 'Could you fix the window in my room? It's sticking.'

I was amazed at her temerity. I wondered, 'Why me?' I am five foot seven inches tall, and so no doubt looked capable, but surely there were people around – housekeeping staff – who would do this kind of thing. I followed her to her room and realised that the window frame had become warped. I managed to close it but, as she was bound to want it either opened or shut again, and as there was nothing I could do to permanently fix the problem, I suggested she contact the office to deal with it.

Years later, as I prepared to write this book, I asked two of my closest friends from college, Lisa and Marjorie, how I appeared to them during those far-off days. They took a moment to consider and I gazed at my two pals, now middle-aged women like myself, though in my mind's eye we were all three of us young again and about to embark on life's adventure as adults. Their answer warmed me.

'Well, you were vivacious, lively, full of fun,' Marjorie said.

'Yes, yes I agree. You were outgoing, confident, very friendly if anyone looked left out. You were always trying to help. You looked out for other people,' Lisa responded.

'That's right.' Marjorie looked at Lisa. 'She always included everyone.' Turning back to me she continued, 'Yes, you always did that. And you weren't a lazy student. You always seemed so enthusiastic.'

'And privileged! I remember one time you were in the laundry doing your wash. You had a gorgeous red knitted dress . . . remember?'

I smiled and nodded as I remembered a favourite dress I had managed to ruin that day.

'Well,' Lisa continued, 'we had this twin-tub machine and you were standing over it holding up this strangely shaped material saying, "What on earth have I done to this dress? Something's happened to this dress. It's not rinsing itself." I knew straight away that you were used to an automatic machine. In those days they were very expensive and only well-off people had them. Anyway, because you'd taken the dress from the first tub without setting it to do the rinse, and you'd put it into the second tub which was the spinner, you ended up with a very shrunken and matted dress.'

My friends and I laughed at the memory before I asked, 'Did you notice that anything was wrong with me? Was I odd or different or . . . anything?'

'You were different only in that you were so lovely, so

outgoing. We were the quiet ones and you were the extrovert. There was nothing to suggest that you were unwell. You were so confident, so good at making and maintaining friendships and relationships,' Lisa said. It was true I was skilled at fitting in with people; the condition makes you hypervigilant so that you learn to watch and mirror others.

Margie laughed. 'You were very slim, athletic. You had a gorgeous body and all the guys would look at you and quietly go "Whoa!" When you took up with Gerry, you broke a lot of hearts.'

This was of course lovely to hear, but I hadn't questioned them just for an ego boost. I really wanted to know whether my friends had had any inkling of my inner turmoil. I smiled but persisted. Surely they'd seen something? 'Are you sure there was nothing out of the ordinary, nothing odd?'

My friends looked at each other for a moment and then Margie said, 'There was one thing I remember that astonished me greatly. Well, it must have, as I never forgot it. One day you said that your mother sunbathed in the nude outside in the back garden and hoped no one noticed. I was in total shock, but you didn't seem to notice and you were so matter-of-fact about it. Later I just thought, "Maybe that's how some people are about stuff like that", but I never considered anything else.'

Lisa chipped in. 'I remember one day I was a bit upset because I hadn't heard from my mother and father for a while. It was the longest time I'd had no contact with them and I was getting worried that something might have happened.' Lisa raised her eyes to mine. 'You said, "For heaven's sakes, what's your problem? It's just your parents." Your response surprised me because I had seen you with your own parents and you all seemed perfectly friendly and comfortable with each other. I didn't understand the inference that you wouldn't care if you didn't hear from them, but of course in hindsight it was a missed clue and your reaction then makes perfect sense now.'

Part of me was amazed that even my friends hadn't noticed anything odd about me. But by then, of course, I had become very skilled at concealing my alters and their behaviours from the world. And, as my life went on, I got better and better at it. One of my tricks was to sing to myself as I walked along, which helped to suppress the many voices inside me.

My teacher-training course lasted three years, and I managed to live in the halls of residence for all of that time. Most of the others stayed for just the first year, then found houses to rent outside, but I had spent so much time cleaning, cooking and so on that I wanted a break from that. Living at the college meant that I could eat in the cafeteria. The cleaners kept my room in order and all I had to take care of was my laundry. There was a laundry room nearby so I didn't have to go far to deal with it. Everything I needed was to hand. However, there were episodes occurring that frightened me. My habit of losing time was becoming more frequent and I would find myself in various parts of London, or on the tube, without any idea of how I got there. I began to feel more and more that I was mad. I obsessed over my mother's mental deterioration and hospitalisation. I became obsessed with the inevitability of my own descent into mental illness and possible future hospitalisation and I cringed in fear every time I considered this scenario.

Despite these fears, much of this period was a fairly happy time for me. Thanks to my mother's instruction, I was able to make my own clothes, and that allowed my grant money to go further. I found that my work schedule wasn't arduous. Except for English, lectures weren't compulsory. My specialist subject was geography and my training would allow me to teach at both junior and secondary schools. I attended all of the lectures I could physically get to, for I soon realised that my ability to retain information was outstanding. I suspected that the other beings in my life were helping, but I didn't know the extent of this. If I thought something was super boring, there always seemed to be another who wanted to lap it all up. As a result I wrote essays and did other projects quickly. One tutor asked for an essay on teenagers and authority figures. From the lectures I attended, I was able to approach the essay from five quite different perspectives and so I (and my alters) sat down and quickly produced five different essays. We got top marks for all of them. What no one knew was that, in addition to listening to the excellent lectures, I had for years been observing myself, my siblings and many of my friends – particularly those at boarding school – and looking at the differences in our attitudes, how we perceived events and reacted to them. I therefore had some understanding of the kinds of expectations parents, peers, teachers and so on placed on young people and how these pressures affected them physically, socially, and mentally.

Later, when I met Gerald, the student who would become my first husband, and compared my learning style with his, I discovered something else. After a lecture, Gerry would go to the library and research his coursework, something I simply couldn't do. Personally, I hate libraries, always did. When I was a child, my mother used to make me go to the library and choose her books for her, four at a time. The problem was that I couldn't always remember if she had read them. If she had done so already, or didn't like any of the books I had chosen, she instantly fell into one of her rages. I became so worried about not getting it right that I began to hate the libraries themselves: they represented my stupidity and fear of what would happen when I got home. The fear stayed with me and I continue to avoid these buildings. Reading also seemed to leave me cold, perhaps because Mum so clearly enjoyed it, and I wanted to be as little like her as possible. Instead I lived for the lecture, which brought the material alive for me, and I forgot none of it.

Gerry was a friend of a friend who I began meeting for coffee and then dating. He was over six feet tall and was a quiet, unassuming man with whom I immediately felt comfortable. He seemed dependable and level, which appealed to me. Living with the constant upheaval of my alters and their chatter made relationships with more demanding friends hard work, as it required all of my concentration to maintain even a simple chat. Gerry demanded very little other than my love. He didn't even require much by way of conversation, which was like a balm to my soul, for here I could be in a close relationship with someone who demanded little in the way of mental energy from me.

My physical energy levels were quite different, as noted in a report made by one of the lecturers, who expressed his amazement that I was 'always alert' – and he was right. I was always on the go. I didn't appear to tire easily, and Gerry found it hard to keep up with me. My alertness might have been further emphasised by the fact that so many of my partying peers could hardly keep their eyes open during lectures. But I was energetic and alert during the day as the alters that had arrived from the time I was in boarding school seemed to think they each had a different body, which was fresh when they emerged. As I was switching from one to the other, it was tantamount to my body having just awakened.

The switching between alters was not something I could control. When someone wished to make an appearance, she simply did. At night, I slept deeply, recharging the single body that was now home to at least nine alters, and there would be days when people spoke of thunderstorms during the night that woke them, not realising that they left me slumbering on.

Because I didn't need to spend hours revising and doing library research, I always had plenty of free time, and I received many invitations to party with other students. After the first few events I realised that alcohol affected the senses in an alarming way, and I saw students who experimented with alcohol, drugs and other intoxicants become completely different people. They often became people I didn't know or like – or on occasion even felt afraid of – and I quickly made the decision not to mix with that crowd. I had too many lapses, periods lost to time where I had no idea where I was or what I was doing. I lost control involuntarily. There was no way I would even dream of doing it voluntarily. So I kept away from them and their stimulants.

I also kept away from promiscuity, which was fashionable as always among some students. I got a reputation for keeping my distance, but I didn't care. Gratuitous sex would hold no magic for me, and if I found someone who could respect that it would be a bonus for me, for it would signify to me that he saw something more of me than just a body. Gerry, who made no demands of me whatsoever, completely fitted the bill.

Despite my reservations, I was determined to have as many friends as I could, and forced myself to be cheerful and outgoing. It was an act that was constant and debilitating, especially as, deep down inside, I was filled with depression, particularly as the realisation hit me that my parents were different from other parents I'd met. It never occurred to me that perhaps other families had secrets too, for the parents seemed so comfortable with their children, my friends – and vice versa – that it would have been impossible for me to believe anything other than that they were good, normal people.

Yet on some level, I knew that I could not be the only one. Everyone knew about disadvantaged children – orphaned, abandoned, neglected – and although in those days there wasn't the widespread knowledge of child abuse that we have today, these children were likely to be abused too. It became my vocation to turn the bad in my life into some kind of good for these children. I would turn their lives around and would likely turn my own around as well. So strong was my need to help that I focused my training on helping children seen as difficult, unhappy, disadvantaged loners.

I began to take psychology classes, but as little then was known of MPD, I learnt nothing that would help me make sense of my own condition. I did learn about schizophrenia, and even had to write an essay on it, for which I got excellent grades – all I had to do was use my mother as my inspiration.

In addition to Lisa and Margie, my best friends at college were Gerry and Andreas – or Andy, as we called him. He was a most delightful friend of ours, a Greek Cypriot. He was responsible for introducing us to Greek cuisine and the delights of dishes like marinated leg of lamb, which he slowly roasted until the meat was about to fall off the bone, and *dolmades*, or stuffed vine leaves. For a brief while there was also Judith, a clingy, homesick young woman who needed mothering. She was always asking for something, like help with her make-up, checking her clothing was on properly or some such thing.

'Ruth, can you help me? I can't manage.'

'What's the matter? What can't you manage?'

'My hair. Could you brush it for me, please?'

My own hair had always been kept long, except for a brief period in childhood when Mum had cut it all off, much to my despair. I never had any problem dealing with my hair and I couldn't see why the task of doing her own was beyond Judith. I always felt obliged to do what she wanted as she seemed so much in need. On this occasion, I really didn't want to do it, so I persuaded Andy to do it, which he seemed happy to do.

Another time Judith made it clear that it was *my* assistance she needed for some other trivial task that required personal contact. Although I was quite generous with my time, and I felt satisfaction whenever I helped someone, I was uncomfortable with Judith's needs. I felt very sorry for her, but I also found that I felt uneasy around her. I did what she wanted as it was not in my nature to refuse, but her demands made me feel obligated in an uncomfortable way. I started to avoid her whenever possible. One day she collapsed, screaming, and the administrator who came to see her promptly called a doctor. He in turn called an ambulance after giving her an injection. I never saw her again, and though I felt sorry she had been so unwell, I was also relieved she was no longer at college.

Yet somehow I got a reputation for being someone who was always prepared to help. People were always asking for advice and assistance, which I increasingly found very upsetting as I was just about managing to hold myself together. I was being pushed in this role of universal mother and helper, when I was the one that needed help

Finally the time came when I could begin teaching practice, the practical component of my course, in a real classroom with real kids. Using dance and drama, techniques for both of which I had learnt at college, I found to my delight that I worked well with the children who were described as having 'special needs'. It was a great way to get through to my young charges and they opened up to me. As they warmed to me, and I to them, I was able to communicate, to empathise with them. I could give them support and confidence and, in each child, I saw some version of me – even in those who had not been sexually abused. I saw their frailty and their strengths, their needs and their generosity, their need for closeness and for aloneness. I reached out to them with compassion in my heart, and became delirious with happiness when they reached out to me. This was what my life's experiences and education was for, and I would not fail them. I *could* not fail them, could I?

Training to be a teacher opened my eyes to the worldwide phenomenon of abuse, and naturally I was particularly interested in child abuse. The defining day came one morning in one of my lectures. My alters had been particularly noisy and distracting. I cannot remember the cause but suddenly there was a

Hush! This is important.

and I had a sense of becoming aware of the classroom.

'. . . fingers.' The lecturer was turning away to draw something on the blackboard.

'Pardon me, Mr Jordan. Could you repeat that last bit, please? I didn't quite catch it.'

Mr Jordan turned back and said, 'Which bit didn't you catch, Ruth?'

'The bit about the fingers.'

'It is one of the signs of physical abuse in young children.

Sometimes the abused child will refuse to write anything. Its fingers will be badly swollen. The problem is not always caused by arthritis, as some parents will tell you, but by the child having its fingers badly twisted. If a child is right-handed and only the left hand has "arthritis", or vice versa, it is a clue that the parent is aware enough to not want the teacher investigating why a child won't write. However, we do see "accident-prone" children presenting with many injuries and just about all their fingers twisted, in families who don't realise that their abuse leaves clues.'

'Have you any further examples?'

'Yes, many. You will see some of them on the handout I will give you at the end of this class, but personally, my most difficult memory is of a young boy who was forever coming to school with long burns on various parts of his body, some of which were quite nasty. I requested a visit from his parents and they came along to the school with him a couple of days later. As soon as I saw the family I realised that this was an abusive father.'

'How can you tell it was the father and not the mother? We men always get all the blame.' One of my fellow students was clearly annoyed.

Mr Jordan sat on the lip of his desk facing us. He gently swung a grey trousered leg whilst twiddling with the stick of chalk.

'There were major clues, Bryan. The mother was a thin, frightened-looking woman who was sporting a black eye. Father immediately told me that she was as "accident prone" as his son and had walked into the proverbial door. His son, who was fidgeting somewhat and was clinging to him with a fervour I thought unusual in a six-year-old boy, had "fallen on an electric heater". When I seated the family around me, I tried to seat the boy near to his mother, but they were clearly both trying to distance themselves from each other, which I also found to be telling. There were other smaller signs, too. Father was a powerful-looking, well-fed man who clearly believed in his own self-importance. He was urbane and pleasant, but I couldn't help feeling that he was a coiled rattlesnake waiting to strike.

'Young Richard, that was the child's name, seemed in even more discomfort than the burn on his thigh should have been causing. He had not taken off his school blazer and, when I asked him to, I saw that his shirt had stuck to a bloody area on his back. Although his father tried to brush aside the injury as "just one more, he'll get over it" I insisted on taking a closer look. But Richard was so distressed by my touch that I insisted he needed medical treatment. That was when the father began to bristle. He stood up and I too made myself tall and stared at him. You could imagine his consternation.'

There was a general tittering in the classroom, as Mr Jordan was a tall, athletic-looking man.

'When I smiled and asked him if he would like to join me in the boxing ring one day as I had quite a useful amateur career before I became a teacher, he immediately remembered a meeting he had to attend. As soon as he had gone, the boy went to his mother.

'To make a long story short, he had been battering both his wife and child. The boy was punished every time he was seen to be showing any affection to his mother. He was also punished if he did not show affection for his father. His punishment was to be pressed against an electric bar fire and his latest burn was quite a serious one. He too had the twisted finger syndrome, and to show you how nature tries to help, I will use diagrams to . . .'

Mr Jordan walked to the blackboard and began to draw. I kept an eye on the diagrams, which showed how bone-building cells caused the swelling around the damaged fingers, and other bone-sculpturing cells made the fingers look normal again – another clue of a child suffering physical abuse when their 'arthritis' was intermittent. My ears listened as my younger alters talked animatedly about some sign of mine that they thought my own teachers should have acted on.

My feelings at hearing of this awareness of other children being abused were, as usual, mixed. On the one hand, it gave me some kind of relief to know that my family was not the only one that was so twisted. This seemed to somewhat assuage my sense of isolation. There were others outside my family who suffered and who could understand my suffering. My next feeling was shame at my initial relief. There was no way I wanted others to endure such a life and I wondered if, in my relief, I was becoming some sort of monster. Then a powerful hate emerged at the evil people who could do such terrible things to children, and for a brief time I daydreamed of how we, the abused, could turn the tables on our tormentors. Next came resolve as I determined to help all the children who showed signs of abuse. I was an adult. I had power that no child has. I was a teacher. I had power to help any child in my care. I would do it. There was a chorus of

Yes,

yeah,

let's do it

in the background and this, plus my thoughts, combined to send me into reverie.

After this lecture, and as a young teacher in the early seventies, I read a lot of material on child abuse and the reasons why it occurs. I noticed that much was made of socio-economic factors, such as education, poverty, job description, employment status and so on, all of which are facets of social class. According to the information available, it appeared that many people with abusive childhoods came from poor and working-class backgrounds. This was the way in which the 'intellectuals' seemed to excuse the poor and cruel behaviour of adults from certain social strata, apparently completely oblivious to the cruelty and abuse that goes on among the 'higher classes'. Of course that led me to think seriously about my own background, as the data sometimes allows us to think abuse doesn't happen in middle-class families. We are led to believe that people from poor and uneducated backgrounds don't know any better. Naturally I don't go along with this point of view because of my own background. My parents' heritage was working class, but they were upwardly mobile and I and my siblings definitely had a middle-class lifestyle after I was five years old. Eventually my father would become a senior sales manager in a large international company. My parents had dinner engagements at the Savoy and other well-known hotels in London.

When it comes to rearing children, to drug and sexual abuse, it is the working classes that tend to attract most attention. I don't want to debate the truth of that statement but to say why it matters. No one – not our neighbours, our doctor or our teachers – ever helped any of us. Even though they might not have realised the extent of it, they knew we were all being abused. At school, although most of our bruising was hidden by our clothing, teachers definitely saw the red, purple, yellow and eventually black fingermarks on all of us, courtesy of my mother's habit of grabbing us by the neck and squeezing until we passed out. Perhaps the fingermarks seemed clearer to me because I knew how the bruises on my siblings' necks were made, but I don't really believe that. Mum was all but leaving her fingerprints etched into our skins. The teachers would tut-tut at the bruises they saw whenever we changed into our gym clothing. But they never appear to have made any comment to my parents, the police, or anyone else who might have helped us. I get so angry sometimes when I think about their lack of involvement and the fact that they turned a blind eye to it all, especially after I learnt that – even in those days – teachers had *some* degree of training to spot abused children. School could have been a place of safety for me. It could have been a place where I could escape from my fear and the violence at home. It wasn't, though. I vowed to become the kind of teacher I had wanted myself when I was a child.

The failure of teachers, neighbours and the doctor to act is almost unbelievable. If they had acted when they saw the injuries on us three older children, they might have prevented my youngest brother and sister suffering as we older ones did, and could have put a stop to the abuse we were still enduring. If they had acted, we might not be so damaged. As an adult I learnt that I was not the only one who felt hated. We all felt that way: all of us thought that we must have been very bad children. It is a belief that is hard to get rid of.

On the plus side, I can never allow any hint of abuse I see to go unreported.

They could have helped us, Liz said with a shudder.

They could have stopped the pain, Jenny began to cry.

Jenny please don't. That was me, Ruth, but Jenny didn't stop crying, and in her distress I slid further back.

The memory of my grandfather's first abuse is still so clear in my mind. I have never forgotten it. What still hurts most is my mum laughing and laughing about it. They knew what had happened and thought it funny. My father shrugging his shoulders, saying, 'As long as you enjoyed it', as he looked at me in the driver's mirror. To this day I hate it when someone looks at me in the driver's mirror. I have used taxis a lot over the last few years and I always sit in the back. The drivers use the mirror to see you as they talk with you. I can't look back at them through it and I try to look over the seats at them when I respond.

Hairdressers do the same, watching your reactions in the mirror – I hate it. I feel so uncomfortable, so ashamed. It feels as though they can see what happened to me all those years ago. The mirror and 'viewing' became for me a powerful symbol of my abuse. Every time I was sexually assaulted, I stood beside myself and I viewed what was happening, as though I was looking in a sort of mirror. To view, to look into the mirror gave knowledge of the terrible things that happened to me. I was embarrassed and ashamed when I saw myself being raped. I felt that somehow it was all my fault. I was embarrassed and ashamed when I saw my father's knowledge in the car. I am embarrassed and ashamed every time someone's eyes meet mine in a mirror.

My granddad spoke nicely to me. He had given me new clothes and shoes. I had liked them. He said I was beautiful, was pretty. He whispered to me, kissed me. He was prickly. Even now I am very reluctant to kiss my husband Jamie if he has not shaved. If anyone with a beard or who is unshaven greats me with a kiss I have real difficulty in not recoiling, as it instantly flashes me back to my grandfather and his perverted sexual desires.

I blame Granddad for my illness. I am aware now that I dissociated as a three year old when he abused me. It might have been the first true dissociation, but I doubt that, as the two babies were there for a reason. When I was their age, I scarcely saw my father; I lived at Granddad's and would have seen him every day. So whether I was halfway to four years old or possibly just about a year old, it was he who started it all.

Even now, at the age of fifty-seven years old, I feel sick as I write this. Of all the sexual abuses I endured, this for me was simply the worst. It was such a betrayal of trust, and when it was followed up by the horror of my parents' reaction and the fact that they clearly got some sort of enjoyment from it, then my father's own abuses, I am surprised that my psyche was not completely destroyed.

It's strange how certain things stick in my mind. Those shoes with the silver buckle! How I could only walk up one step at a time and needed to put both feet on the same step; how steep they seemed. My new socks – to this day I am certain they had a frill around the ankle. How everyone in the room was staring at me. The fear! I was so afraid even before he started kissing me. What was different? Who was warning me that something bad was going to happen? Then, standing outside my body and looking across at me, feeling so safe there on the outside, so sorry for the little girl on the inside.

Why weren't they stopped?

Now my career was giving me the opportunity to be the person I had so desperately needed as a child. The sense of purpose was incredible and it helped to ease the despair and resentment I felt when I thought back to my own childhood. I was still in agony much of the time, still terrified of being mad, but life was moving on.

10

Shaky beginnings

I had finished college, but Gerry had decided that he wanted to do a fourth year of training in order to get a degree in education, which meant that we would be remaining in London. I found a teaching post near Gerry's college. I was upset to discover that he would live on campus, which meant that I had to find a room in someone's house for that year. I didn't like it, mainly because I found it disorienting to live with strangers, even though they were nice people. I ended up spending most nights with Gerry in his college rooms. The friends we had made at college had all found jobs in different parts of the country, so we were cast somewhat adrift – neither of us had been brought up in London and we knew no one. I was completely lost. I needed some kind of familiarity around or I became anxious, and when I became anxious, we all did.

Things didn't go well for me. There was so much dissonance in my life that my stress levels rose sharply and my alters began to switch and switch again. On the plus side, I liked my students at the school for children with special needs. They were sometimes wild and difficult, but as I recognised some of their behaviour, having seen it in myself and my siblings, I could empathise with them. What I found interesting was that they very quickly picked up that I was there for them. However, because my alters were so twitchy, some days at school were simply awful . . . they were completely lost to me. I would remember getting to the classroom and having the children get their books out. I would sit at the desk . . . and then somehow it would be twenty minutes later. The classroom would be partially or completely empty. There would be an irate head teacher, Mrs Jonas, in my face, yelling at me for not keeping better control. But I would have no idea where I had gone. This happened several times a week.

When I 'blanked out' like this, the children would wander out of class and run up and down the corridors, disrupting other classes even if they hadn't wandered into their classrooms. Not surprisingly, the head wasn't amused.

'Miss Dee, I know you can control them. I watched you yesterday and could not fault you. Then you let them run wild again today. What is the matter with you? Why don't you try? Focus more?'

If Mrs Jonas was annoyed, I was terrified. I had no idea about MPD, and losing these long periods of time left me feeling distressed and distracted. As time went by and things did not improve noticeably, my relationship with Mrs Jonas deteriorated to the point that Mr Chatsworth, the deputy head, tried to intervene.

'What is it between you and the head? Some kind of personality clash?'

There was not much I could say except deny that it was a personality clash. In my heart of hearts I knew that Mrs Jonas was right to be upset with me. *I* was upset with me.

Gerry noticed nothing amiss. When I walk into a room, I notice everything, as I automatically look for anything that could be dangerous to me and seek out the exits. Gerry, on

the other hand, is introverted and not particularly emotional. In addition, at the time of my developing troubles, he
was deeply immersed in his studies and, unless my problems
hit him on the head with the force of a sledgehammer, he
tended not to be bothered by them. He was a quiet, studious
type who seemed to find his contentment from somewhere
deep inside but it was this apparent calm levelness that had
attracted me to him. Now, because of my great need for
him, I briefly wondered at his withdrawn demeanour. I
wondered why we didn't have a home together. Even a
small bedsit would have sufficed. I didn't understand why
he never thought of keeping a bit of food in his room,
knowing that, when I finished work, I would return to him
rather than go to my lodgings. I always had to get something to eat on the way back, as he ate in the cafeteria and I
– no longer a student – couldn't.

Even as the questions I wanted to ask were forming, he'd
tell me, 'You're a good teacher, Ruth. You were great in
college and you're great now. It's their problem, not yours.
You shouldn't worry about what they think.'

And with this vote of confidence, he'd return to his books,
leaving me stunned and surprised. In a way, I really couldn't
blame Gerry for not noticing my plight. I too was at fault
here. I tended to hide my problems, aided and abetted by my
alters, who'd chorus, *We have to stay strong. We mustn't let
them know we're afraid.*

Even observant people tended not to notice that I had needs,
and part of me even expected this attitude. After all, wasn't I
nothing? Wasn't I conditioned from childhood to believe that
no one would be interested in me? Why, then, should they be
interested in my problems? So I never asked for more, and I
never got more.

I began to develop major problems with claustrophobia. When I was in the teachers' training college, I had been able to travel on the tube, even though I found that I 'lost' time. Now I began to fear the crowded carriages of people being hurried to work as the teeming mass of flesh pressed hard against me. Not being able to get off the tube when it stopped in a tunnel, which it often did, reminded me of being locked in the cupboard as a small child. My stress levels rose, my other selves became distressed and chaos ensued in my head. It was difficult to remain, at least outwardly, composed, as my panic levels went sky high. I was being hurled back into my childhood, into my sixth year in this world, and the young ones would set up such a cacophony of screams that I feared I was going to be mad like Mum and that the panic might make me run up and down the carriages.

'Run! Run! He's coming to hurt me again,' Jenny would be screaming.

'We're always getting hurt! What did we do? Why does everyone hate us?'

'Run! Run!' Jenny was shrieking, high pitched and terrifying.

'Who do they think we are? Why can't they leave us alone?'

'Kick them where it would do the most good!'

'Please don't hurt me. Please don't! Why didn't you run? Why didn't you?'

'Leave her alone! She's only a little kid.'

'Aaaaaaaah!'

I was switching in and out, from one to another and back again. Round and round and round we went. With all the terror, pathos, anger and determination to fight, I struggled to remain seated. Then I had moments when I thought I might simply hold my head and scream too. However, knowing that would be the quickest route to the nearest psychiatric hospital, I started travelling by bus. But the alters were still switching and during my journey to work I would lose time, just being aware of the 'highlights' of what was happening for the brief moments I was allowed to be myself. I began to arrive for my teaching duties late.

Although Mrs Jonas was exceedingly unhappy about my tardiness, she did try to be encouraging regarding the frequent occasions when I was unable to control the children. I was a puzzle to everyone as, on my good days, I showed the promise of the good teacher I would eventually become, and it was clear that I could empathise well with disturbed children and get to the bottom of their concerns. For example, there was a little girl who never spoke because of her disturbed background; her father was a murderer. I was able to get close to her and, as the child developed a strong attachment for me, she began to speak again. She would take my hand and follow me wherever I would allow her, and one day she came to me in assembly, and insisted on sitting with me, which left my colleagues looking quite amazed.

The head teacher spoke with me several times about my progress and, in addition to her admonitions about my inability to keep control in class, she also had praise for my successes. At the end of my teaching year she gave this final assessment:

'Ruth, you can be an excellent teacher if only you can be more consistent. I have just gone over the test results for your class and they are beyond what my expectations were at the beginning of the year. Overall, their reading levels are much better. I am impressed. There have also been improvements in the children's behaviour generally. It is only on the occasions when you relinquish control that they become disruptive.

Unfortunately, I am going to have to make this inconsistency in your abilities clear in any references I write for you. You do understand, don't you?'

I understood her all right, and if she thought it had been a bad year for her it had been a nightmare for me. When I wasn't switching, I could see the alters all around, some clearly, and others like ghostly shadows in the background. No one commented on any changes in my behaviour, which made me think that – except for the tube episode – it was the older alters, from Alex the teenager upwards, who were largely dominant. It was clear that my interactions with the other staff were adult enough not to cause eyebrows to be raised. Eventually, as the school year was drawing to a close, depression set in.

Gerry passed his exams with flying colours and, armed with his brand-new degree, we made our plans to leave London and move north. London was too expensive for two youngsters just starting out, and Gerry didn't wish to go as far north as his home town, so we stuck a pin in the map. We settled on Leicester, which was approximately midway between his parents' home and London. Both of us managed to find jobs there. It was harder for me, as my references were not terribly encouraging. Nevertheless, I found a headmaster who clearly read between the lines and invited me in for interview.

'I am Ian Darling,' he said when we first met, and indeed he was darling enough to give me a chance. He looked as if he was in his fifties, and his neatly trimmed dark hair was peppered with white. His moustache was full but discreet. By that I mean that it was not a pencil type, nor was it bushy. He wore wire-rimmed glasses, and bright blue eyes sur-rounded by laughter lines twinkled at me from behind them.

I liked him straightaway. We were sitting in his office and he had my application and references on the desk in front of him. He muttered as he read through some points in the reference, then said more clearly, 'incomprehensibly inconsistent', and he looked at me over the top of his glasses.

He asked why I thought I had not performed as well as Mrs Jonas had hoped, and I ventured to explain.

'I know I got a poor reference, Mr Darling, and in a way I deserved it. I was having the most dreadful year personally, and the additional stress of it being my first job and wanting to do well didn't help.'

'Yes. I know nervousness can be disastrous. Mrs Jonas also says that you have a good touch with the children emotionally, and that has impressed me. Many are chosen but few have the gift, and she seems to think that, with time, everything will come together for you. I am of the opinion, therefore, that with careful supervision, all will be well.'

I was made to feel so much at home that I shed my depression and many of my fears as if taking off an overcoat. Gerry and I found a flat to rent temporarily, until we could buy our first home, and we had plenty of time to plan everything and get it all sorted out before the school term started. It was wonderful. I was comfortable and adjusted well to the new surroundings. I got on well with my colleagues and, as now I wasn't switching often, and then not for more than a few short moments, I never again lost control of a class. There was simply no time for it to become disorganised. I enjoyed being with the children, rarely lost my temper, and whenever I felt sorely tried by one or more of them I was firm but fair. They quickly learnt that I was no pushover. I managed such an impressive year that I was given a promotion to take into year two.

Gerry and I settled into our routines and I continued to value his lack of demands on me. I had already recognised that our relationship was not one based on passion; I saw his cool, dispassionate steadiness as a prerequisite for what I needed at that time in my life: a secure, undemanding relationship. Ours was typical of the male/female relationships of those days, with a clear demarcation of our roles. I tended not to do the heavy stuff and he didn't cook, do laundry and so on. Between us, all went well. We married at the end of that first year.

Initially he had got on well with my parents. I still saw them whenever I went home for holidays from college, as I had nowhere else to go and I still felt a need to check on my younger brother and sister. Mum was still dominant and Dad seemed puny and harmless to me now. As they were always polite with outsiders, I risked introducing Gerry to them, ensuring that for the two or three times we were with them, we always met in a public place and for a comparatively short period. We certainly didn't stay long enough for Mum and Dad to get tired of their act. I hadn't told Gerry anything about them at all, which I suppose someone else might have thought a little odd. But Gerry, being who he is, never seemed to notice. Later, cracks would appear in his relationship with my mother as her true nature emerged with longer exposure.

My parents insisted that we should have a bigger wedding than Gerry and I were considering. It was described by some of my friends as a 'posh' wedding, and certainly my parents pulled out all the stops, making all the arrangements, inviting more people than I would have done – and paying for everything. As usual, they were showing what they could do, and were effectively stamping their class on Gerry's parents. Recalling my Christmases at home, I was eternally grateful that nothing got broken as the day progressed. We were married in church and the reception was held in the grounds of a large and prestigious restaurant near the river running through the town. It was lovely in the garden, and we enjoyed our slap-up meal as the insects buzzed around us and rays of the sun blessed our day. My day was all simply perfect, and for a change my parents did nothing to spoil it.

Instead they waited six weeks to tinge my happy memories with a large splodge of sadness. Six weeks later Mary also married, but as Mother didn't like Dennis, her fiancé, my parents didn't pay for this wedding, even though by now they were very well off and could have afforded it. Mary and Dennis did their best with limited resources and managed a buffet meal for their guests, but their wedding was so much more low-key than my own and Mary was distressed at our parents' lack of interest. I too was unhappy. Why did they do this? I simply did not understand it. I would happily have had a much less extravagant wedding so that my baby sister could have had a more upmarket one. Why did they shut her out? Disliking her choice of husband didn't seem like any sort of justification for me and I hated them for upsetting Mary.

My sister hid her distress and didn't allow the snub to affect her relationship with me, since thankfully she recognised I wasn't to blame; but neither did she let it destroy her relationship with our parents, who surely had much to be blamed for. Having discussed it, we decided in fact that our mother, who had instigated the whole thing, actually wanted to cause a rift between us sisters, and we were determined not to dance to her tune. She had played us one against the other so often as we were growing up that we tended to recognise her machinations and refused to let her destroy our friendship. My little sister had grown up to be a truly lovely woman.

Gerry and I bought our first house, which we got at a reasonable price because of the amount of work it needed to make it comfortable. He enjoyed working with his hands and was good at DIY. For him, working on the house after a hard day at school was a balm. I did what I could to help, but he would have been happy even if all he got was the occasional cup of tea, and for me to hold something or other when he needed another pair of hands.

I had many promotions and new job titles over the next few years. I became the only woman in the management structure as I was promoted over the heads of several older and more experienced men. When I became one of the heads of department, and therefore part of the senior management team, many colleagues saw me as a young upstart who had done nothing to deserve the post. Even so, I wasn't prepared for what happened when, at my first senior managers' meeting, a much older deputy head, Marcus Hatton, asked for a quiet word.

'Yes of course,' I responded as he took my elbow and led me to a corner of the room. I was unhappy about his touch, but I managed to hold the terrors down successfully. He was a colleague and we were in a room full of other people.

'You're just a kid. There are a lot of good men who could have done with this job. You've only got it because you're sleeping with the headmaster, aren't you?' His tone was snide and, as I looked into his cold, hard eyes and registered the downturn to his mouth, I wrenched my arm away and said loudly, 'I am a married woman. Why on earth would I want to do that?' And I laughed as coldly as I could as I walked away.

Somehow, I'd had the presence of mind not to mention the headmaster, because I wanted there to be doubt in the minds

of all the people in the room. I suspected that they all knew
what he was accusing me of, but the uncertainty in several
pairs of eyes after my indignant remark, and his own shocked
reaction, would cause some to always wonder whether he was
propositioning me himself. With an air of genuine disgust, I
rejoined my colleagues in the middle of the room.

Although I appeared calm on the surface, I was seething
inside. What right did he have to speak to me like that? Why
would I do that? I had a husband and had never chosen to
sleep around. Of course, the men in the room with me didn't
know that. None of them knew me well and they most
certainly didn't know of my background. Yet still they felt
able to judge me negatively, even though all I had done was do
my job well. I was highly offended and Marcus Hatton knew
it. It did nothing for our working relationship and I believe
that he grew to dislike me intensely. The feeling was mutual.

I had always wanted to have children and hoped to have four
of them, two boys and two girls. It was what married women
did – that's how I and my peers were brought up to think, and
when I became pregnant I was simply over the moon with
delight! I had so much love to give to this child and I talked to
my baby from the moment I found out I was pregnant.

'Hey, Munchkin. What do you think of this then?' I read the
article from a magazine on the benefits of exercise in pregnancy and asked my unborn child for an opinion.

'This is Vivaldi's *La Notte*.' I would say the name of
whatever piece of music I was playing and Baby would give
the required response.

I would talk to my ever-expanding tummy, play music to it,
and when I was rewarded with the baby kicking I felt such
happiness that I thought I would burst! In this way, I learnt

that my as-yet-unborn son liked Mozart, Schubert, Elgar, Tchaikovsky and Rachmaninov, but turned his nose up at Wagner. He loved Handel's *Messiah*! He also enjoyed a little jazz and the Beatles!

I didn't at this point think too much about the actual mothering of my baby. I knew it would come naturally, as I would simply do for him or her the things that I wanted done for me when I was young. I was also not worried because I had already experienced the rigours of childcare with my own brothers and sister. It wasn't until just before the impending birth that I began to worry. This would be a tiny baby. What was one supposed to do? Did I need to be extra careful? How? Would I make them happy? These fears were swept away as the day of the birth approached and they were replaced by other problems.

In those days teachers were given about seven weeks' leave before the birth. I thought I might have an enjoyable time preparing for my baby's arrival, but my problem was that I had too many energetic alters and too much time on my hands. I was suddenly – and for the first time in my life – on my own for long periods of time and with little to do. For someone who was used to waking hours lived at full throttle, it was horrendous. I became disturbed and was enveloped in a constant haze of fear. I didn't have any friends who weren't at work and I tried to occupy the free time reading. I began to experience a lot of 'floating'.

I floated around the house vacuuming, or cooking, or doing whatever jobs needed doing. I 'floated' down to the shops to get the groceries, or to get things for the baby. I even 'floated' to the antenatal classes, and as I did my exercises. I 'floated' as I waited for Gerry to come home. I needed his presence as a comfort. He never knew that I was somewhere just short of the ceiling as I put the dinner on the table. I had no fear of the pregnancy itself, or the impending birth. Instead I was scared of the *difference* between a full and active life in which I was constantly occupied, and this semi-life where nine or more people were doing chores for one. As I became more and more unsettled with the idleness, I began switching as the alters became more active. They were staying longer, doing what I don't know. Time was being lost to me again, and in large quantities. I began to be scared non-stop.

The day for the baby to be born came and went. I was at home but the midwife trusted me to know when the baby was coming, even though it was my first. That was a sign to me that – whatever else I was doing – I continued to appear capable and in control to others. My parents were making a permanent move to the coast down south at that time and they had arrived to spend an evening (and night) with us before going to visit Gordon who lived near the Scottish border. They intended visiting all of the children in turn.

The next morning, I realised that my baby was preparing to make his appearance. I was terrified! Not of the impending birth, but rather that my parents would want to stay for it. I didn't want either of them near my baby, especially if I was in no state to defend it. Therefore, when I realised that the baby was coming, I said nothing and watched with immense relief when they got into their car. I waved cheerfully as they drove away. In a way, I wondered why I was feeling so relaxed. I should have known. How could I have forgotten that I was not alone? Although it was late spring, it had begun to snow. I shut the door and turned to my husband.

'My contractions have started. The baby is coming.'

Gerry looked at me, panic touching his eyes briefly before he smiled and said, 'No it's not. You're having me on.'

'But it is. Honestly. I'm not joking.'

'No! You're not in any pain. You have to be in pain. That's how you know it's coming.' My husband was an expert obstetrician all of a sudden. 'They won't thank you for going in too soon,' he continued, 'so we'd better wait a while. Especially in this weather.'

So I went upstairs, lay on the bed with a book and waited for a few more hours. When I began to feel that it would be dangerous to wait any longer, I walked downstairs, picked up my packed bag from near the front door and called to him, 'I'm going to the hospital now. You can come with me or not.'

Within seconds he was standing in front of me. 'But you're not ready yet. Look at you. You can walk without problem.'

'Gerry, if I wait much longer, you are going to have to deliver this child. Are you ready for that?'

He paused only a moment before he said, 'Let's go to the hospital.'

At the hospital, the 'sister' midwife examined me and declared that I was well into labour. She checked the baby's heartbeat, then carried out a few other checks before attaching me to the monitor. Her brows furrowed as she looked at the monitor, which showed my contractions coming fairly close together. Then she looked at me lying there looking inquisitively at everything she was doing. She walked to the monitor, thumped it sharply on the side and continued to stare at it for another minute or so.

'Have you much pain?' she asked.

'No, not really, but I could feel the contractions,' I replied, half amused at the apparent preoccupation with pain. First Gerry, now the midwife.

'I think I have a defective machine. Your reactions do not match what the monitor suggests is happening. I'll just get it changed.' She said all this as she was detaching me from the machine.

She picked up the supposedly broken machine and disappeared, leaving me alone in the room. While all this was happening Gerry, who was very calm, sat with me and spoke encouragingly. He had thought he would be hanging around for hours waiting for me to give birth, and he had brought some sandwiches, in case he had no time to get a meal. As the nurses had told him I would be in labour for ages yet, he went outside to eat. While he was away, the midwife returned, and I was reattached to another monitor. She frowned again. A nurse midwife came into the room and she called her attention to the monitor. I felt the fear coming.

'What is it? Is something wrong with the baby?' I asked.

'No. No. Don't think that, the baby's fine.' The ward sister had returned to me and was lifting the sheet to begin an examination. 'It's just that the monitor indicates that you are far along into childbirth, but your lack of pain reaction suggests that you are still in early labour.'

'No. I'm not. I've been in labour for hours,' I just managed to say as I began to 'float'. I heard a rush of air that told me that an alter was with me and had experienced a shot of pain.

'Heavens!' she exclaimed, 'the crown's showing. The baby's coming.'

They called to Gerry, who came back into the room just in time to see the baby's head appear. He began to bounce up and down in his excitement, causing my hand, which was in his, to bounce up and down too.

'Okay. She needs to push now,' the midwife said.

'Push!' Gerry ordered.

I pushed.

'And once more,' the midwife said.

'Push!' Gerry said again. He gripped my hand hard in excitement.

'One last big one.' That was the midwife again.

I heaved and felt the surge as I expelled my baby. Gerry looked from me to the nurses, who had moved away briefly with the baby. Within seconds, I heard the lusty bawl that would dictate my life for several weeks to come. The midwife spoke and smiled. 'It's a boy!'

'It's a boy!' Gerry shouted, as though somehow he thought I hadn't heard the nurse. He kept looking at the baby and it was clear to see the pride etched on his face. He looked as though all his Christmases had been rolled into one. He held our son, only for a few minutes, but he gazed at him with delight.

Within minutes, Jack had been cleaned up and was placed in my arms. From the first moment I saw him, I fell deeply in love with him. I cradled him in my arms, there was a satisfied chuckle, and I sensed another pair of strong arms around my own. Several other pairs joined in, until I believed that all of us, including the tiny alters, were in contact, all of us holding our newborn baby son.

Well done, Ruthie. Well done. My smile grew wider as I gazed at baby Jack.

Gerry hurried off to phone everyone – family and friends. People said later that they were surprised to hear how excited he was about the baby. He was clearly a doting father, even though – in the spirit of the times – he was very unlikely to pick his son up or do any of the caring things that so many fathers do for their children today.

They took Jack away to the nursery, which he clearly found not to his liking. He cried virtually non-stop. He was always hungry, it seemed, and even when he shouldn't have been, he continued to cry.

'Perhaps if he could have his cot beside my bed,' I asked, albeit hesitantly because I knew that it was not permitted. All babies had to be in the nursery. The rationale in those days was that the new mother would be more able to rest if she didn't have the baby beside her twenty-four hours a day.

'No. That's not on,' the nurse replied. 'If I do that, who knows? All the other mothers might want the same.'

So Jack cried on, disturbing all the other babies in the nursery. It is an unusual thing that human beings so young can feel the pain or distress of others so intensely that it changes their behaviour. Instead of the calm, sleeping infants they were before, almost every baby in the nursery began to cry. Jack was therefore moved to another room so that peace could once more reign in the nursery. But he screamed even more, it seemed, and as he was now nearer to the nurses' own office, they were not very happy.

Eventually one of them, a burly middle-aged woman who had little patience, brought him to me. The look on her face alone warned me of her displeasure.

'This child is hungry. He needs feeding again. Clearly you are not producing enough milk to satisfy him. I'll show you how to give him a bottle.' The aggression was streaming out of her and Jack, apparently sensing it, began to howl his rage to the world. Still holding him, she walked to a trolley that stood not very far away, and picked up a sheet. She then proceeded to swaddle him tightly. A younger nurse arrived with a bottle of milk, having been clearly dispatched to get it before Nurse Aggressive came to my bedside, and she darted away again.

The nurse tried to force the baby to drink, but by now he was so enraged that he was turning a horrible puce colour. For the next minute or two it was a battle of wills between the nurse and the baby – and Jack won. Fed up, the nurse handed him and the bottle to me and stalked away.

I loosened the swaddling and, cooing to him, I offered him my breast, which he took almost immediately. Peace reigned as he fed. The nurse returned, pushing a small trolley on to which a cot was fixed. Jack had won more than the right to be fed the way he wanted to. He was allowed to stay by my bedside too, where I fed him on demand. Although he later showed himself to be a baby who needed little sleep, something the nurses commented on with some surprise, he never found a need to cry incessantly again and settled down well beside me.

One nurse amused me by her reaction to his not sleeping much.

'Why isn't he sleeping yet?' she said. 'Are you keeping him awake?'

'Er . . . no,' I responded, slightly taken back.

'Well, I'll be back in a half hour and I expect him to be asleep by then,' she said as she walked away. I grinned and looked forward to the next half-hour, for I had already begun to understand my son and this would be a battle he couldn't lose.

I had spent much of the time during the experience of childbirth watching myself. I was watching myself when they cut the perineum to allow Jack to be pushed free and I saw the midwife who was also the ward sister look sharply at me as I happily pushed. After the 'It's a boy' moment, she had looked at me for a longer moment with a frown on her face as I was being stitched up. I didn't understand her reaction as I moved up to peek at the baby who was lying on his tummy on my chest. What I did understand was that, as I was outside watching all this, a 'mother' alter, Kathy, was taking the pain of childbirth and holding our baby. Soon after that, she let me rejoin and I could enjoy the magical moment of us all cradling our baby.

When I left the hospital, the ward sister who attended me for that birth, and who I'd seen observing me closely, wrote to my general practitioner that something was wrong with me. She could not put her finger on it, but she suggested that the GP kept an eye on me. On my first postnatal visit to him, he told me about her concern and laughed.

'You must have been difficult,' he said. 'They always write something like this when the patient is a problem. Were you? Did you have a falling out with them?'

'I don't think I was a problem and, except for Jack crying such a lot, I didn't think I was that bad a patient,' I answered. It was an opening I could have taken, but the need to keep the 'secret' was so strongly ingrained in me that I didn't take the opportunity to say that I thought I was probably mad, that I saw and spoke with others within me.

The GP began to make a series of joking remarks to which I responded in kind, even as my mind gnawed away at the news of the ward sister's actions. I was pretty sure that she was not referring to me being 'a problem' as such, but rather that she had seen something in her close observation of me during childbirth to puzzle her. I even suspected what it was that she'd noticed. Both she and Gerry had been surprised by my lack of response to the pain of my contractions. She was watching me, both when the perineum was cut and then when it was being stitched, as I cheerfully ignored what must have been excruciating for others. Later I realised that she was watching me when I sprang out of bed and strode down the corridor. When I realised that all the other new mothers could barely crawl out of bed and had to hobble down the corridor,

I began to understand something of her scrutiny whenever she was around.

The fact is that I leapt out of bed because I found it less noticeable than slowly getting out of it. My jauntiness walking down the corridor was a reflection of my natural cheerfulness and my pleasure with my new son. What no one knew was that an alter had taken over and prevented me feeling physical pain. However, the realisation that she had spotted something and was interested enough to be keeping an eye on me caused my anxiety levels to shoot through the roof and I began switching non-stop. This would have given her more opportunities to notice the differences in my personalities and behaviours, and although she might not have understood clearly what she was observing, she had become concerned enough to ask my GP to follow up.

'Anyway, Mrs Bradley, you seem eminently unproblematic to me, and little Jack's fine. A bonny little boy. As for the ward sister, they need to be kept on their toes sometimes or they'd be caught flat-footed.' Completely ignoring the very valid concerns expressed by the midwife, the doctor made his last inane joke before I left his surgery.

I had remained in the hospital for ten days before being allowed home. I and my new alter, Kathy, spent a lot of time caring for Jack. In addition to the usual tasks of baby care, we played with him, cuddled him, loved him – and just generally did all the things for him that made for the kind of relationship I would have loved to have had with my own parents.

Jack quickly began to sleep all night, but refused to do so during the day. This didn't bother us and, as we finished our household tasks so quickly, we spent all our free time with him. I would have him on my lap, propped up against my chest as I read the daily newspaper aloud to him and 'discussed' any items of interest with him. When he was old enough to lie on his stomach and hold his head up, I used to settle him on a portion of the paper and I would lie over them both. Then I would point to the words as I read, or show him items of interest in the photographs. I was also reading children's picture books with him.

By the time Jack was six months old, he had begun to speak, something that startled everyone, but I realised that it was because of our reading sessions together. He was showing such an interest in the pictures that, although he was so young, I bought him some crayons and began drawing with him. By the time he was eighteen months old, he was drawing in 3-D. People began to say that he was gifted, but as a teacher, I always knew that he was simply responding to the quality attention he was getting from *both* his mothers.

Whenever my baby cried I hated it, as it had the power to return me to a small girl listening to her siblings' screams. Fortunately Kathy, the alter who took my birthing pains, didn't hold any of those memories and she was a more than capable and loving mother. She was always with me as I interacted with Jack.

My role model as a mother was myself. I thought of all the things I had wanted from my own mother and what the children within me also wanted. The result was a child-friendly mother who was prepared to go the extra mile to ensure her child's happiness. I was always asking my selves:

What did I want as a child? What should I be doing for him? How can I best meet his needs?

I knew what *my* needs for all of my children – Jack, Barry and Kate – were. I wanted my children to grow up to be comfortable with themselves, to have consistency and to be considerate of others. I wanted them to feel and to be secure, to know what they were good at and to feel proud of themselves. I took them to meet children with special needs so they could learn that their comfortable existence was not universally shared. I answered their questions about some of the kinds of things that could affect small children who were alone in some way, either because they had withdrawn from their environment or because they had been left physically alone by adverse circumstances. I did this because I wanted them to be rounded adults who considered others, and they didn't fail me. Everyone thought that I was eccentric as always, but my children never seemed to notice.

My husband didn't notice either. When Jack and I returned home, Gerry was quietly pleased with his new son. He was never a demonstrative father and had little to do with any of his children. My feminine roles became even more strongly demarcated, as did his role as the man of the house. He took this role seriously and, having restored our home beautifully, he was on the prowl for an older property to renovate. He found a four-bedroomed, two-hundred-and-fifty-year-old house, which we moved into when Jack was just eight weeks old.

I had no say in the matter, as it was not a 'woman's decision', but I wasn't very happy about moving house with a brand-new baby, particularly as the place needed a lot of work. But it was by then early summer, and I eventually fell in love with the house, which Gerry was redecorating with both enthusiasm and good taste. The area was also pleasing as it had plenty to offer mothers and young children. Even with my mother–child duties, and the bits I did to help Gerry and my general housekeeping chores, I was still brimming with my over-abundant energies, and I found all manner of tasks to do both at home and in the community. My alters continued to keep me busy.

My family continued to grow. I had another son, Barry, who arrived when Jack was eighteen months old. He arrived more quickly than Jack did and we bonded immediately. When a woman told me in a pitying tone that it was a shame I'd produced two sons, I was understandably highly annoyed, but I bit the angry words back. *What right had she to say that? Who does she think she is? I am so pleased to see my strong, healthy baby . . . he's beautiful and I am very happy with him.* I couldn't understand how anyone could think I would be sad to have a healthy baby boy.

My next child was a little girl. Kate beat Barry's record and was simply adorable. I had originally wanted four children, but by now there were serious cracks in my marriage as far as I was concerned, and I decided that three children under five years old was enough. A fourth baby, no matter how much wanted, would put an unbearable strain on what was already becoming a tense marriage.

Gerry had still been working on the house through Barry's birth and I was pregnant again with Kate when he started on the kitchen. He literally pulled the thing apart. The house had been designed so that the kitchen was the central room. In order to get to any other room, one had to walk through the kitchen. The place was a complete mess, and, having grown up amid such strict cleanliness, I hated it. The problem was that I had become obsessively tidy. I was not quite in my mother's league, but I liked things to be in the right place.

We had no kitchen for nearly a year, as Gerry was a conscientious schoolteacher and he was building the kitchen in the odd bits of spare time he had. For me, pregnant and coping with two young children, without a kitchen and with other building work going on all around us, was trying at times. We exposed beams, renovated old fireplaces and stripped all wood back to its original state. I tried to keep it a fun experience, especially as my sons were fascinated with it all, and to get involved in the work. I became good at plastering small sections of wall, at paint stripping and tiling. It took up much of our free time, but it was satisfying to see the house transform slowly into a homely old cottage.

Although I was outwardly coping, actually I struggled to stay on an even keel. It was all very stressful for me, even though I was not teaching at the time. I tried not to show my unease, though, and it seems I was successful, as Gerry continued in his own way to fulfil what he saw as his role in our marriage. I had never told him about my childhood abuse and the effects it had on me, and I knew I never would. Unburdening myself seemed unattractive and pointless to me. Deep down inside, I sensed (perhaps wrongly) that Gerry wouldn't be able to come to grips with either the abuse or the alters. I didn't understand the alters' appearances myself. I only knew that they were there, that they generally helped me in times of stress, that no one could see them, and that other people did not appear to have them. I decided I would just have to get on with it.

Then my mother came on a short visit. Although we children tried to avoid too much contact with our parents, we did take it in turns to have them to stay once a year, and we would also take turns to visit them again perhaps one further time during the year. With five children, this kept my parents feeling fairly satisfied, in so far as they could ever be satisfied. On this occasion my father was away in Europe and so Mum came alone. Needless to say, I was even more on tenterhooks than usual about the visit.

Gerry had already experienced my mother's need to be instantly obeyed and in control, but he wasn't really moved by that. He said we should stand up to her. He was of course right, but I was already conditioned to do what she wanted. My mother registered his reluctance to do her bidding shortly after we were married and, by now, really disliked him. The day after she arrived, Mum came in from doing some shopping.

'Gerry and Ruth. My shopping's in the car. Bring it in, will you?' she ordered as she walked through the door.

Gerry stayed where he was. I did as I was told.

'Why isn't your husband helping you?' She looked at me as I struggled in with a load of things. 'Why aren't you helping her?' She looked towards where Gerry was sitting. He ignored her. I ran out for another load.

She spent a few hours shouting about how dreadful Gerry was. He continued to sit where he was. As my mother paused to take a breath, he turned to me and said clearly, 'When she ordered you about like that, you shouldn't have moved.'

At the time, I found this difficult to handle. He was right, but I was still so afraid of my mother. After that incident she always openly criticised Gerry, saying that I shouldn't have married him. Everything about him made her angry. I had lived my life in constant fear as a child and that had continued throughout my adult life. This sort of situation just made me more afraid. I didn't tell Gerry how I felt. I just said it was best to humour her. How could I tell him I was afraid of her? I was an adult! I didn't even know what I was afraid of now. I was a strong woman, used to giving other people their work orders and being assertive when necessary, yet inwardly I was constantly living in fear, and my mother's presence always made it worse.

I learnt to switch off my feelings once the fear got too much. A couple of hours would go by in a second as an alter took the opportunity to occupy what I had voluntarily left. Of course I didn't tell Gerry about this. What would I have said? I didn't have an explanation for it, nor did I have the language to explain it. What could he or anyone do to help me? And why on earth was I still allowing my parents into my life? I simply didn't know why and I still don't know.

My daughter, Kate, was born just as we finished renovating the house and we now had three children under five years of age. I adored my children and I believe that my love for them helped me to carry on, despite all the stresses. I had hoped that Gerry would help me through this period by showing some support. Perhaps he could have cleaned up after himself, or at least left less cleaning for me to do, but he was clearly completely oblivious to my needs. It was around this time that I found myself becoming irritated with him. I hadn't minded his coolness towards me before, because it went well with the even stability I needed from him. However, he also seemed oblivious to his children's need for him to participate in their upbringing. He loved them. I knew he did. I sometimes saw him looking at them with an expression of beaming pride on his face. He just never touched them for more than the briefest of moments. He didn't hug them, or play with them, or spend any quality time interacting with them at all. If they needed anything, it was, 'Go to your mother. She'll sort it out.'

I didn't feel as though I could approach him about this. He was always a kind person and he worked hard to provide for us. In addition, the renovations took up all of his spare time and I could hardly complain. I thought I would wait until the renovations were complete and speak with him then, and in due course the time came when the house was finished.

'Gerry, it is wonderful!' I congratulated him. 'I can see that we'll be really happy living here. I love it and the children love it, and I know you must be proud of all you've done.'

However, unbeknownst to me, Gerry had made the decision that the house was too small for us all and that we would make quite a lot of money if we sold the house and bought another one to do up. He wanted us to keep on doing this, as it was a good way to make money and move up the property ladder.

'We're not staying,' he told me, abruptly.

'What?' I was puzzled. Whatever did he mean?

'We're not staying. I've started looking for another house.'

'What?' I was aghast. All those years of living on a bombsite and he was thinking of selling it. And why wasn't I worth consulting?

Biting back the anger that was rising within me, I agreed to move. I didn't voice any real concern. I wasn't *really* being forced to do something I didn't want to do, as I could see the logic in his argument. Our family was growing quickly. His teacher's salary was not bad, but I was not working, so more money would be welcome, as would a larger house. Still, I would have liked to have been consulted about a decision this important. But despite my apparent equanimity, the whole business of doing up a house again and living in all the chaos it created made me inwardly quake. I told myself that I wasn't being sensible. Gerry was a kind person who never tried to hurt me. I couldn't thank him by reacting negatively to his efforts.

Why hurt this kind man when you couldn't hurt those who were cruel?

What is there to get worked up about? He is doing his best to get us the ultimate home.

I was a logical and sensible woman. I could make this work. I should be able to cope. I had three wonderful children and a husband who both brought home the bacon and would provide a nice nest (eventually). What was my problem? Why did I feel so afraid all the time?

Do not be afraid. We can do it. Don't show any fear to anyone. Not even to this kind man. We will cope. The alter soothed my concern. Liz? No this was someone else. Then I recognised her. It was Kathy. She was the one who took away the pain of childbirth, and mothered my children with me. I trusted her as I trusted Liz.

So neither Gerry nor I thought that he was forcing me to do something I didn't want to do. My voice was pretty much emotionless, as my alters tend to be the emotional ones. They have taken the burden of stressful emotion away from me. They hold all my fear, pain, depression and anguish, so that I, Ruth, never learnt how to show these emotions. If there is a powerful emotional reaction from me, then I'm not at home. Someone else is in charge. Whenever I felt strongly enough about something to make a comment, it would be so matter-of-fact that Gerry thought I was just stating a fact that could be swayed by logic.

And of course he made sense. I simply couldn't open up, especially to him, but really to anyone at all. I knew that if I had said to any of the people who knew me, professionally and otherwise, 'Look I am seriously depressed; I think of suicide a lot,' that my external demeanour would lead them to make a joke of it, saying something like, 'Yeah! I know what you mean. I get that way every time my husband starts to sing.' And we would laugh and change the topic.

So the house-hunting went ahead. We were gazumped a couple of times, and I was beginning to hope that we would be at our lovely home for some time when Gerry came home full of excitement, 'I've sold the house. It's a good offer. I've already signed the papers and we have a month to get out.'

My mouth fell open. 'Wha—?'

He interrupted me. 'I've been looking at a couple of old houses with great potential.'

My heart fell. I realised I really wasn't ready to move. I had hoped that we would have a bit more time in this house, and to me it was all happening too quickly. People who knew us thought I was the dominant one, as at work I was so assertive and I did fight as hard as I could for my young charges. I was the one who was so confident and lively and he was always so quiet and withdrawn. That was far from the truth, as at home he was the 'man of the house' who always got exactly what he wanted. I knew that if he'd made his mind up, I had no option but to go along with his plans.

'But . . .' I tried again and again he shut me up. This time he said, 'We made a huge profit. We're going to be able to get something really good . . . with a huge garden for the children. I have my eye on something. It's huge, and has a prime spot in this lovely little village. It's three hundred and fifty years old and a bit derelict, but when you see it, you'll like it. It has great potential.'

He was so enthusiastic about the house that, within the hour, he bundled the children and me in the car to go to see it. Even as we drove into the countryside, I was wondering how I was going to get around, given that we just had the one car. I'd have three children to keep me prisoner in the lovely little village. He was right about its potential, though, and I could see that straight away as we parked outside. The house was huge, old, and was set prominently in the village. However, it was pretty much completely derelict. It would require a lot of work, and we had young children for whom living on a building site could be dangerous, but Gerry jumped out of the car and moved towards the house purposefully. I decided to leave the children in the car while I had a look at the house. It seemed silly to get them out just to stand outside the building, which had once been a combination of a forge and a home for the blacksmith's family.

Within days, Gerry had made an offer and the house was ours. I discovered that the stairs were rotten and there was no electricity upstairs, no inside toilet and – with the exception of a single sink downstairs – no indoor plumbing. Mould was growing up the walls. It seems that the elderly blacksmith and his wife didn't 'hold with those modern conveniences' and thought an indoor toilet was particularly unhygienic. We had less than a month to find somewhere to stay. Fortunately we had good friends, a farmer and his wife, who said we could stay in their old and unused farmhouse in a nearby village while our new home was being renovated. I gratefully accepted.

The farmhouse we stayed in was in the middle of a working farm and, to my horror, it wasn't much better than the house we'd bought. When it rained, the water came in and, because it appeared not to have a proper foundation, everything was quickly sodden. It was also infested with mice, which had no fear of humans and would run boldly across the table when I was preparing our meals. When I found mouse droppings in Kate's cot, I was beside myself, but Gerry thought the whole thing was just funny. I began to work myself into a tizzy, for I knew that a rat's bite carried a disease deadly to humans, and I worried about whether mice did too.

We had to cross the milking yard each morning to get Jack to school, and the children's boots would be covered in cow manure, which needed to be wiped off before they could get into the car. Jack was then a sparkling five year old; Barry, who was four, was always full of mischief and unstoppable curiosity, and baby Kate was just one year old. I might have had reservations, but the children all loved the farm. Calves were born while we were there and they 'helped' in a birth. They watched the milking and ran around a lot in the surrounding fields.

We had builders do much of the structural work at our new house and Gerry and I did the rest with the children helping. Despite having some problems with the builders, the house made steady progress and was becoming quite a beautiful place. I spent many of my days at the house watching the builders, electricians and plumbers at their respective tasks. At the weekends, Gerry and I stripped wooden beams. We discovered two original inglenook fireplaces, which we restored to their former glory. Everything was done to our own specification and we ended up with quite a luxurious house. Even better, it was completed within our budgets and we had no more than a reasonable mortgage to pay.

During the entire process, alters were switching in and out, giving me an apparently inexhaustible supply of energy. Kathy, the mother alter, was particularly active, taking care of the children whenever I was beginning to feel overwhelmed. Even Alexis, who was more likely than not to be angry, pitched in and helped, grumbling under her breath as she did so. Liz was also there a lot, soothing, soothing everyone, including me, and keeping my anger to manageable proportions.

The end product was well worth the wait. I really loved the house's atmosphere, which was welcoming, warm, old and beautiful. It was in a quiet, pretty village, which was safe for our children to grow up in. My three children were happy and healthy. My husband loved me. I felt that I must be as happy as everything suggested I should be, and in many ways I was. I had what I had always dreamed of: a family. It should have been heaven for me . . . a place where my alters could settle and quietly disappear, but all was not right with me. During that time, the decibel level in my head increased as the alters chattered incessantly. The switching restarted as I floated around fulfilling my role as wife and mother, and undertaking all the other duties that now occupied me. I felt what I could only describe as 'hysterical' inside. In order to focus on something else and to hold the alters at bay, I also threw myself into the DIY with Gerry. It was something extra to do that would help me pretend nothing was going on. I would cope somehow.

Incredibly no one noticed, as usual: not my friend who owned the farm we stayed at, or her husband, or my husband, for that matter. I thought it was incredible, because I was sure I was going quietly mad. I was certain that, because I was switching so much, and – judging from the amounts of time I lost – for long periods, someone would surely notice a different me . . . but no one did. Outwardly everyone thought I was happy. Friends saw me get angry with the builders and tense from time to time as building work took longer than anticipated, but this was nothing unusual. Problems always occurred with projects like these. But I knew! I knew I wasn't all right. I knew that my head was all wrong, that inside my head didn't feel normal, and you must remember that normal for me included seeing my alters, hearing their voices. I was mentally in chaos and deeply distressed about it. I kept trying to stay in my then present time, for there was nothing to upset me and a lot to be happy about. *So why was I slipping back? Why were my alters taking me there?*

Finally the day came, not long before Christmas, when we moved into the home we'd named 'The Old Forge'. It had taken six months for us to complete the main house. Although Gerry had done his usual fantastic work and it was magnificent, there was still a lot left to do as he was, with the help of the builders, now constructing an extension. There was a piece of plastic sheeting separating the newly built rooms in the extension from the main house. There was no security, just this thick piece of plastic. As a result, it let in the cold, and dust. My anxiety, which had been high for ages, now began to overwhelm me. Something was building up inside of me.

It's all so dirty. Just look at the dust in here.

Not to mention the mud tracked into the house every time the builders come in for a cup of tea.

And the garden is a tip . . . all that rubble and mess.

It's not safe for the children. They could easily fall over something dangerous.

What about the diggers in the garden?

What about hygiene? You know we are a tidy freak!

Stop it, please. Don't go on and on so!

We must! We must! Yes we must! They were beginning to sound like a pit of vipers hissing at me. Day after day.

One evening, after the children had gone to bed, I walked down the stairs and moved towards the extension. I had already tried to clean the most affected areas a half-dozen times that day and the cacophony in my head was completely out of control with its repetition.

Dust, dusssst.

It's a mess. A messss.

It's not safe. Sssssafe.

We must. We mussst . . .

Almost like an automaton, I walked to the sheeting, pushed it aside and I walked into the extension itself . . . and all hell broke lose, as the darkness in my head descended on me.

Dusssst.

Messss.

Sssssafe.

Mussst . . .

Hahahahahahahahaha!

'Oh, please God, don't let the horrids come back! I thought they went away at boarding school!' I fell to my knees crying.

Get up you nasty little person. Do you think you can escape me so easily? I'm here to show you that you can't!

It was too much, far too much, and it all came spilling out in a loud guttural scream that tore at and burned my throat. I went completely berserk. I ran round the room screaming and, to his credit, Gerry ran to me and grabbed me. He held me close as I continued to scream and, after a while, calmness returned to me. But nothing had really changed and nothing was better. I was terrified.

My husband never said a word. He never asked me why I was running around screaming, and I suspected he thought it was simply the mess that was getting me down. I'd already indicated several times that it was annoying me, and was constantly trying to clean it up. I never said what was wrong because I didn't know for sure myself. Why were these horrid alters back? What was going on? The episode was never mentioned again by either of us, and life went on. It was extraordinary and, even I, convinced that I was mad, marvelled at the 'usualness' of our lives.

The next day, Gerry went to work as usual. When he returned home, he sat down with the newspaper and I gave him a cup of coffee. As usual, there was no conversation to speak of. I walked out of the room and into my bedroom.

No conversation?

What are you, mad?

What about me?

Me?

Me?

I'm not mad! Go away! I'm not mad!

Just who do you think you're trying to kid? Horrid voice 1 said.

I'll just settle in and wait for the right moment, Horrid voice 2 said.

Yeah!

It sounded like a sigh and the hairs on my skin rose in terror.

11

An ending

The next few weeks were a terrible struggle for me, trying to keep the *horrids*, as I was now calling the destabilising alters, under some degree of control. Both Liz and Kathy, the mother alter, realised that I was under stress and worked hard to soothe me. At the time I had no idea that they were unaware of many of the other alters and certainly did not know of the *horrids*. I suspect they knew something of each other and it may be that Kathy is the adult version of the Liz in me, what she would have grown up to be. Under their influence, and as the work on the house progressed and finally ended, I finally regained some sense of my old self.

I decided I would go back to teaching full time and would look for a permanent job. Both boys were at school now, but Katie was only two years old. Gerry agreed with me that getting a live-in nanny would be a good solution. I know this sounds very grand, but in fact at that time it was no more expensive to get a live-in nanny than it was to pay for a child minder. We had the room and there was a college in the nearest city that trained nannies. We interviewed quite a few and found a good one. The children liked Ailsa a lot and she was good with them.

Having her there meant I could relax in the mornings and enjoy my children before going to work. As Ailsa helped get the tea in the evenings, I could enjoy family life with my children then too. She had her own car and we arranged that she went home at weekends and in school holidays, something that pleased both us and her. Although we had to pay her the same amount as if she stayed all year round, it meant we got our privacy.

Things improved somewhat when I began working again as a supply teacher at a nearby special school, which catered for students who had both learning difficulties and physical problems. I loved it. I wasn't aware of it at the time, but Jean, Carol and Val had joined my team of alters and they were all incredibly efficient, playing tag with each other and with my body. When Jean had done her work, Carol took over, followed by Sarah when Carol was done. It just depended on what jobs needed to be done and when. With apparent boundless energy, they made me a teacher who showed inventiveness, compassion and utter professionalism in my daily work. Jean was a proficient manager and negotiator. Carol was an efficient organiser, not simply of the children's activities, but of my own tasks and duties. Sarah enjoyed being with the children, encouraging them to be more daring in their efforts. She was also the consummate socialite, who went to dinner parties and a myriad of other social events with me, helping me with my various roles. She was always watching to see that I made no social or professional gaffes and ensured that I was always efficient and friendly. During my average work day, I eschewed the normal breaks and free periods that most teachers took. When they were relaxing from the rigours of teaching their classes, I was attending meetings and any seminars that might have been on offer. I started work promptly and, although I tried not to stay late too often because my children needed me and I them, I volunteered for responsibilities that both challenged and invigorated me. Soon I would return to management, where my own real skills were added to and reinforced by Jean.

In the evening, I would go home to relieve Ailsa, and Kathy would emerge, feeling completely fresh, to care for us all. After the children's bedtime, I would do whatever marking was required whilst relaxing with a soothing drink. At my own bedtime, I would sink into a deep and dreamless sleep – healing recuperation for a body that housed so many different people. These were the years in which my alters and I were truly functioning to the best of our abilities. I was making a success of all areas of my life, and my career went from strength to strength as I was promoted several times.

All was not completely well, though, despite our hard work. On the home front, Gerry became more taciturn and withdrawn. It wasn't just me he excluded. It was all the family. I didn't know why Gerry was so introverted and could never find out because of his taciturnity. I believed then, and still do now, that he and his family had a perfectly happy relationship with each other. I do know that looks can be deceiving, but in the years I'd worked as a teacher, I always seemed to have a sense of which children (even adults) were disturbed because of parental cruelties, and I never had this feeling about Gerry.

Because of his lack of interest in my past, I could never tell him of my parents' constant fighting and the torrent of invective I and my siblings had had to live with. Indeed because my parents were always polite to others, he mightn't have believed me. I could never tell him of my mother's cruelty, of her 'madness'. I could never tell him of the sexual abuse I suffered at the hands of my grandfather, father and numerous others. I could most certainly never tell him about seeing the alters, living with the noise of their existence, indeed of allowing them space in and use of my physical self. If our experience that night in the extension of The Old Forge had not even evinced the merest flicker of curiosity, my past would not make for interesting listening for him.

In a way he was quite a hard man. I recalled stories he'd told me in the early days when we were still quite young. Apparently on one occasion his grandfather had been out shooting rabbits. He had a dog with him who was supposed to retrieve the dead animals. After having bagged a rabbit, the dog ran off towards it but didn't return with it. Gerry's granddad was so angry that he shot the dog.

'But that's awful,' I exclaimed as he finished speaking.

'No it wasn't,' he'd retorted. 'It was the dog's job to bring the rabbits back. He was no good and so wasn't worth keeping. Granddad had no time for an animal that wouldn't work, so he was right to shoot him.'

So even if he had been the most garrulous man in the world, there was no way I could have admitted to him that, during many periods of our life together, I had been just hanging on by a thread.

I did try to speak with him about my need for us to communicate, but he wasn't interested.

'Gerry, please can we have a little chat?' I asked as I brought him a snack. It was quite late at night and the children were long since in bed. Gerry was sitting in his favourite chair doing that day's crossword. Until I got up to get his snack, I had been flicking listlessly through the few television channels we had in those days, looking for something interesting to watch. Finding nothing, I decided to try to engage him. It was an activity that I tried from time to time and, although I needed to try, I had few expectations that it would succeed.

'No.'

'But we never speak.'

'I know.' He filled in the answer to a clue on his crossword.

'I can't cope with your not talking. I am so very lonely.'

He nibbled complacently at his pen, then raised his eyes to mine. 'I know.' His eyes returned to the crossword. He frowned in concentration.

'Will you do it? Will you speak with me?'

'No, I can't. Sorry.' This time he hadn't even looked up.

I sighed and went back to my place on the couch, thinking about this man I'd married. He was a good provider and he never did anything to physically hurt us. His DIY activities and his work were his life. Outside the home, I considered him to be a brilliant, conscientious teacher who was well thought of, and that was the sum total of him. Nothing more. Nothing else fulfilled him. He was not a husband and father in the true sense because, after meeting the needs of his two loves – 'house-building' work and school work – he had nothing left to give. The tank was empty. There was nothing left for anyone or anything else.

I, on the other hand, had my children, my work and a social life of sorts in the village. I believed that marriage should mean, at the very minimum, companionable friendship with one's spouse, but Gerry was so turned inwards on himself that I was lost and afraid. My going back to work hadn't helped my marriage, but it was exactly what I needed to feel as though I was maintaining some degree of control over my life.

Several days later, he looked up from his newspaper. 'I don't like working at that school,' he said.

I looked up from the dress I was making for Katie, startled by the sound of his voice.

'What do you mean?'

'I don't like working there. It's not right for me. I'm not happy.'

'Why don't you leave then? Get another job you like better.' I broke a thread with my teeth and smoothed the material on my knee.

'Okay.'

The conversation was over and I wondered later if I had imagined it, until the day of our next real conversation several weeks later. Apparently, after much soul-searching, he'd decided it would be best if he did some additional training.

'I took your advice, sort of.'

As I wasn't in the habit of giving him advice, I knew immediately what he was referring to. 'What do you mean "sort of"?'

'I've applied to do another course.'

'A course? But—'

He broke in, as was his habit whenever he decided to hold a conversation, as though he had to say whatever it was he wanted to say before he ran out of words.

'I'll be going to college in Milton Keynes for a full year to do another course. The school has approved it and will pay for the course. I'll also continue to draw my salary, so we'll be all right. You and the children won't starve.' He laughed awkwardly at his little joke, knowing that even if he never made a contribution to the housekeeping, we wouldn't starve. He returned his attention to the book he was reading.

Rather than commute daily to Milton Keynes, which he could easily have done, Gerry wanted to go to the college for the duration of the term, with the occasional weekend break at home with us. He wanted the time saved to study.

The idea of further study seemed to stimulate him, but by now I'd had enough. We had grown apart with all the silence and I wanted to separate, but I hadn't said anything to him about my feelings yet. I made another attempt to engage him a couple of days after our conversation. Despite wanting to separate, for the sake of the children I was prepared to try to hold the marriage together. It was a weekend, and Ailsa had left for her break. The children were in the room we used as a playroom when I seized my chance. I truly felt that I would be less lonely on my own with the children than I would be staying with him, but I had to try. He was sitting in his study working on some papers.

'Ger, your going away to Milton Keynes . . . is this really what you want?' From the way he looked up at me, it was clear that my enquiry was an unwanted intrusion.

'Yes. I need to do it this way.' His response was curt.

'But why? Why can't you commute? It's not that far away.'

'I need the peace and quiet to study. Surely you can understand that?'

'No I can't. You have a perfectly good study here and the children won't bother you. I'll see to that. It's just that it would be nice to have you home . . . for us to chat about our days.'

'Why on earth would we want to do that? Look, staying in Milton Keynes makes good economic sense. Why would I want to waste money in unnecessary fares?'

'The amount you'd save on rent would more than cover your fares.'

'No it won't. You can't change my mind about this.' He turned his eyes back to his marking.

His attitude hardened my own. 'Then I suggest you go up there and stay there,' I said. 'This is not a marriage and hasn't been for a long time. I'm better off single.' In financial terms, this was definitely true. I was by then again in management and earning even more than my husband.

'You don't mean that,' he said, sure of my commitment to him.

'Yes I do. I—'

Just then the children came noisily into the room looking for something to eat. After I'd seen to them, I took Gerry aside and spoke to him quietly and clearly. I wanted him to be under no illusions. For me, it was the end.

'This marriage hasn't been working for years,' I told him. 'You work, you come home. You treat this place like a hotel and I am your chef, launderer and general factotum. You do nothing to help with childcare and you don't even speak with me or the children. We cannot go on like this. Now you want to go off to Milton Keynes for a year even though you can easily do the commute. As far as I can see, there is nothing for me with you in my life. So if you really want to live away from us during this time, it would be the best time for us to separate completely. If you want me to remain as your wife, commute to your course, help in the house some more and, most of all, talk with me. If that's too much for you to handle, then go! Do your course, and don't come back. I wish you luck.'

Gerry gave me a long, careful look then shrugged.

What's that mean? Is he leaving? Staying? I wanted to ask him but he left the room, got his coat and walked out of the house. Over the next few days, it seemed to me that we saw even less of each other than usual. I was tied up with my workload and my children, and Gerry – well, it may have been that he was avoiding me.

It wasn't until a couple of days before he left for Milton Keynes that I knew what he'd decided.

'I'm sorry,' he said. 'I have to do this. We'll work something out.'

His idea of working it out was to do nothing. For him, nothing had changed. My concerns were seemingly not important enough to derail us. I was his wife and that, for him, was that. He expected me to be at home waiting for him whenever he came back, which he did some weekends. When he did, he made no effort to be any more communicative. He came, he ate, he went to bed. However, having made my decision, I wasn't going to go back on it. I was distant but polite whenever I had to deal with him. I continued to prepare his meals and so on but, as far as I was concerned, the marriage was dead. I 'left him' emotionally and concentrated on my children and keeping myself sane.

As I look back, I wondered if he had really taken in my decision that we should separate. I spoke with him several times about it, or rather I spoke *at* him because he did not respond any time. I really thought he had understood what I was saying and somehow, even through his lack of response, he had taken it all 'on board', but when we finally separated he was so shocked and distressed that I felt incredibly guilty.

'Look, I know that I could have been more communicative, but can't you see I have problems?'

'We all have problems, Gerry. Why don't you simply talk about yours . . . ?' I stopped suddenly. I didn't speak of mine. If he wasn't open to me, I certainly hadn't been trusting enough to tell him of my troubles . . . but then again, I wasn't letting my problems place such strains on my relationship with him, or our children. That was certainly the way I felt at the time. Gerry had always been so uncommunicative. But now I see more clearly that, since I was concealing so much of myself – of my selves – then that must have had an effect on our relationship too.

'I can't. I can't.' His voice faltered and for a moment he sounded piteous, then he spoke more forcefully, 'You might have picked a better time to leave me.'

'Better? For whom? Neither I nor the children have any of your attention. We have been waiting for years for you to show some ability to communicate. How much longer do you expect us to wait?'

'Well, you could have waited till I sorted myself out.'

'I don't think that time is anywhere in our near future. I'm sorry, Ger, but all these years while I was waiting, my love for you as a man trickled completely away. All I can offer you now is my friendship.'

'You're taking my children away from me!' His tone was anguished.

'No I am not. You are their father. They need you as much as I think you need them. They love you and would not be best served by losing contact with you. And I will do nothing to cause harm to our children. Surely you know that?'

'Yes. I suppose so. So what happens now?'

What happened next was that, after eleven years of marriage, we were to divorce. I know that, in his own way, he truly loved me and our children. He cried the evening he finally accepted that I meant it, and he went back to the university campus till the end of his course. To this day I am sorry I had to make that decision. It was the right one for me and I think for our children, but to break up a family and to upset another person that I really cared for was hard. I still love him in some way and will never forget that he is my children's father. I moved myself and the children out of the house, which was then put on the market. Gerry was very upset about the whole sorry mess.

We got houses only a couple of miles apart so that he could see the children every day if he so wished it. They stayed at his house whenever it was convenient to us all. I had a series of 'conferences' with the children during these difficult times, for I wanted them to understand fully why I had left their father and what the future was going to be like. They needed to know that they weren't losing a parent. Indeed, they were gaining another home that would hopefully be a sanctuary for them. I truly wanted our children to have good access to their father and he to them. They needed to grow up knowing their father and knowing he loved them. It was difficult for us all to adapt at first and things were initially strained, but eventually they did settle down into an easy routine.

I applied for a new job not long after the divorce and became the head teacher of a school that was newly opened after three schools had amalgamated to become one. This meant that initially I had to travel from school to school. The effect of this was that I was now also working closely with Gerry, who had finished his training and unknowingly got a job in the new school. Our new situation was something that was embarrassing to us at first, but we were professionals and just got on with it. However, the first day he realised what the situation was, it came as a bit of a shock.

'What on earth are you doing here?' We had bumped into each other on the way to a meeting that I was chairing.

'I'm the new head teacher of the amalgamated special schools and I am here for a meeting.'

'But . . . but that makes you my boss.'

'Yes it does.' I watched as he raked his fingers through his thinning hair. I was sure he would accept the situation gracefully, and I was right.

'Well, we'd better get on with it, hadn't we?' He walked forward, opened the door, then stood back for me to precede him.

Fortunately I knew Gerry was a good, conscientious teacher and he had always thought I was a good manager. Even so, to my surprise, he showed the same quiet pride in my progress as he does in our children's, and I came to understand that he'd moved on from the bitterness he'd felt at the time of the divorce. I was further amazed when I found that in the school environment he was a completely different person who focused totally on his young charges. It left me perplexed as to why he couldn't save some of that energy for his own children: the saying 'it's only the cobbler's children who have no shoes' seemed rather apt for him. I pushed aside the annoyance this made me feel and we gelled well as colleagues; so much so that when he was promoted to the role of one of my deputies, I was happy for him. Our working relationship worked extremely well for the nearly five years we were together as colleagues.

I hadn't reverted to my maiden name, and we had not confided to our colleagues that we had been married to each other. It was clear, judging from the looks that they exchanged when they heard our names, that they were intrigued. When they asked Gerry whether I was his wife, or his sister, he retreated into his shell and simply but truthfully said no. One day we were in the car park when he called to me, 'What shall I give the kids for dinner tonight?'

'Pizza is easy. Katie will show you what to do.'

Unknown to us, another teacher was nearby, and before long all the staff at the school knew of our conversation. In order to stop the speculation, I explained to everyone that we had once been married. Fortunately, as my ex-husband and I worked so well together, we received nothing but praise for our ability to leave any animosity and be nothing short of professional.

During the weeks and months that followed, I learnt to have a new appreciation of my ex-husband, and the feeling of failure I'd felt at the time of our separation and divorce became a deep-seated sadness that we couldn't achieve even a part of what we were managing to do as colleagues. I wondered if I should have tried harder, even as a new fondness grew between us, yet I knew instinctively that, if I had stayed in that relationship, it would not have boded well for either of us. My alters took the separation and divorce well once we had got used to the idea of it, though there was the occasional comment from the one or other of the horrid ones.

Who would love you?

You're a bad girl.

No one could love you. No one would!

Eventually I learnt to accept that my ex and I were now both happier people as friends and colleagues. In my head, I believed that Gerry's inability to show a more loving side to me was exactly as the horrid ones reminded me – he couldn't love me. It was all to do with me. I was not the kind of person who could be loved. That was my life and my destiny.

But the fates have a way of throwing our words, our beliefs, right back into our faces and – unbeknownst to me – fate would soon take a hand in my love life, changing it completely.

12

Love and a revelation

I was attending one of the numerous meetings I chaired before the closure of the old schools and the opening of the new one, when I noticed an attractive man. His name was Jamie. He was just another teacher on my team, but this was the first time I had met him. Slightly taller than me, he had very fine blond/light brown hair, a slightly aquiline nose and searching blue eyes. Although there were laughter lines around his eyes, his face was otherwise unlined. He walked as though he had been a soldier and stood erect to his full height. He wore tan boots with a heel, which increased his height further. Even as he marched into the room, I sensed a challenge. He wore a brown and white checked shirt with the sleeves rolled back to just below his elbows to display his very hairy arms. The shirt was open at the neck and showed a fashionably hairy chest. The legs of his dark trousers crumpled untidily over his boots. He tossed a disdainful look at me, his lip briefly curling up before he threw himself into one of the soft chairs and placed his feet (and the aforementioned boots) on one of the low tables. He cast another brief look in my direction and I found myself wanting to smile, for it seemed to me that he was thinking, *Oh no. Not another woman coming to gum up the works. Well you might be my manager, madam, but I'll show you who the boss is.*

I kept my own demeanour as neutral as possible. I had no desire for open warfare and this man intrigued me. I also knew well enough that there are more ways than one to skin a cat so, even as I studiously ignored his challenge, I began to plan my campaign for a peaceful approach, knowing that I was not interested in anything but complete capitulation.

We were introduced and I was noncommittal in my inter-action with him. I went on to chair the meeting, where I outlined what I saw as vitally important changes to our approach to teaching and the profession generally. There were groans of dismay. Many of my colleagues didn't want change, didn't see the need for it, and they resisted me vigorously. Some even became malicious and aggressive. They made it clear that to them I was just an outsider who'd been brought in to disrupt their lives before moving on to another area. Fortunately, I seemed to have an ally in Jamie. He had long recognised the need for change and accepted my propo-sals without a problem, probably because they were just the sort of changes he would have proposed if he had been in my place. The result was that he saw me with different eyes and, although he didn't know it yet, capitulation was on the horizon.

These were difficult days for me, as the opposition of so many colleagues to change placed stresses on me that caused my alters to return. I was back in the dark place called 'they hate me', but my alters shielded my vulnerability from my detractors. If I was less than competent and persuasive, my position would be jeopardised. My alters Jean and Carol helped me in these types of situation. They were both efficient and protective types, but whereas Jean was kind and giving, using persuasion to change people's minds, Carol was firm and dealt more with facts to get her own way. They helped me to press on regardless, because the changes were necessary to improve services for the benefit of the children.

The teaching relationship I had with Jamie was companionable, and somehow I recognised that he was not as confident as he first appeared. However, he turned out to be a great source of good ideas and I began to think of him less as someone who needed my support and more as someone whose support I welcomed. We developed an easy friendship that was entirely platonic, but after working with him for about a year, I found that I could talk with him about most things. I still didn't speak about my past or the visual and auditory pseudo-hallucinations, but I found it easy to discuss my concerns for the profession, to tell him if I felt unwell and so on. In fact, he became so astute at reading me, that he often told me before I recognised it myself, when I wasn't well. He would see when I was struggling and was very supportive and encouraging. Slowly our friendship deepened, and before long we knew that we had fallen deeply in love with each other.

Our relationship grew in strength and understanding. For example, Jamie was always amazed at my ability to 'switch', as he called it, from the passionate, private person to the consummate professional. One of us sometimes picked the other up to drive to work, and occasionally we might have been having a heated discussion in the car en route, but as soon as we'd parked and I stepped into the building, the professional alter took over. It was Jamie who first used the expression switching, and he likened me to a light bulb.

'One minute you're there, the next it's like you're a different person!'

Fearful that I would lose him if he realised the truth, I responded, 'Oh come on. Anyone can do it. You can too if you tried.' I genuinely believed other people could do it, as at this stage I didn't understand how different my alters made me.

It was difficult for him at first but, in my ignorance of MPD, I insisted that if I could do it, he could too. I didn't want him to know that for me it was child's play, but he really tried and in part he succeeded. He learnt to suppress his natural inclination to be passionate right up to the resolution about whatever was bothering him, and learnt to stop demanding that I joined him in his passionate arguments as he could see that it was not in my nature to do so.

Jamie was and is a very affectionate man. He enjoys cuddles, holding hands, or putting his arm protectively round me as we walk. He has never changed and is like that now with me and the grandchildren. We decided to move in together, which wasn't as simple as it sounded, because he had a wife and two children. It was a difficult start to our life together. During this time, Jamie was understandably volatile so I sold my house and we bought a larger house together, sharing the expenses, to accommodate my brood and his when they visited. My three children were delighted to have new friends who came to visit and stay over, and Jamie's two settled in quickly whenever they were there.

For me those were especially happy days, despite the problems. Jamie is such a lovely man that even now when I think of him I feel a warm glow and find myself smiling. He is a great talker and I spent hours listening to the sound of his voice. I say the sound of his voice, rather than what he was saying, as often someone else was taking in the conversation, allowing me the pleasure of focusing on the wonderful feeling of love that listening to him made me feel. I learnt to enjoy arguing with him, which we did often after that, sometimes about some intellectual topic, other times about some triviality, as is normal when people live together.

At first I was frightened when he became angry, because he got so passionate about it. He would slam doors, muttering to himself, something which could tip me back into childhood. But I soon learnt that if he was really cross about something, he would leave the room to return later, calmer. Sometimes the argument would continue in a more reasonable manner, but often we recognised that whatever we'd been arguing about wasn't really worth the effort, and we would return to loving ways.

Our children got on so well together and I made sure that I included them all in everything I could. If his two were with us when I bought clothes for my three, I bought clothes for them too, and when they were not with us, my children were not allowed to play with their toys or indeed use anything that belonged to them exclusively. Then, because of the constant anguish and bitterness of the divorce that Jamie and his children were experiencing, their visits stopped.

If this upset me, Jamie was devastated. This was probably the worst time of our lives together, as Jamie's moods were explosive and I became volatile too. Alters began to flash in and out but I hoped with all the pain that Jamie was experiencing, he wouldn't notice that something was amiss.

I was wrong, of course. He did notice something, and whatever he saw clearly warned him that delicacy was required.

We had just finished washing up together after our evening meal when he dried his hands, took me in his arms and held me close.

'What's the matter?' he asked gently.

'Nothing.' I spoke to his chest.

He took me by the chin and raised my face to his. 'You should know me better than that by now, and I know it's not "nothing".'

I began to tremble, only slightly, but he noticed.

'Long story?' he asked. The look of concern was so strong that the tears came involuntarily to my eyes.

'Come,' he said as he led me to the lounge. He made me sit on the settee where he joined me and snuggled me into him. 'I'm here for you, you know that, don't you?'

I was terrified, but I knew that if I was ever going to tell my story, then this was the one man I could confide in. I was exhausted by my struggle to maintain normality. Suddenly, I knew that I wanted Jamie to hear everything, to understand what I had gone through. Only a few minutes passed before I dropped the first bombshell. 'My grandfather raped me.'

Bit by bit I told him the story of my childhood abuse. I heard him gasp with pain when he heard of my parents' involvement. His arms closed round me tighter and I could feel the tension in him like a wound-up spring. Every time I slithered to a halt for fear of an explosion from him, he stroked my hair or face and whispered, 'Go on.'

There was an explosion all right, but of love, support and understanding from Jamie. The relief I felt was enormous – my trust had been amply rewarded by this wonderful man who believed me utterly. We became stronger as a couple. We had been living together for some years and it was at this point in time that we decided to get married. This was a registry office wedding with my children there. We invited a couple of family members and some friends to the service. Afterwards on a wonderful warm summer's evening we held a party in our own garden for all our friends. It was a lovely intimate wedding.

Not surprisingly, however, his knowledge of my story led to an intense dislike of my parents that he did not bother to hide from them on the few occasions he saw them. By now I was seeing very little of them as they lived so far away. My commitments, both as a full-time mother and educator, meant that there was not enough time to include them in my life, and we only met perhaps once every other year. By now my children were growing fast and, as my parents were virtual strangers to them, they had no real need or desire to spend any time with them, something which pleased me, because I had no intention of leaving them alone with their grandparents.

Although Jamie now knew about the childhood abuse, I still hadn't told him about the alters, for even at this stage I had not known exactly *what* they were or *why* they were there, now that the abuse was long gone. I had no comfortable diagnosis to fall back on. All I knew was that I danced daily with 'madness', for want of a better word. I saw and conversed with other versions of me that I knew weren't really there. The only people I'd heard about who saw things had been diagnosed as schizophrenics and therefore in the eyes of the world were 'mad'. They believed that the things they saw were there. I knew mine weren't, but I also knew that my mother had been labelled 'schizophrenic'. What's more my father's words still reverberated in my head when the stresses piled up on me.

You're as mad as a hatter. Just like your mother.

I didn't want Jamie to think I was as 'mad as a hatter'. He was a wonderful loving man, but would this be too much for him? I struggled to keep this truth from him, but for some reason all the stresses of my life chose this time to start applying the pressure. Often, when we were alone, I would begin to pick him apart. Every tiny little fault I could find I took up, worrying at it like a dog with a bone. Naturally my criticisms stung Jamie and we would have the most blistering arguments. I could see myself doing this and knew I was completely out of order. I tried to stop myself but, whoever was in control, (and I didn't know her, though I was beginning to associate her with the 'horrids'), was too angry . . . and too strong. I didn't understand. *Who was she? Why now? Why here?* My heart was breaking because I was allowing all the deeply buried anger that had been eating away at me for so long, to overflow and spill out. And I was unfairly attacking the one person who had shown me nothing but love and complete understanding. I had aimed at and was demolishing the wrong person!

We were having one such argument and I could see that Jamie was reaching the end of his tether with me when the phone rang. I was standing closest to it, so I reached over, picked it up and switched! The woman who answered the phone was calm, rational, friendly and able to carry out a witty intelligent conversation with the teacher who was at the other end. I was watching Jamie in the mirror above the telephone – this alter had no horror of mirrors. He had turned away when the phone rang, but now he was turning slowly around again. I dropped my eyes so I would not see his.

When I rang off, I turned around to see Jamie leaning against the doorframe, with his arms crossed over his chest. He was frowning and his mouth had fallen partially open. As I watched him warily, he stood up straight.

'Who are you?' he asked. As he did so, his eyebrows disappeared under the fringe of hair that had fallen over his forehead. 'Who are you?'

'What do you mean?' I was relieved that it was the real me

who answered. The angry alter had vacated the premises for a while. I couldn't sense her anywhere.

'I mean who are you? How do you do that? You do it all the time. Sometimes you are sweet and playful, then you're cool and professional, then you're a harridan blazing away at me, then you're a lovely woman again . . . Sometimes you are different minute to minute. What on earth is happening? *Who are you?*'

'I'm Ruth. What a silly question. I'm just Ruth.'

'Come here.' I walked into his opened arms and we spoke quietly for a while. I was thinking of how to explain myself to this wonderful man, when the angry one literally burst out of me and continued where she had left off.

As she tore me out of Jamie's arms, he reached out and grabbed me again, holding me tight against him. He looked into my eyes and said clearly but firmly, 'And you can get out. I want my partner back.'

I felt the struggle within me and she slowly trudged away.

'I'm sorry,' I said. Jamie released his hold slightly.

'Ruth, when you switch, it's so quick. Tell me what's happening. What's happening to you? And don't tell me "nothing". I know something is wrong. Sometimes living with you is like living with a score of different women, and I want to understand why.'

'I'm scared.'

'Don't be. Whatever it is we'll deal with it together. You're the woman I love. I'm here for the long haul, so we share everything, right?'

'And if it happens again?'

'I'll cope. Somehow I'll cope.' He tried to hide it but I heard the desperation in his voice, and of course, I was quaking. *What if he couldn't cope? What if he left me? What if . . . ?*

The question I should have really asked myself was: *What if I was the luckiest woman in the world right now and had truly found my knight in shining armour, my heart, the man who was a giant amongst men?* Because I had, and much later, after I had started therapy but had some reason to ask a similar question, he laughed mischievously and said, 'Well, it's not every man who could sleep with a handful of women, sometimes in as many minutes, and still not be cheating on his wife.'

I didn't tell him everything that first time we spoke about my problems, but I was surprised when he immediately made a connection between my childhood experiences and my 'idiosyncrasies'. He didn't realise that I was really several personalities; it was more that he rationalised that my responses were simply learnt in order for me to cope.

I had hoped that with Jamie on side I would cope better with my alters, but I had another job change that counteracted all the good he did. I moved from the school I was at, and got a job as a head teacher in a larger one forty miles away. That meant that I got no relief from the amount of travelling I was doing. Indeed this increased, as did my workload. All my old fears of the unfamiliar resurfaced with a vengeance. I began to dissociate while driving and I watched myself navigate the car to whichever workplace I was heading to. The alter who drove was expert and never caused any accidents and I was immensely grateful that there were no problems. I would get into the car, drive for an hour and a half, and get out of the car again, thinking I'd only just stepped in. It was only my different surroundings that made me understand that a considerable amount of time had passed.

Although people I had arranged to meet did not see my fear, they were amused at my anxieties which demanded that they provide very detailed and accurate directions to get to whichever building we were due to meet in. In addition, often en route, the alter acceded to my mute request that she/I stopped at any important landmarks and made notes about them on a pad we carried, so that if I ever replaced her/me at the wheel, I would recognise something of where we were.

I continued to chair meetings as necessary, but this time, although my alters continued to function expertly, I was losing so much time to them that, even with the carefully written notes to keep me in touch with the main points of the discussions, I began to lose touch with the proceedings. I began to talk out loud to my alters and would pass it off as 'just thinking aloud'. I developed the strategy whenever I returned to the discussion at hand by going around the group asking participants what they thought they were there to achieve, or to recap from their perspective what had been said so far. If other participants seemed sceptical, I would get any misunderstandings cleared up there and then.

I, or an alter, always asked for the secretaries to produce a summary of the meeting's main points for me to take away with me. These would include the item under discussion, the main points that were raised, as well as the recommendation and actions to be taken and by whom. This was fleshed out later when the full minutes arrived. That way I just about managed to keep on top of things, but it was becoming harder to juggle everything.

Even so, my colleagues were often complimentary, praising me for my 'clear thinking', 'decisiveness' and 'judicious' decision-making. Apparently I could see the wood despite the trees, and cut to the chase very quickly. I was often completely confused because I had no idea what they were talking about, unless they went on to say something else that made things clearer for me, or until I looked at the minutes of the meeting.

Someone else said, 'You are always the same. When you come in, you're ready for work. You're not like the others who might need a coffee or something before they start. You just get on with it.'

I now recognise that I could do these things because my alters had just the function they came for. It was *they* who never changed. Whether they had come to take my pain, mother my children, be assertive on my behalf or do my job, that was all they did. Jean and Carol had nothing else to do in their lives but be efficient managers. They didn't have to worry about relationships, or child rearing, teaching or being a lover. They had never been abused and had no other stresses. They were just there for the job and could pour all of their energies into it.

When one needed a break, or if my duties required a different approach, another would take over. When they came in they were always fresh and didn't even seem to recognise that they didn't have bodies of their own. They were generally assertive and very clear thinking, logical and unperturbed about any problem at work. They loved having to deal with a so-called 'insurmountable problem' and had excellent problem-solving skills. They were also honest and plain speaking – Carol in particular was too plain speaking sometimes, as, like Alex, she too didn't suffer fools gladly.

I recall one person who was truly inefficient and she tried to place the blame for some error on me. I'm not sure, but from reports I heard from amused colleagues about my dealing with this particular teacher, I suspect that team alters jumped in and really let fly!

Yet they, and I, could be nurturing and gentle. I always

loved helping people I thought were struggling, and we managed to combine my assertive, professional and caring selves into a package that worked hard to bring out the best in ourselves and the colleagues we managed.

That was their reason for being. No wonder they were good. There was no baggage like most people have. Their minds were clear. They/I would reach a solution almost immediately, while other people had to go through the slower process and work their way there. We had to learn to wait for others. We were dealing mostly with male colleagues, and one or two of them would suffer bruised egos if the woman manager solved the problem first. I had learnt the hard way that being too accurate or too quick brought out resentments I'd rather not deal with.

Sometimes someone would say that I was psychic, as I responded to their questions so quickly that it was almost as though I'd read their minds and had an answer prepared. Even one of my brothers, years earlier, had asked me whether I was a mind-reader. Again I now know the alters were responsible for that. It was almost as though, with their intense focus on the job, they were not only able to anticipate many of the problems and produce the solutions, but they were also skilled at anticipating the questions that might be asked and produce the answers. Even so, the more compliments I got, the more it emphasised my difference from other people.

During these times, Gerry continued to be supportive and helpful, and he and our children spent as much time together as their combined schedules allowed. I had resented Gerry's isolation during our marriage, but I hadn't realised just how confused the children had been by his lack of reaction to them. They seemed to take it all in their stride, responding to him when he spoke and getting on with their lives when he didn't. Their true feelings of perplexion were only brought home to me when I was chatting with them as adults.

'Why doesn't he talk with us?' Katie asked.

'He does try,' I said. Jack snorted and Barry laughed.

'He does!' I insisted. 'Your father is one of these men who doesn't speak much. You know, the strong silent type.'

'Yeah! Just like other dads?' Jack said.

I didn't respond. Even then it was important for me to let my children understand that they were always very much loved – by both of their parents. It is important for me that they are secure in that knowledge, even now.

'Not everyone can show their emotions,' I told them. 'Some people find it quite difficult. But I've seen the look on your father's face when he looks at you even now. The pride, the joy in being your father, the love . . . it shows. It's all there. It's not just me saying it. Know it. It is hard enough for your dad not being able to talk about his feelings. Don't make it harder for him by doubting his love.'

Kate added, 'Mum, I love him to bits, really. I just wish he would *talk* to me sometimes.'

Today, all three children have a good relationship with their father. They meet him often for a drink and he visits Jack, who is now thirty, and who moved to the east coast when he finished university, for a couple of days at a time. Barry is now twenty-eight and has a long-term partner and they have two children. They live in the same village as I do. Kate is twenty-five, single, and moved back to the village after finishing university.

My children are my proudest achievement but my pride in bringing them up well was eroding. The knowledge of their concerns was added to the pool of underlying worries that

began to plague me almost non-stop, and an old refrain began
again:

Failure.

Failure.

Naturally a failure.

Soon after that, my sister Mary became ill and, on a visit to
her, I had the greatest shock. I had gone to see her shortly after
visiting my parents, as my father had been diagnosed with
lung cancer and was to be moved to a hospice as the cancer
was fairly aggressive. Mum had been distraught and needed us
around her. After we'd finally left her, I was spending a few
hours with my baby sister before returning home. Naturally,
our conversation focused largely on Daddy, and perhaps this
helped her to drop her bombshell. I hadn't been the only
daughter Dad abused. I can remember the exact look on her
face as she told me. The bleakness matched that buried deep in
my soul. I was so upset I could have cried, but it would have
been unfair of me to have thought of my own emotions at that
time. Mary was mentally ill and was having difficulty coping
with her memories and her life in general. I remained im-
passive and just listened.

'Do you believe me?' She had looked at me with such fear in
my eyes and I felt the end of my nose burn the way it does
when tears are threatening.

'Of course I do. I do, little Mary. I do.' To me, she looked
so frail and small as she told me of the horrors in her life, and I
once more saw her as the small child I tried so hard to protect.
Somehow I never imagined that they would hurt her in this
way too, because I never saw her as having the same kind of
evil in her as I apparently did. She also didn't seem to talk to
herself or display any signs of having 'others' around her, as I
thought of them in those days before I was sent to boarding

school. As I associated my abuse with the alters and she didn't appear to have them, I imagined that the sexual abuse couldn't be happening to her.

I didn't feel it was right at that point to tell her I had been abused myself. I don't know to this day if that was a mistake or not. Would it have been better to have told her so she knew she wasn't alone? I was just about holding my life together at the time and I knew Mary needed all my support to help her through a difficult time in *her* life. If I started to tell her or anyone else about the abuse I would have been in no fit state to help her. I couldn't face the truth and talk about it, so I said nothing.

Listening to Mary talking about her experiences caused a lot of internal turmoil for me. I spent more time at home and work, finding that hours were passing in seconds. I began having nightmares. I would wake up screaming, disturbing Jamie in the process. I always woke thinking I couldn't find the way out of my bedroom and had to really concentrate to find the door and windows. I was also finding that during the day I couldn't picture my present home, that is, the house I currently lived in with my husband and children. If someone asked me where I lived I couldn't answer. I just couldn't remember. I would picture the house I lived in when I was six or thirteen. Although this had always happened to me in the past, it was happening more frequently now. The impact of my sister having a breakdown was to increase all my problems. I am certainly not blaming her for this. I wanted to be there for her. As I had failed as a girl to protect her, the least I could do was to help her now when she was finding life so very hard.

A few weeks after this, Mary phoned me at work.

'Ruth? It's me. I've just had a phone call from the Macmillan nurses. Daddy has about five hours to live. They want us to go to see him. He's dying.'

'Will you be going to see him?' I asked.

'I-I-I don't know. I'm still having problems coping. I think maybe I should, but to be honest, just the thought of it makes me ill. Will you? See him I mean?'

'No. I don't think so. To be honest, I can't think of anything I could say or do that would make him feel any better about himself. I cannot be hypocritical and comfort him with words of love, because I feel nothing of the sort for him. I'll be thinking of you though, especially if you decide to go down there. Do the boys know?'

'I'll call them now. I wanted to speak with you first.'

'Mary, remember, you must take care of yourself. Don't do anything that risks your health. Only you know how strong you feel deep down inside. So do what is right for you, okay?'

'Okay.'

With his passing, I had hoped for an easing of my spirit, but life is never that easy. I did not visit him in his last days, nor did I go to his funeral. I have no regrets about those decisions whatsoever.

The effect of my energetic and heavy workload began to take its toll on my body. My two sons had grown up and left home, the elder for university and the younger to start work. Then it was the turn of my baby girl who, like her brothers, had suddenly grown up and left for university. Although I was no longer as occupied as before, the extra free time was no boon. I fretted about my departing chicks. I agonised about my sick sister and I worried about the pressures that drove her into madness and seemingly wanted to push me headlong there too. The free time worked against me as it had done before, years earlier, when my children were very young . . . and once more gave free rein for my alters to emerge with greater ease. I began to slide inexorably towards the meltdown that awaited me.

13

Meltdown

More than fifty years after the alters first emerged to protect me, it was time to pay the bill. I do not know how or why, but perhaps they too were losing time when I was myself or some other alter was in control. Perhaps they too were becoming frustrated and upset with the semi-life they led. Whatever it was, I was losing increasingly longer periods of time as one or other invaded and stayed much too long. I would sit down to watch a favourite programme on television. Some time later, and judging from the clock, I knew that the programme had come and gone and I had not seen one second of it because someone else had been enjoying it. Sometimes I would sit down to read a book and become aware that I was driving my car, heaven knows where, possibly because someone wanted to go some place and, having been there and done their business, had started back and decided to let me drive home. As I didn't know where we'd been, I would 'come to' in a panic, and would remain there (together with any of those who empathised with panic), until I reached some familiar place or a sign indicating which way I had to go to get to my village.

I would find myself running, not knowing why, and im-mediately thought the worst, but perhaps the alter who had just vacated me was simply enjoying a little jog. There were times when my heart would be pounding so wildly that I had to force myself to breathe slowly in the hope of lowering my blood pressure and pulse. This began to happen so often that I became somewhat hypochondriac and thought I was dying. I was always in and out of the doctor's surgery looking for a cure for my physical ailments. Then, when these periods of 'illness' and blackouts began in earnest, Jamie realised that it was not simple forgetfulness, but something rather more serious. His concern was so touching that I didn't want to miss a single moment of our life together. I began to be terrified that one day the alters wouldn't let me back. *I*, Ruth, had probably been becoming weaker ever since they began to cover for me, but all anyone had seen was the illusion of strength, of efficiency.

I began to wonder. What if they needed so much time in me that one or other of the adults who were working so hard for me decided that the one who was the strongest should have control? What if, in my easy acceptance of them and the benefits they bestowed on me, they had come to view me with contempt? What if one of the strong ones was jealous of the life I had and decided she didn't need my particular personality around in anything more than minute amounts? Could she kill my personality off completely, that is, integrate me into her so that I existed only as a part of her? Would I want to be a completely new personality? One who experienced none of the horrors of my childhood? It was a tempting thought, until I learnt that none of them was whole. Each held only a tiny part of me. I was the real being! I and I alone. What would life be like for my beloved Jamie and the children if the strongest was a woman who knew only how to manage others? And what would happen when the time came inevitably for her to retire? Then a thought hit me. What if the strongest one turned out to be the raging virago, who knew nothing but how to rage? Why, my family would have to be with someone who was eerily like my own mother. That was the clincher! I was me, and no alter, no matter how much I respected and cared for her, was going to usurp any more time from me. It was time to take back my body!

I went back to my general practitioner and this time I asked to be referred to a psychiatrist.

'Why? There's nothing wrong with you.'

'Precisely, doctor. I have been here so often, absolutely sure that I was seriously ill, dying even, and you've found nothing wrong. That must mean the problem is psychological.' I lost my nerve and ended lamely, 'Hypochondria . . . perhaps.'

'Mrs Dee. There is absolutely nothing wrong with you. It is true that you've had a few panic attacks, and you're rather anxious. But you're going through a difficult time in your life. Your body is still going through the menopause and your hormonal levels are fluctuating. We do not refer people for psychiatric treatment for simply having a midlife crisis. All this will pass. Don't worry.'

Of course. The menopause. I had not considered its effects before and so, somewhat reassured and believing that now I had some kind of explanation and I could beat this thing, I returned home.

However, things got worse. I know that I must have been switching several times a day because in addition to being 'out of it' most of the time, my body became chronically tired as each new switch brought in a completely fresh, energetic alter. It appears that I wasn't eating properly because I was simply too busy. I was running around here, there and everywhere, appearing normal to others, but in fact I had often been pushed out. Whenever I was allowed in, I felt chronically tired and depressed. I returned to the doctor.

He did some tests and decided that I was 'run down'. He diagnosed ME and sent me to a specialist who confirmed the diagnosis. During the next year or so of treatment, my physical symptoms disappeared, though the anxiety and other psychological phenomena remained. I began to sense the struggle for my physical self begin again and I went to my GP and begged him again for a referral to the psychiatric services. This time I told him about my childhood abuse. I could see his surprise even before he spoke.

'But I would never have guessed. You hide it well.'

'I had to. My parents made sure that I believed the consequences of "telling" anyone what happened would be far more terrifying than what they were doing to me.'

'Even so, you have dealt with it very well. Are you sure you need a psychiatrist?'

'Yes, doctor. I am positive. It's all getting on top of me, and if I don't get some kind of control over this, I'm afraid I'll be lost.'

'All right. I'm still not convinced, but you know how you feel . . .' He pulled a pad towards him and began writing.

On my first visit to the psychiatrist's office I almost burst into tears. Here I was, standing in front of a psychiatrist's office door, truly fearing that I was insane. The past came welling up with the threatened tears. 'You're as mad as a hatter. Just like your mother.' So my father had been right about me all along. If he was right about this, then perhaps he was right about every other horrible thing he said about my general lack of worth. I saw others. I heard their voices. I must be mad. Feelings of suicide swamped me and I almost turned around and walked away. All of the depression that I had managed to hide successfully over the years came roaring out like a tidal wave, as all the alters seemed to release into me the memories they held of our damaged life. In the background, the screams in my head rose in crescendo before fading away. I was a bad person. Everyone hated me. I had no worth. I was ugly. I was dirty. I was mad just like my mother. I was mad. I was mad. I was mad. Granddad is on top of me hurting me. There's a frill round my socks. Mummy is running up and down the street screaming. I'm in the cupboard. No, it's Gordon. Philip and Mary are in the cupboard again.

I don't want to do this with him, Daddy – he smells.

The devil and the bogeyman are going to get you.

Run! Run! He's coming! Run!

I could see the pictures, technicolour on orange, behind my closed eyelids. A kaleidoscope of memory, like a quickly moving film, but disjointed and out of order, some pictures repeating themselves.

He's coming! He's coming! Run!

I felt my muscles bunch, ready to run, then the telephone in the secretary's office rang, and I remembered where I was. Somehow I found some strength.

Go away!

No! I won't!

Yes you will! Do you want to end up in an asylum? Do you want them to put electrodes on your head and fry your brains?

No answer.

So go away. It's for the best.

No it's not! Nobody likes you. You are a useless lump . . . good for nothing!

Get away from me! That is not true!

I decided I was not having any more of that alter.

I have worth. I am a good teacher. A good mother. A good wife (by now Jamie and I had married).

I was also an adult, I told myself, and no one would ever assault me again, physically or sexually, without facing the veritable tiger I would become. It wouldn't be worth their while, for I had worth. I was not mad. Whatever was wrong would be put right. Wouldn't it?

I opened my eyes. The psychiatrist was standing in the doorway observing me. When he realised that I had registered him, he gestured for me to enter. He offered me a seat in an armchair, sat opposite me in another, and without further preamble I took a deep breath and said, 'I need professional help.'

'Yes! I could see that,' he replied as he settled down to listen to me.

When that session was over, he told me that I would also need to see a clinical psychologist for psychotherapy. He would listen, diagnose and generally direct my treatment. The psychologist would somehow help me negotiate the minefield of my life, helping me develop strategies to deal with any unexploded bombs. He wrote to the GP who prescribed me some antidepressants, which made me quite ill; we never managed to get the dosage right for me.

A second visit to the psychiatrist was arranged for me to be assessed for psychological counselling, and this time I saw a woman. I had to go through the process of repeating everything I could recall about my childhood. After a couple of hours or so, the psychiatrist said, 'You are very matter of fact about it all, aren't you?'

I shrugged. 'It happened. I had no power to stop it then and I can't do much about it now. I have taught many children who have also had very disturbed childhoods. Sometimes parents let you down. It's sad, but it happens. You just have to get over it and deal with life as best you can.'

It was this psychiatrist who actually referred me to the clinical psychologist, and another interview was set up for me to meet him. Again I had a two-hour interview and once more I had to recite the litany of childhood abuse, despite the fact that he must have had all of that information from the psychiatrist. However, he gave no indication of having had any knowledge of my history.

'Hmmm. I am rather curious about you. Why aren't you showing any emotions? You sit there and describe what happened as though you're reading a report,' he said.

'I have thought about what happened to me so often, and this is the third time I have talked about it in a fairly short time. It's all in the past. There is nothing I can do about it now except to deal with the consequences as they affect me now. With regard to the panic attacks, I believe that if I can understand how they work, why they are happening now, I'll be able to adapt somehow to be able to deal with them. It's just another problem for which there must be a solution.' I was telling him what had been the basis for the logic that I'd always used.

Then came the wait. I was put on an eighteen-month waiting list as in his opinion I was clearly not 'mad' enough to require immediate treatment. I had good days and bad and, although my eccentricities increased and began to show more at work, my colleagues saw nothing that caused them to worry. I had somehow developed my mother's ability to have, on the whole, an acceptable public face – but, as in my mother's case, that was soon to become very different from the private one. At home, even though I continued to function, I began to get progressively worse. One morning I was in the bedroom tidying up when the chattering began. It rose to a deafening roar and panic quickly swelled within me. I started to look around, my eyes darting here and there when, with the sound of a cannon exploding, I heard Jenny shout,

Run! Hide!

I knew what was coming. Granddad was going to hurt me! I had just been bathed and dressed. All those people were staring at me.

Run!

Aren't you a pretty little thing?

You're just beautiful.

I looked down at myself. I saw the pretty blue dress edged with lace. I saw the socks, the frill round the top, the black shoes.

Granddad lifted me off the table. I hugged him and kissed his nose.

Granddad put me down on the floor and took hold of my hand.

RUN! RUN! HIDE! PLEASE!

I looked round once more in complete panic and I ran!

'Ruth! Ruth! Where are you?' I sat in the dark place and listened to Jamie call my name.

Shh! He's going to get us!

'Ruth? Where are you?'

He was coming up the stairs.

I know him. That is Jamie's voice. He wouldn't hurt us.

That's what you thought about that man who was your father!

No! No, Jamie's different.

I vote we stay here. We have to hide. I vote we stay.

Me too.

Me too.

Me . . . me . . . me . . . me too . . . me too . . . The echo was growing in my head.

There was a stab of light.

'Ruth! What on earth are you doing?' Jamie pulled me up from my position at the bottom of the wardrobe, dropping his jacket on the floor and holding me close. He swayed gently with me and I heard tears in his voice as he whispered, 'Oh my love. My poor, poor love.'

Other than increase the medication, which in any case was not helping me, there was little we felt we could do. I was terrified of being admitted to a psychiatric ward as my mother had been, and Jamie wasn't about to let them take me away. We would wait as I moved slowly up the waiting list for treatment, but Jamie became adept at checking the wardrobe, under the bed and a myriad of odd places whenever he came home and I was not to be found, even though my car was parked outside and it was obvious I must be in the house.

Finally the day came when I started psychotherapy with Fingal. The wait had been interminable but I had been so scared of what the diagnosis might be that I had not been completely honest with the doctors, which had probably hampered the pace of my referral. Fingal was a rather distinguished-looking man with salt and pepper hair and gentle deep-set blue eyes. When he smiled, he showed even, well cared-for teeth. His Irish brogue was musical and I found it very soothing. Everything about him exuded calm and safety and, within a few short months, I trusted him implicitly. I thought he was absolutely wonderful. Our meetings lasted fifty minutes and they began and ended promptly. He settled me into a routine and was endlessly patient with me, bringing a level of stability back into my life. He didn't say much, but listened intently. In time I relaxed enough with him to mention that I tended to lose time, occasionally even in my fifty-minute sessions with him. His gaze never left my face but he didn't respond.

Whether that was why I didn't go on to mention the alters or hearing voices, I'll never know, but it told me that – much as I trusted him – there was something still holding me back. Perhaps I didn't trust myself enough to let go of them. Perhaps one or more of them didn't trust him or me. Whatever it was, my alters remained a secret. I had still told no one about them, not even my beloved Jamie.

We jogged along with our sessions which I felt were doing me some good, though I was still having problems trying to claw back more time from my alters. Then, about eighteen months after my therapy had begun, I walked into Fingal's office for our meeting. He was gathering my notes up.

'Come,' he said, 'we have to go upstairs. We'll have to use the small interview room in future.'

'No we can't.' I knew the room upstairs that he had mentioned. It was tiny.

He looked at me. 'What?'

'We can't. I can't. I don't want to go up there.'

Did I see a vague look of impatience? Surely not. That was my imagination. He moved towards the door and placed his hand on the knob.

'We have to.' The patient tones were there. I took the plunge.

'We can't: there won't be room for all of them.'

He stood stock still for what felt like a long moment, then he turned to face me. The deep blue eyes found mine and held them.

'All of them?'

What could I hear? What was in his voice except the calm patience? Why did I feel off centre?

'I suppose I should have mentioned them before, but I was waiting for the right time and it never came, though I guess it just did.'

'Mention them now. Please do,' he said softly.

'At the moment, there are at least' – I looked around me and started counting – 'nine other people in the room with us. They need to come to therapy too. There won't be enough room for all of us upstairs.'

His eyes wandered round the room briefly, as though to see the others and as if he was assessing what to do with us all. He took a step back from the door, crossed his arms over his chest and took his chin in his hand. If he had a beard, I thought he'd be pulling at it. He looked at me quizzically as I (and my alters, for even the baby had turned her head to look in his direction) stared back, waiting patiently.

Then he spoke. 'Well then,' his tones were as musically soft as ever, 'perhaps you could leave the others outside the door when you come in for therapy.'

I was devastated. This was a man I trusted. He was the only person I'd told about the others. I risked it because of his position as a professional who dealt with psychological phenomena and because I trusted him. If this was his reaction, what hope would I have if I had to confide in my friends, my children, my husband? My heart simply broke. I had trusted him with this inner reservoir of my being. I believed that I was in the presence of someone who would understand, and he failed me by falling at the very first *real* hurdle.

He didn't want them. Didn't want to have to deal with them. He didn't understand the intricate weaving of our lives.

This was bad. Where one went, we all went, and now that they were so active I was seeing them virtually all the time.

All for one and one for all.

Yes I know. It's always been so.

So *what are you going to do about this?*

I need this therapy. It's important to me, to us.

Why do you need this? Why do you want to get rid of me? Did I not try to help you?

Yes of course. But I'm hurting. We're all suffering. Don't you feel it? Maybe he can help.

The last questions confused me at first and then enlightened me. Although they were all speaking, sometimes at the same time, I began to realise that they spoke only for themselves. They rarely said 'us'. And whenever they did, they seemed to be referring to me and whoever was speaking. Why didn't they speak for each other? It was only Liz and Kathy who did.

But he doesn't want to talk to me.

We can work something out. Can you not just wait outside? It's only fifty minutes.

He talks to me . . . when I take control. But you're right. It's better if he talks to you. That was Kathy speaking.

Will you help me?

Yes, I'll try, but look round you. You 'see' them better than I do. I sense rebellion. What do you see?

She/I was right. They wouldn't give in without a fight. The thoughts flayed me as I, and my selves, reeled under this hammer blow. We trusted him. I knew we did, for I would not have been able to give our secret away unless we'd had some kind of agreement. I blamed myself. I can't even do therapy right. I thought the world of this guy. How could I? Why did I?

I did try to leave them outside the door, to close them out and force them away from me, but I could sense their resistance. Although I didn't see them when I walked into the smaller room, I was never sure whether they were really outside somewhere, or lurking quietly inside me. My sessions began to lose their efficacy, as trust was no longer there. All the progress I had made with Fingal began to disappear like autumn leaves in a howling gale. Without the alters there to help me explain things, there was no more depth to the sessions. Even so, I continued with him for another year because talking with him, even superficially and on a limited number of topics, was better than nothing at all. He never asked me about the others, and I never mentioned them again. Then he told me that he was leaving for another job. Despite the problems I had developed with his therapy, I felt his departure keenly. I felt abandoned. He had become a part of the routine, a kind of anchor.

I was once more hopelessly adrift. Dissociation, which had abated only slightly in the last couple of years, began to bother me at full blast again. To my distress, Fingal had signed me off before he left, saying that I was well enough and didn't need any more therapy. What I didn't know at that stage was that he had been telling Jamie after my sessions that he was worried about my state of mind. According to him, I was suicidal, and should go to the Accident and Emergency Department to get additional psychiatric services. Neither Jamie nor I knew what to make of this apparent contradiction. If he knew I needed help, why was he signing me off?

I was now entering meltdown. I was constantly switching and, as I lost track of what I was supposed to be doing, I began to miss days at work. At home, Jamie would suddenly find himself talking to a small girl who lived somewhere in the south west of England. He knew about the alters by now, as a result of two things. One was the aftermath of the episode with Fingal, which gave me the strength to consider telling him. However, the clincher happened when one evening we were sitting watching television. I cannot remember the programme, or even what actually happened, but Jamie told me when I had returned to my body.

'Oh! Your television is in colours.'

Jamie felt his mouth falling open as he looked at Ruth. For a moment he thought it was a small child speaking.

'What on earth are you talking about? Of course the television is colour.'

'Ours isn't.' Ruth was focused on the screen. She showed the raptness of an excited child.

'What do you mean ours isn't? This *is* ours!'

Ruth turned to look at him and he saw the shock register in her eyes before she began to look frantically around her. Spying the door, he saw her bunch her muscles in preparation for flight. He managed to grab her arm as she tried to get up and away, running to the door.

'Ruth! Ruth! What's happening! Ruth!'

No! Let go of me! Please! No more!

Jamie heard the screams of the terrified child his wife had become, and struggled hard to hold her tightly to him. Suddenly she stopped struggling.

'Jamie! What on earth are you doing?' He slowly loosened his arms, ready to hold tight again if necessary. He looked into her eyes and saw . . . Ruth.

When Jamie told me what had happened, I realised I had run out of options. The relief on his face when he understood was almost comical. Even as I explained, I was interrupted by one or more child alters coming out to tell him their stories. He listened to Liz describing horrors in a way I could never tell him. Sometimes Jenny would be sobbing on his shoulder as though her heart would break. He had been used by now to the adult alters coming out but had never, until then, really thought of them as separate personalities. They were simply different sides of me. Even I, at that stage, didn't think of them as separate personalities. When he heard what the children had to say and what they were like, he became disturbed and concerned for my state of mind. He correctly understood that the emergence of these very young and deeply repressed personalities represented a serious deterioration in my mental health.

During the brief periods when I was myself, I decided that I would have to take time off work for health reasons, even though Jean and Carol, the two work alters, were continuing to function well and were maintaining my managerial roles. I was nervous about this and what it might mean for my career. But Jamie was so concerned for my sanity that I agreed to see a clinical psychologist privately to get an assessment and a report on my health. We hoped that this would encourage a more sustained response to my needs from the National Health Service. It would also give me some idea about how I should proceed. I knew that an adverse report would possibly put an end to my career, and I was hoping that the psychologist would say that, although I had mental health issues, I'd always had them, and that they had never adversely affected my judgment, professionalism or performance at work. As I had always functioned effectively, a period of sick leave for rest and recovery was surely all that would be necessary before I would be fit again for work. Retirement shouldn't be the first option, but I would need more flexibility from my employers and in my responsibilities in order to be able to give of my best. That was what I hoped he would conclude, anyway.

The new psychologist was Jonathan and he said that he needed to be able to provide a diagnosis before writing a report. Other than 'panic attacks' and 'depression', I had not been given any sort of diagnosis. Fingal had studiously ignored the possibility of alters and therefore this strand of enquiry had never been taken up. I wondered if I should mention the alters but, judging from the 'expert's' reaction, I was reluctant to bring another adverse reaction on my selves.

Jonathan gave me a three-hour appointment in which I described all my ills except the most important one. The time went quickly and I remember wondering afterwards whether I had switched. When Jonathan asked for another three-hour session, I was taken aback. I thought I had given him enough material to work on but, as it was so important, I readily agreed. During this next session, the time went even more quickly and it seemed to me that just a few minutes had passed before I was suddenly aware that he was sitting forward in his chair, staring at me with a look of intense concentration on his face. A deep frown was making a double furrow lengthways above his nose. I frowned too. I had switched. I knew I had! What did he see?

He remained still for a moment, watching me closely as I tried to marshal my thoughts. After what seemed like a long time, he sat back and said almost casually,

'Have you ever had a diagnosis?'

'Panic attacks? Depression?' I replied hesitantly.

'No. I mean for the other problem. Have you ever heard of multiple personality disorder?'

With those words a blinding light had been switched on. *Multiple personality disorder? Why, that described it perfectly. They have a name for this? That must mean that other*

people . . . other people . . . there were more like me. Why
else would they . . . ? My mind was reeling.

'Are you there?'

'What? No. I-I-I mean yes. Multiple personality disorder?
What's that?' I leaned forward and I was completely there.
My mind was clear and I was focused.

'I think you have multiple personalities, that is, more than
one personality is inside you.'

'Yes. Yes.'

He smiled briefly and went on. 'The last time you were
here, I noticed small gaps in your demeanour and saw brief
glimpses of someone else. That was why I wanted to see you
again. I had brought some specific tests that I wanted to do.
Within minutes of this session starting, one of the gaps
appeared and I was able to engage what I thought was a
different personality. I began to run a number of state-
dependent memory tests, which separate out alternative personalities: different ones have different memories. About two
hours into the session, something remarkable happened and I
spoke briefly with a small child. Multiple personalities start in
childhood and, as you are probably already aware, they come
to protect you from terrible abuse. The psyche dissociates
from whatever the situation is and the condition is sometimes
called dissociative identity disorder. In my opinion, you have
multiple personality disorder and my report will reflect this.'

The questions poured out of me and he answered patiently
and as fully as he could, given that I was not a psychologist.
He also pointed me in the direction of further information. I
was experiencing such a mixture of emotions that I couldn't
identify them all, but elation was high on the list. *I know*
what's wrong! There is a name! A diagnosis! Other people
have it too. I'm not alone and I'm not really mad. And if they

knew what was wrong, maybe they also knew how to put it right!

He gave me the most welcome news that his report would reflect that I would need some time off work and that, as my workload was placing too many stresses on me, perhaps some adaptations could be made in order to allow me to participate as fully as possible without jeopardising my health. I went away feeling much happier . . . until I started researching MPD. The more I learnt, the more petrified I became. This was not a good illness to have. The prognosis seemed to be worse than anything I'd imagined. So I stopped reading about it and, until the report was prepared, I continued to try to concentrate on work.

Unfortunately, the switching continued with increasing ferocity, and now it was affecting my ability to work. I couldn't keep up with all that was happening. My strategies were no longer working. When the report came, I took some time off and returned to see the NHS psychiatrist who was still prescribing me antidepressants. I gave him the psychologist's report, which he read and agreed with. I felt annoyed that he'd perhaps known what was wrong with me all along, but had never said. Instead he suggested that Fingal's departure had intensified my symptoms.

'Ruth, until we can decide what treatment to provide for you, I think it would help you to attend an acute psychiatric day unit.'

Psychiatric unit? What was he suggesting? I looked at Jamie, who had come to the session with me, and saw the look of distress on his face.

'No,' I replied. I don't think so. I'd prefer to stay at home and have therapy sessions as needed.'

The psychiatrist was probably in his late thirties. He had

thick, black hair, calm brown eyes and spoke very quietly. He slowly opened my file and began to read through some pages. Then he wrote some notes in it. Somehow, I knew that this performance was designed to give me time to change my mind. When he had finished writing, he carefully put his pen down, lining it up against the blotter and, as I had not added anything to my rejection of his offer, he said coolly, almost as an afterthought, 'I do think you would prefer to attend the day unit rather than have a residential place.'

I felt my eyes open wide as I looked over at Jamie. He seemed stunned at this turn of events. Then I flashed back. I saw my six foot tall mother struggling under the burly male staff the day she attacked the man who thought he was Jesus. She was screaming the place down and those screams reverberated in my head now. I looked at the psychiatrist again.

'Just for a few weeks or so. Maybe six weeks,' he said reassuringly. 'I'll sign you off work. There won't be any problems.'

I realised I had no choice and that the doctor had my best interests at heart. There was a sense of relief, too, as I knew I could no longer maintain a front at work. As I was due to start at the hospital on the Monday and this was the Thursday, I went into work on the Friday. I had to explain why I needed six weeks' sick leave and to give the certificate the psychiatrist had given me. One of my deputies, a woman teacher I'd 'mentored', asked me what was wrong. She was truly concerned. Still, it was a difficult conversation for me.

'I have to be gone for a while.'

'Why?'

'I have some mental health problems. I start treatment at a day unit on Monday.'

'But why? You don't look ill to me.'

I was pleased at least that she hadn't noticed anything was wrong with me, despite having worked alongside me for several years. 'I have Multiple Personality Disorder,' I explained to her. 'I can't cope any more and must have full-time treatment.'

I smiled reassuringly to cover the embarrassing pause before she managed to say, 'Oh, I had no idea. I'm really sorry to hear that. Good luck.'

I returned to my office and picked up the telephone, arranging to meet with the two most senior governors in the organisation. Soon I met Irene and John in a small meeting room.

'Ruth! How are you?' We all exchanged greetings, shaking hands before settling into chairs. Coffee was offered and declined and I took a deep breath.

'I just wanted to let you know that I will have to leave work for a few weeks. I am being admitted to hospital.'

'Oh dear! What on earth's the matter?' Irene had a worried frown on her face.

John looked surprised. 'Are you going to be all right?' he asked, recovering quickly.

'I hope so. I have Multiple Personality Disorder and I have to go into a psychiatric day unit for about six weeks.' The fact that I had a name to put to my condition was both liberating and comforting; I felt a huge sense of relief that I could finally explain what was happening to me in language that other people could understand.

They stared at me, completely lost for words.

'You were always different, Ruth.'

'You never know, do you?' John said reflectively.

'Over the last few months things have been getting on top

of me, and I only recently got a diagnosis.' I explained what had been happening to me.

There was a moment of stunned silence, then they both spoke together, 'Is there anything we could do to help?' They stopped and looked at each other.

'I'd appreciate it if you would tell the rest of the senior staff. I want the truth to be told.'

'Are you sure about that?' John asked.

'Yes. If I, a head teacher of a large special needs school, can't be honest about mental health, who can be?' I responded.

We spent a few more moments chatting before I returned to my own office. I tidied up my desk and went home for what I thought would be a few weeks. I never returned.

During the next days and weeks before I entered the day unit I began to switch backwards and forwards frequently – much more so than ever before. The child alters were now switching most aggressively. They were virtually always with me and I felt constantly fearful, even when I had not switched. I was losing a lot of time. Whole days and nights would go past without me making any real contribution to the life that was mine. I would wander away from the house any time during the evening or night as a child alter tried to find its way home. I was also having major nightmares and waking up screaming in the night. Whenever I, Ruth, emerged, I would peer into the hidden places for my stash of pills and gaze longingly at them. I needed to end my life. Death was preferable to this constant state of fear and hopelessness. Could I do it? Certainly the child alters preferred it, were desperate for it.

Jamie watched me like a hawk. He knew what I was contemplating. It helped him in a way that I was in a zombie-like state because of all the medication and so couldn't easily evade his scrutiny. He also knew when the child alters were present as we often had conversations like this.

'May I have some sweets, please?'

'Yes of course, would you like some Smarties?'

'Are there any liquorice pipes or purple violets?'

'Oh, we couldn't get any in the shops today, but I have an idea. How about a nice ice lolly, or a Magnum. They are new!'

And they were too, for my childhood in the 1950s included no Magnums. Jamie was also constantly having to leave work and come to collect me from wherever I had found myself. At home, he was hard pressed to keep up with who I was at any given time. The Sunday night before I was due to go into the acute psychiatric day unit, we had gone to bed, and as usual did some reading before turning off the light. After a few moments, Jamie put down his book.

'I don't feel well,' he said.

'What do you mean? What's wrong?'

'It hurts . . . under my arm. I can feel the pain going up my neck and across my chest.'

'Shall I phone the doctor?'

'No, don't panic.' He sounded irritable and that worried me. I watched him as he rolled over and crouched on all fours on the bed.

'Jamie!'

'Oooh! That hurts. The pain is bad.'

'I'm going to call the ambulance. This is worrying.'

'No, Ruth! Stop fussing!' He yelled at me as he got out of the bed and managed to stagger downstairs.

I was surprised that he was rejecting my help, though not at his irritability. He has always been the type to flare up, then, once the tension was gone, he would be fine again. I waited for a couple of minutes but worried that he was really in trouble, I decided to follow him downstairs. He was lying on the settee looking deathly pale. Suddenly, I felt a sense of great calm and I realised that one of the adult alters was with me. I dialled 999.

'Yes, my husband is having chest pains . . . yes, in the chest, neck and down his arm.'

'What's your address?'

I supplied all the information they asked for.

'All right, stay with him. The paramedic and an ambulance have been alerted and they are on their way.'

'Thank you very much.'

They stayed on the phone talking with me until the paramedic arrived, just five minutes later.

He set about checking Jamie's vital signs, while I got on the phone again to tell my daughter what had happened. Of all my children she lived the closest and I knew she would be over to help me as soon as she could.

When I rang off, the paramedic said, 'I think you're having a heart attack.' He was talking to Jamie but looked frequently at me. Jamie closed his eyes, looking grey in the face, and I felt my momentary panic immediately vanish as the alter increased her presence. The paramedic gave Jamie some medication and put him on a heart monitor. Within another ten minutes, the ambulance had arrived. They worked over Jamie for a while longer, ensuring that his condition was fairly stable before taking him to the hospital. I remained outwardly calm as my alter continued to soothe me. Strangely enough she did not take over completely. It was as though she understood that Jamie needed me, Ruth, to be there with him, so she worked effortlessly in the background.

By the time the ambulance was ready to leave, my daughter Kate had arrived; she drove me to the hospital where we waited in A&E while they admitted Jamie. He would remain in the hospital for ten days before being discharged but, as it happened, I would remember very little about those days. I know that Kate took me back home and stayed with me all night. The next day I was due at the unit, which was attached to the same hospital, for my own all-day treatment. I visited Jamie before going into the unit the next morning. Escorted by a nurse, I also saw him at lunchtime and before going home later by taxi. I would do this every day for the ten days he was hospitalised. Despite being able to see him and to see that he was recovering, I was terrified that I would lose him. I was also frightened by having to attend the psychiatric day unit, but in the circumstances didn't want him to see too much of my fears.

Somewhere in my mind, which was no longer mine for more than scant minutes, I knew that the stresses of caring for my illness had triggered Jamie's heart attack, and I was wracked with guilt. It was simply too much for one person to cope with and I know that he found it difficult to manage a full-time workload and care for me. He had never been ill before and had been a fit, healthy man until my problems brought him down.

Kate remained with me while Jamie was in hospital. Every evening she took me to visit Jamie before he went to sleep. When he was discharged, she drove him home and stayed with us for a few more days before returning to her own life. I continued to attend the unit during the day while he recuperated. Fortunately, Jamie made a full recovery, and reassured me that he would support me through my own illness. But it was a very long road ahead. I quickly had to give up any idea of going back to work – my meltdown had simply been too great.

For the next year and a half, I continued to attend the acute psychiatric day unit, outwardly appearing to cope but inwardly struggling to remain in myself. Each day brought the same private war. Then one day in early 2004, eighteen months after I had first started attending the unit, I lost a major battle.

I looked around me, first puzzled then fearful. It had happened again. One minute I was doing something familiar, the next I was in a place I didn't know, had never been in before. *How did I get here?* The corridors stretched before me and I hurried down them, noting as I did that I was entirely alone. If this was a school, no teachers scurried to and fro. No students laughed and pushed at each other. *Where was I?*

In the distance I saw a woman and hurried towards her. She was a nurse! But my babies are born . . . *Why am I here?* Then it came to me. 'Jamie! Oh my God! Jamie! Please, please don't die! He's here. Somewhere, Jamie's here. He had a heart attack last night. They brought him here. Please God, don't let him die. Don't take him from me,' I prayed as I rushed headlong down the labyrinth of corridors. I saw another woman, then a man. I became aware of others here and there, appearing and disappearing. Then I finally found the place. Apart from an A4 label on the glass panel on the door there was no hint of the existence of the place in this enormous hospital. The label said *Psychiatric Unit*. I trembled with dread.

Mum? Mum! Are you in there? I've come to visit!

The door was of Georgian glass, the stuff with the wires set in it. I opened it and walked into the room. There was no reception, no welcome and no face to reassure me that this was really the right place.

I was on my own. I switched. Jamie was here, but not in this room. He was in a different part of the hospital.

How did I know that? Why was I here? Why am I not rushing to his bedside? What's happening to me?

The room was full . . . all the people were in here. No, that's not true. I could now see many shadows of people as they walked past the door to the labyrinth. I looked around the room. There were nurses and doctors over by a large desk. To get to them meant that I would have to walk across the room past all these people, a few of whom were staring at me with knowing looks on their faces.

Who are these people?

Other than the starers, there was little curiosity from the rest of them. There was a low hum of conversation that soothed me somewhat.

'You'll have to wait. Take a seat and someone will call you when they are ready for you.' I was somehow at the desk and the nurse responded to my query.

What did I ask her?

I found a chair, low and soft and with straight smooth wooden arms. I looked round and smiled.

That's what you do, isn't it? I must try to make them feel all right about me.

As I gazed around the room I began to notice more. Two people were checking their mobile phones and, after reassembling them, began to dial each other and speak: they were sitting next to each other!

The door opened and a woman walked in. I recognised that walk. There was depression and medication in every step. Her shoulders were slack and her eyes were looking at nothing.

Other people sat as I did, but seemed deep in their thoughts, completely isolated. Off to one side of the room, I saw a kitchenette . . . *so there are 'facilities'. I must bring my own mug.* There was a table with an untidy pile of magazines and old newspapers. From where I sat I recognised *OK* and *Hello* magazines . . . full of the 'beautiful people' – but that untidy stack is out of place here.

There were motivational pictures on the wall and what looked like examples of one or more untutored artists. There was also a stand of old books. As I stared at the people around they began to fade in and out. In and out. I switched again. I sat up, feeling every hair on my body standing up stiff. My vision blurred then cleared and, when it did, I was alone and the room was vast!

No! No! Help me! Please! Not again. Not again! Granddad, No! Don't!

A hand touched me. I switched. It was a nurse. She was saying something. I couldn't hear what she was saying.

Why can't I hear her?

Her face grew larger and more grotesque. Then it shrank back to normal. I switched and the lights went out!

God help me!

I heard the screams in my head growing louder by the second. So loud that my head felt as if it was going to burst. Then suddenly everything stopped. The screams stopped. I could hear nothing. I was deaf. As there was no light, I was also blind. The air was gone. I couldn't sense it, nor feel it. I even tried to taste it, but there was nothing. Nothing but void.

Then something came back. High-pitched and terrified. I heard my thoughts, my alters themselves, screaming.

Where is this place? What are we doing here? What do we do now? Don't let him hurt me! Where do we go?

I was lost and, except for the screams, completely alone. Then my own thoughts joined in the melee.

No, Granddad, no! What's happening to me? Where's this place? Who am I? Please, tell me, who am I?

I tried to speak, but the words did not come.

14

Finding myself again

Some time later, I became aware again. I was sitting on a bed in a small room, wondering how long I'd been there. As I began to get up, the door opened.

'Mum? Mum. It's me, Kate.'

I looked up and to my astonishment I saw my daughter, Kate. The tears began to roll down my face.

'Katie!'

As we hugged each other, she said, 'Mum, thank God you're back!'

And with that one statement, I knew that I had been away for a while. I am Ruth, and I am back.

The door opened again and Jamie walked in with a pair of bags hanging from each hand. As I drank him in with my eyes, he walked over to the bedside table and began emptying squash, chocolate and fruit from his bags. Then suddenly he froze, then he turned around slowly. I do not know what alerted him. Perhaps it was the total silence, for neither Kate nor I spoke but, as he turned, his eyes sought mine out, a look of expectation on his face.

'Ruth?' he whispered.

I smiled and through the tears that were gathering in my eyes, I saw that his were full too.

'Hello darling. I'm back.'

That was the beginning of my reawareness and my journey back. Although I would still lose time, I was never so deeply out of it again, always having some awareness. I took great pleasure in thinking about my family who were incredibly supportive. My eldest child, Jack, now lived and worked such a distance away that he was unable to visit me regularly, but he made up for this by sending me the most beautiful letters. I have one much treasured letter in which he told me what a great mum I was and how I had given them all super child-hoods. Every time I read this letter, I am filled with such joy. Despite all my baggage, I had done this most important task right! Barry, my younger son, lived with his wife and children locally and, like Kate, who was still at university, he visited me often. My children accepted my illness completely. As parents we always think that they are too young to under-stand, which they might be, but they are never too young to see and, as they teasingly told me, I had always been eccentric. That probably stemmed from me switching between myself and Kathy, the mother alter who helped me care for them, but they had always taken any 'eccentricities' in their stride and responded appropriately.

I had been on that ward for about three weeks when I finally re-emerged from wherever I'd been. No doubt the alter who inhabited me thought that she was needed for my protection, and when she realised that I was safe enough, allowed me to come back, or perhaps I simply managed to struggle through. Within another week, I was well enough to be discharged and I returned to the psychiatric day unit, which meant that evenings and weekends, I lived at home.

I continued to attend the acute day psychiatric unit five days a week, from 9.30 in the morning until 3.30 in the afternoon. As before, the unit sent a taxi to collect me and to take me back home, and occassionally when I was not well, I would have a nurse accompanying me on the journey. I was in a pretty bad state. Although I now had some access to my body again, I was still doped up and switched constantly. That first year, I was unable to sit in the group work or relaxation sessions for long. Then the time came when I was switching less often. I continued to be fearful and wouldn't leave the house to visit friends or even have people come to visit. We would arrange to see friends when I was feeling okay, but often on the day of the visit I would be ill again so we would have to cancel.

In the day unit, other patients recognised when I switched and would alert a nurse, who would then persuade me to go to a room with them. I would often come round to find myself on a bed in a side room covered with a blanket. The nurses were always very caring. They were especially understanding of my young alters and treated them very gently. I always woke up as Ruth and I began to appreciate that, when I switched, the alter needed to get away from wherever I was, because somehow we, the alter and I, were back with Mum, Dad or the bogeyman. Being in bed under the covers had obviously remained a place for me to hide.

In these days and weeks following my return, my feelings were very mixed; in fact they changed almost as fast as my alters switched. It was all overwhelming and I ran the full gamut of emotions. My first feeling when I thought of the day of my breakdown was one of embarrassment. I was embarrassed because I had lost control . . . and because one minute I was a professional head teacher, and the next I was a patient in a psychiatric unit. I was terribly confused as I would switch several times in a single hour. I was frightened because I couldn't figure out where I was even when I, Ruth, would briefly emerge. I moved from one home area to another in random order between my grandfather's house and my current home. I could be different ages and degrees of maturity all in the space of an hour or so. Mostly, no matter who emerged, we were *angry.*

What am I doing here? Tell me!

No more Mummy, please! No more. You can't do that!

What's happening to me? Who are all these people? Get your hands off me!

Where am I? I should be in the art class! Why am I late again??

Run! He's coming! Run! Stop it Granddad! Stop it!

Why am I here? Why doesn't someone just say???

Why can't I control myself? Stop being mad, Ruth!

Duck! Hide! I won't! I'll fight you!

It's not right. I'm fed up of growing good. You can get somebody else to stand outside your door!

You're mad! Just like your mother. See? Look around you.

With you as a father, it's not surprising! You can just go straight to hell!

It's not fair. Come on! We just have to get on with it!

We, and especially I, Ruth, were also scared. Yet, despite all our fears and doubts, we all knew deep down that *I* needed to be here. I would be safe here. But in our fear we continued to think,

Dad was right. I really am mad.

I must be in a really bad way to be here.

Yes. I must be really ill. Just like Mum.

I began to deteriorate again. I could not hold a conversation or complete any tasks. At home I did nothing – no cooking, no cleaning, no nothing. Even washing myself became problematic. Jamie had to run a bath and encourage me to use it, as I was constantly switching back to childhood, mostly to the three year old, the six year old, and the teenager. As these switches were occurring so quickly I couldn't recall anything, and I'm not sure how Jamie coped as he was faced with the terrified children or the bolshy teenager in me, but cope he did.

Some days I would feel complete panic. If I were alone at home, I would call someone at the day unit and he or she would calm me down until the taxi arrived to take me to the unit. The hospital used special firms and the drivers were really very good. This was particularly important as it was a twenty-minute ride to the unit – longer in rush hour – and I would occasionally panic in the taxi.

At first the experience of being in the unit was surreal. For example, it was strange queuing for lunch at the unit. I would then eat my meal with the rest of the clients. There were no problems there, as the more aware among us tended to look after each other, but it was strange for me to be eating with so many people, some of whom might begin to shout, or simply wander away from the table. Those who could provide some support understood about my switching from personality to personality and, on the many occasions when I tried to leave the building, they would prevent me from doing so. One of them would chat with me while another got a nurse.

'Hey Ruth! Hang on a minute. Where are you going?'

A strange woman had reached out for my arm. I pulled it away from her, terrified.

'No please. Please don't touch me.' I tried to edge past her but fear wouldn't let me.

She did not try to touch me again, but stood between me and the door.

'I'm sorry, but you can't leave.'

'Oh please, I have to go.' I was wringing my hands in agitation.

'Why don't you wait a while? The nurse wants to have a chat with you.'

I looked around warily but saw only a group of people sitting in the large room.

'What nurse? Please let me go. I am scared. I have to go.'

'Ruth! Ruth! Are you there? Ruth! Come back! Will you leave before you finish your painting for Jamie?'

The nurse knew exactly what to say and the memory of Jamie jerked me back into the present and my anger dissipated immediately.

'Wha . . . What's happening?'

'Ruth, we were about to start your new painting.'

'Painting? Where's Jamie?'

'He's at work and you'll be seeing him when you get back home in a couple of hours. Come, have a cup of tea and we'll work on your painting for him.'

'Okay.'

My therapy included belonging to a number of different groups. I was in music and motivation groups, healthy living and literature groups, film, painting and other groups. Each one aimed to discuss problems and find solutions to them. For example, we would read or watch a film together, after which we would discuss the topic. All of this was designed to get our concentration going, and my concentration was particularly bad because of all the switching.

I had marvellous carers. Anita was my key worker. She and I would meet every day for a chat that lasted between ten minutes and one hour. We also had a brief chat before I went home in the evening. She was reassuring and supportive, was never judgmental and always listened to and encouraged me. In time I began to trust her.

Gradually I began to overcome some of my problems. For example, I often used to get lost when I had to travel somewhere – like to the shops at the weekend. If I switched to the six year-old Liz, I would be thrown back to 1956 when I lived in a completely different part of the country. I would therefore have no idea where I was. Anita encouraged me to write down the origin of my journey, and my ultimate destination, on my arm. I also always wore a medic alert bracelet, so that any official who had to deal with me could read about my diagnosis and telephone the unit or my doctor.

I was still on massive doses of antidepressant, anti-anxiety and tranquillising drugs and, although they made me tired all the time, my fear levels dropped off considerably.

Jane was my main psychotherapist and the manager of the unit. She took an active interest in my health as none of the other carers had a lot of experience with MPD, and they weren't sure how to approach my care regime. Jane was the only one who had experience of a client like me before. Within the groups, she began to work with my alters, which would prove difficult because I was no longer getting the individual psychotherapy I had been getting before my meltdown. The people at the psychotherapy unit refused to treat me. Their rationale was that I was too high a suicide risk for them to see me and that I ought to be receiving psychiatric care at this stage. I was, indeed, storing tablets all over the house, *just in case*. It was a decision that all of my selves had taken as soon as I was more or less aware again – *just in case*. The view of my care team was that without the individual treatment I was even more of a risk. In addition, I needed to know that I could access individual therapy to avoid the situation becoming a 'just in case' one.

Back at home I was absolute hell to live with. I was constantly angry, crying or making demands. Some days I didn't know where I was. Other days I wanted to sleep all the time. Sometimes I'd suddenly get into rages and begin to throw things. I simply wanted to get the noise out of my head. It was total chaos and my behaviour was extremely erratic. Soon afterwards I began self-harming. Mostly, I cut myself. I used a craft knife and began carving things into my stomach – SHIT, HELP, PAIN, DIE. I'm not sure why, but the blood made me feel real and the slight pain I felt seemed to give me some pleasure. As I was switching a lot in these days, it meant that I did not feel the pain too much. However, I did feel some, and it too made me feel as though I was alive, acting as a salve for the dead feeling that lived with me every time Jenny recalled some dirty old man labouring above me.

The first time I cut myself, Jamie became alarmed and called an ambulance, which arrived with a police car, because a knife was involved. By the time they arrived, I was calm again. The police took the knife away from me and I was taken to hospital. My wounds were not life-threatening, but it was the beginning of a period of self-harm where I would continue to carve words, mostly into my abdomen, with a nail file or a craft knife if I could get it without Jamie seeing me. I would often cut myself in the bath, then cover it up to hide it from Jamie. However, sometimes the cuts became infected and I would need treatment. Jamie and Jane worked with me to face this new activity. In the time it took for me to stop this behaviour, I'd learnt to tell Jamie whenever I hurt myself. He had been told what to do; to keep any wounds clean and dry in order to avoid infection and promote healing.

My behaviour was accepted in the unit as just another phase of my illness. Anita would ask me if I'd self-harmed the night before.

'Did you cut yourself before you came in? Last night or this morning?'

'Yes.'

'May I see it?'

Initially I used to say 'no', but she would be calm and persuade me and dress my wounds with sterile dressings, and as there were no recriminations, I began to talk about my self harming.

By this time, I was well into group therapy and there was a weekly group review. As goals were achieved, new ones would be set. There was never any blame. Everything always moved forward. Eventually I began to be more aware, then we began setting goals for the day. For example, *get up, shower, dress, breakfast*, etc.

I was put on an enhanced care plan approach (CPA), and I had a team to help me. This consisted of a psychiatrist, Anita my key worker, Jane my therapist and Barbara, who is a psychiatric social worker. Jamie and I completed the group, with Jamie picking up the slack at home. A meeting was called with the psychotherapy unit I'd used before the meltdown, but they continued to refuse to see me. Jamie and I lodged a complaint and it was agreed that I should have a second opinion from a psychiatrist from another trust. In the meantime the psychotherapy unit agreed to assess me three weeks later. Having attended that assessment, I was referred for yet another reassessment three weeks after that, and finally for a third assessment in a further three weeks. This was exceedingly frustrating and a complete waste of time for me.

* * *

When the psychotherapist's report finally arrived, it described me as 'very depressed' and said that the depression had increased with every assessment. To me it seemed quite clear that my getting the runaround was what was causing the depression. This time they recommended that I should attend a residential therapeutic community unit for eighteen months. Jamie and I were both livid as this was not the most appropriate place for me, but the psychotherapist insisted, and so I agreed to attend this unit for their assessment, which would take a few hours. My team were not happy either, but key worker Anita accompanied me to my first assessment.

We were shown into a waiting room, where we sat patiently for a few minutes before a harried-looking woman dressed in a brown suit, pink blouse and sturdy brown shoes arrived. She walked up to Anita and said, 'Ruth? Thank you for being so punctual. Come with me, please.'

'Oh no. You've got it wrong. It's not me. You don't want me.'

The woman reached for Anita's elbow, 'Please come with me,' she repeated.

'Actually, I am Ruth Dee,' I cut in.

'Oh, I do beg your pardon.' She abandoned Anita's elbow and grabbed at mine before leading me into her office. I couldn't help smiling at Anita's amusement.

After a couple of hours, the assessment was over and she looked over the top of her glasses at me briefly before saying, 'I am not sure that we can help you here. However, to be fair, I will discuss your care with the team before making a final decision. Could you come back for a further assessment?'

I sighed. I was getting very tired of the constant assessments. I'd already had three by the psychotherapy unit and now the therapist, having just done one, was requesting another.

'Why can't you help me?' I asked.

'Well, the main problem is your age. Most of our clients are in their twenties. You are approaching your mid-fifties – twice their age.'

'Supposing you accepted me, what would I get out of being here?' I persisted. I felt that, as I was here, I might as well give them a chance.

'Very little, I think . . .' She hitched her glasses up her nose with her middle finger, 'though you do have something in common with them.'

'What's that?' I asked, curious.

'Many of them are mothers, as you are.'

'I suspect that most will have had their babies taken away from them. Anyway, I've got grandchildren, which makes me even less like them, so I can tell you that I would not be comfortable having to come here.'

Once again I felt a great sense of disappointment, for although I was relieved not to have to be at the residential therapeutic community unit, I still needed specialist care to help me overcome my problems. I needed to be back in the psychotherapy unit where I first met Fingal. Though I was trying hard to maintain the progress I had made so far, I began to slide back. Depression was now always with me. It stupefied me during my waking hours and wrapped me in its folds like a warm blanket at night. Shaking it off was like trying to get out of a warm bed into a cold room on a winter's day. I fought it as hard as I could one moment, but hugged it close the next. The 'comfort' that hugging it close brought often won, and soon I began to feel the complete hopelessness that only the truly depressed can feel.

If we can't get the treatment by now, what's the point?
Have we got the pills?

Yes.

Yes. We do.

Shall we take them?

Yes.

Yes.

No! No! We can work through this. Do you really want to die?

Yes. No. Yes. Err . . .

It's not time yet. We don't all agree.

Okay. Sigh!

In addition to the group work, medication, and so on, people with multiple personalities really do need intensive, long-term individual therapy. The prescribed psychotherapy in many cases involves individual sessions two to three times a week for upwards of seven years. I wasn't getting any of this as they couldn't sort it out, and I was spiralling downward again. The only positive for me was that, although I was now switching often, no single personality stayed around long enough for me to find the stash of pills and take them. However, there were many other negatives. For example, I lost my driving licence after one particular escapade.

One of me got into the car, slammed the door and started the engine. We drove down to the Accident and Emergency Department, parked outside the entrance and walked into the department.

'I wish to enter the day unit.'

'I beg your pardon?' The woman looked flustered and it was clear she didn't know who I was.

'I demand to be let into the unit,' we shouted. 'Now!'

'What's your name?'

'I have absolutely no idea. Don't you?' Our response was mild, puzzled.

'I'm sorry. I don't.'

'Well why don't you find out? I'm not going anywhere.' With that, we began to wander around A&E. It didn't take them long to notice that I was barefooted and, from my demeanour, that I clearly had a mental health problem. They quickly reviewed their security cameras and saw that I had driven myself there. They phoned the police and gave them my car number. The police in turn called Jamie, who came down to the A&E after calling my team. When I was myself again, I found I was in a small cubicle with a psychiatrist who was clearly assessing me.

She was a pleasant-looking woman who spoke gently. She had also clearly been told something of my history. She seemed taken aback when I emerged.

'Hallo. And who are you? Or am I still speaking with . . . ?'

'I am Ruth.'

'Oh hallo Ruth? Are you all right?'

'I don't know. Where am I? How did I get here?'

'Don't you know?'

'No.' I felt close to tears.

If I knew, why would I be asking? Who did I switch to? And why did she bring us here?

'I'm sorry, dear. I know it can be confusing, but you drove yourself here . . . to the A&E. Do you remember doing that?'

'No. Sorry.'

It never crossed my mind for one moment that she would discuss this with my usual psychiatrist who would then ask for my licence to be rescinded. My alters and I had been driving for years and I had never considered that I had been a danger to anyone.

'I think we should admit you to the ward. You need some intensive treatment.'

'No. I don't want to be admitted. It would be better for me if I could stay at home.'

We chatted for several more minutes and finally she said, 'I really think you should be admitted. Don't you? Your coming here today demanding entrance to the unit suggests that deep down inside you know you need to be here. Hmm? What do you think?' She sounded like someone's sweet old granny, but I knew what she was saying. I had been here before. If I refused, she would section me and if that happened, it would be much harder for me to persuade them that I was well enough to go home. As a voluntary patient, I could be back home in a day or two. As a sectioned patient, I would probably have to stay with them for longer. I couldn't bear the thought of being apart from Jamie for so long. Although living with me when I was out of control was hard for him, he and I both knew that his presence was an important part of my therapy, so, once more, I found myself agreeing to being admitted to hospital.

The psychiatrist herself escorted me to the ward, and we were accompanied by two nurses. When I got there, a bed had already been made ready for me. One of the nurses brought me some warm milk and a sleeping tablet, whilst the other found me some pyjamas and tucked me in when I was ready.

When I woke the next morning, I found myself in a six-bedded bay with another nurse sitting beside my bed. Within a matter of hours, Anita, Jane and other members of my team had visited to see how I was and to work with me. I was then moved to a two-bedded room, sharing with a quiet, anorexic teenager. It was all very calm, very quiet, very restful. The only thing I noticed was that the nurses popped in to have a quick chat every ten minutes or so. It wasn't until much later that I realised that I was on a ten-minute suicide watch, as it had all been done extremely subtly. But it was not all easy going. One night I remember waking up screaming. A nurse came running into the room and she sat beside me, stroking my hand, until I fell asleep again.

I was kept in a locked ward and my movements were restricted for almost three weeks. I wasn't even allowed to the main dining room and so I had all my meals on the ward. My days were taken up with sleeping, doing puzzles, reading and talking to other patients. At first I wasn't interested in my fellow patients but later, as I became more myself, I found them fascinating. They had such a range of problems that I couldn't help but be interested. I also had lots of visitors, and everyone was very gentle. My care team never lost a chance to be encouraging. Many friends visited me and showed how much they cared. Heather, who I first met in secondary school and who knew of my illness, was unable to come to see me as she lived too far away. But she has remained a good friend all these years and she has always been sympathetic towards me. She accepted what happened to me and it made no difference to her view of me as a good friend: she treats me as she always has. My lovely family were always there for me too – my dear husband and beautiful children. Surrounded by so much love, I had no option but to try to recover.

Gradually the restrictions on my movements were lifted somewhat and I had a meeting with the team.

'Ruth, we think you have made a lot of progress,' they told me. 'You will now be allowed to eat in the main dining room with the others, and you can go down to the hospital shop, as long as you're accompanied by a member of staff.'

'Actually, I was wondering when I would be allowed to go home and back to the day unit.' I was ever hopeful.

'Do you really feel well enough to do that?'

'Well, I can, can't I? I mean, I am a voluntary patient and I'm much better, aren't I?'

'Yes, that's true, and if you feel well enough to go, you may go.'

'Could I leave tomorrow?'

The psychiatrist looked around the room at the other team members before turning back to me and saying, 'Yes, of course, but if you insist on leaving so soon, you do realise we will have to reassess you before you go.' His voice was gentle as always.

I laughed. I had seen the implications. Clearly they didn't think I was well enough and, if I insisted on leaving, the dreaded sectioning might be used.

'I don't think I am quite ready,' I said hastily. 'I'll stay a little longer.'

The team beamed as, by making that decision, I indicated that I had reached another milestone. I began to go, escorted, to various parts of the hospital, including to group therapy at the day unit. The day of my discharge drew closer. However, all the good work was nearly undone by a silly mistake. Jamie had been allowed to take me out on a Saturday. We were enjoying ourselves so much that time just slipped by. We were brought back down to earth by my mobile phone ringing.

'Ruth? Are you all right? We were beginning to be worried about you. You are due back here you know.' It was Anita from the unit.

'Good grief! Is that the time? We were having such a lovely time that we hadn't realised. We'll start back now.' Thankfully, that slip-up was forgiven as yet another plus in my progress to health; the fact that we were enjoying ourselves so much was seen as a positive. Soon I was discharged . . . back to the psychiatric day unit I would attend during the week.

It was at this point that I was finally assessed by a psychiatrist from another psychiatric hospital, an assessment that had taken almost twenty months to arrange, time in which I had been unable to get the individual psychotherapy I felt I needed.

My care team had not been able to agree whether I was safe enough to receive individual psychotherapy, but the psychiatrists in my hospital agreed that they would abide by any decisions made by this external psychiatrist. This latest assessment was thorough and lasted three hours, and the upshot was that the external psychiatrist said I was well enough to receive two individual psychotherapy sessions each week. Jamie and I were both delighted. We felt that I now had a chance to get really well.

I was assigned Jane as my private one-to-one therapist at the Psychiatric Day Unit, but then the unit got the order to close. Fortunately, as Jane was the only therapist who knew me and understood MPD, she was allowed to continue giving me the individual psychotherapy I needed. She began to work with me twice a week, and at last I was hopeful of a cure.

15

Getting better

It was a roller-coaster period. I continued to get group and individual therapy and a lot of support from some incredibly dedicated people. I felt I was getting my life back – I felt cautiously optimistic.

One day I was at the hospital to see Ian, my new social worker, about some matter or the other. As I left his office, I spotted someone I knew. She was the wife of one of my teaching colleagues. I immediately tried to hide from her, but as I was moving away from her, she spied me.

'Ruth! Ruth!'

Reluctantly I turned back to her.

'Julie! How lovely to see you.' I tried to look surprised to see her.

'How are you? What on earth are you doing here?'

'Oh, I am a patient,' I replied, trying to appear as cheerful as I could.

'Yeah sure! Pull the other one.' She laughed, clearly not believing me.

'No, really. I'm a patient.'

The laughter fled from her face and disappeared from her eyes. It was replaced by a puzzled frown. 'You're serious.'

It seemed to me that our brief conversation became very stilted after that, and soon we said our farewells. I moved away and when I reached what I thought of as a safe spot to look back, I did. She was in the office talking with Ian. Julie was a physiotherapist and it transpired that she was asking to join my care team. Despite this awkward first encounter, she turned out to be an important addition for me, as one of my problems was that I hated anyone other than my husband and children to touch me. When Julie joined the team as my physiotherapist, I had to submit to being touched. I was surprised that when she massaged my feet, I couldn't feel her hands; during the times when I was unwell I had no sensation of my body, presumably because someone was trying to occupy it. Her work proved a breakthrough for me. She taught me how to feel my body again. I would rub my arms or feet. I would clap my hands, not to hear the noise, but rather to feel my palms smacking against each other. I would touch warm or cold objects to identify myself and stay in control.

This new weapon – and my individual therapy which allowed my alters to speak of their anxieties – meant that I was no longer switching at the snap of a finger, but rather more slowly. If I wanted to resist the switch, I could some-times clap my hands or stamp my feet to ground myself.

Initially I would not let Julie stand on my right side, as the alters there, the youngsters, objected. She soon negotiated her way in.

'May I stand here? Is this spot okay? Do your alters mind? Am I crowding anyone?'

She believed in holistic healing and her skills allowed her to become quickly accepted by all of us. Like all of my carers, she turned out to be superb, and a great support to me.

I have nothing but praise for all my carers as they were and are simply outstanding. When I began individual therapy with Jane, I suddenly became embarrassed. I am not entirely sure why, but I suspect that whoever was with me had never spoken up before and it was in fact she who was suffering the embarrassment I felt.

What should I say? What should I not say?

The questions floated in a bubble in my head. When I appreciated this alter's dilemma, I immediately told Jane that I didn't want to know what any alters told her. It was partly to allow any alters who'd kept secrets from me to be able to speak confidentially, thereby reducing any angst they might be feeling, and partly because I wasn't sure whether I could cope with more than I already knew. I also wondered whether I should plan what to discuss with her so that I did not speak for any other part of me . . . but in fact that was all I remembered of most of that first session as the alter took over completely.

I say *most*, as Jane never allowed an alter to end the session and always drew me back in before I left for home. Later it became clear that it was important for me, as the host, to know some of the things the others knew, and the alters eventually agreed to this. Thus, I found that not only was I being told about things that were discussed in the sessions, but that there was complete support for me from my alters and care team.

Talking about my past was exceedingly hard, especially if I had managed to have a good weekend at home. Even so, Jane exuded complete confidence.

'Ruth, know this. You are going forward. No matter how tough it seems. No matter how much you think you're failing, you are not. There's hope . . . a lot of hope. You can and will get stronger.'

She never defined 'stronger', but for me it meant full integration. I'd appreciated my alters' help throughout my life, but I was an adult. It was time for me to be independent. So full integration was my goal.

We worked hard. Each small achievement increased my confidence levels. In addition to being allowed to express their experiences and needs, the alters were being encouraged to move on from the past in which they were stuck. They were used to Jane and the other carers by now, and trusted them. Jane taught me and my alters to imagine a safe place. This place lay in the present and in times of extreme stress I would close my eyes and we would all go there. As this place of safety was a present-day one, none of the alters could slip back into their past.

It took a couple of years of very hard work, but eventually some of the alters began to agree to reintegration. The five youngest left first, but at different times. They told Jane that they wanted to say goodbye. Six-year-old Liz was the first to go and she moved more or less permanently to the safe place. I say 'more or less', because at first she simply spent long periods of time there, coming back occasionally before she left again, apparently for good. Shortly after that, the other youngsters, including Jenny and Alexis, followed her. Before each of these alters left, they moved forward from their usual places on the clock face to stand directly in front of me, facing me. Then they seemed to drift further and further away, before waving goodbye. Within seconds after that wave, they disappeared, and they are all now in this safe place in the present.

This was progress indeed but, as I would discover, every stride forward came with the expenditure of huge energy and, as in this case, a deep-seated feeling of loss. I, Ruth, deeply mourned their passing. I also began to panic more again, as suddenly I was confronted with having to make decisions about and do things I had never done before. They had left me a dark, empty void that I didn't know what to do with. My medication was increased again and I began to suffer side effects, which included nausea. I was unable to eat and so I suffered a dramatic weight loss.

In a way I had returned to a childhood of sorts and my care team often had to visit me at home in order to deal with my insecurities. Jamie, as always, was a great source of comfort, and he would settle me on the sofa in front of the television with what became known as my 'comfort blanket'. If he left the room for more than a couple of minutes, I would become as distressed as any abandoned child. In my more lucid times, I feared that I would never recover, and I confided my fears to Jane.

'I think I will always be in a state of chronic anxiety. I really cannot bear it. I know that it's driving Jamie to distraction and I am frightened it will make him ill again.'

'Ruth, this is just another stage in your recovery. You must see that. You are making marvellous progress. Of course you feel anxious. Several alters, personalities you grew up with, have left. What you are going through now is a period of mourning. That is normal, but you must remember that – although they will hopefully never come back to make you ill again – they are a part of you and are therefore not dead.'

I learnt to focus on my breathing whenever the anxieties arrived. To get me out of the house again, Jamie was encouraged to take me on trips in the car. At first it was hellish for us both. After several attempts, I had finally got into the car for Jamie to take me for a drive into town. We had not gone far when I began to scream.

'No! I cannot do this. Take me home. Please.'

'You have to get used to being out again.' Jamie's voice was gentle, but he did not turn back.

'I don't care. Please, please take me home.'

'Let's do the breathing exercises. Breath in for five, hold for three, out for seven.'

I began to breath as I had been taught, but quickly gave up, saying, 'It's not working!'

Jamie found a quiet spot to park and began to breathe with me.

While I was breathing for the second time, he suggested we get out of the car. Without waiting for an answer, he got out, walked round to my door, opened it and took my arm. I was now breathing in time as though my life depended on it.

'Ruth, don't hyperventilate. Slow it down. One . . . two . . . three.' Even as he spoke, he was encouraging me to step out of the car.

'Four . . . five . . . six.'

'There we go. That wasn't too hard now, was it?' He linked arms with me, locked the car door and, before I knew what was happening, we were walking away from the car. I tried to pull away from him, straining to look back at the car.

'No! No! I'm dying. Stop! I'm dying. Oh Jamie, I'm dying. I'm dying.'

Curious passers-by stopped and stared at us, wondering. After a few moments, I was struggling so hard that Jamie agreed to take me back to the car.

The next day my social worker arranged for me to attend the crisis day unit, where a client could stay for up to twelve weeks. It was either that or hospital admission, which we wanted to avoid at all costs, particularly as this blip was being seen as part of my normal progression to health. I simply had to find a way to deal with my anxieties and to let the remaining alters know that our fears were no cause for them to be alarmed. I had to find a way to stay calm and convince them that there was no longer any war within me, that the present was different.

Occupational therapy was used to help me in this task, but it was not easy. I might be sitting colouring a picture when I would stand and cry, 'I'm dying. I'm dying.'

A nurse would come over and calm me down, only to have me stand as soon as he or she moved away crying once more, 'I'm dying. I'm dying.'

My remaining alters began to have arguments out loud.
Well I know I'm dying.
No I'm not. I just think I am.
Maybe if I go and stand over there, I'll live.
I would then hustle to the safe place. Then,
What am I doing over here? I have to colour that picture.
I'm safe here. I'll die if I go over there.
No I'll not. Stop being silly.
I hurried back to my painting.
Oh, I'm dying. Maybe I'll be safer over there. I should go over there.

And so it went on, with me scurrying backwards and forwards to escape the fear.

I know this must sound terrifying, and in many ways it was. But even when I was in the grip of panic, some part of me believed that I was making progress and that I would be well. I trusted my care team and had had the experience of integrating some of the alters, so I knew the treatment was working. I just had to stay strong. It wasn't easy, though. I dealt with up to seven or eight panic attacks a day. That meant that getting back into the world was a constant struggle. Before my illness had spiralled out of control, I'd applied to do a course, one day a week, at a local college. The course began in October and I was in the crisis unit between September and November. We therefore had to get me to be able to focus if I felt a panic attack coming on. There were a number of strategies I could use. My breathing exercises were paramount here. For example, when I began to feel stressed, I would hurry out of the classroom and go for a coffee. On my way to the café, I would breathe, and count slowly back from fifty to zero.

I can do it.

No I can't.

Yes I can. I must.

Fifty . . . forty-nine . . . forty-eight.

Yes. I must pull myself together.

Twenty-nine, twenty-eight, twenty-seven . . .

Do I need to phone the unit?

No. I can do this. Twenty-six . . .

I could hear the alters breathing with me. If we got too quick, I'd stop and start again. *Fifty, forty-nine . . . Stay calm, stay calm.*

Three, two, one.

Good! We've done it.

Now one more time. Fifty, forty-nine . . .

When we had done it twice without problems, I'd return to the classroom. At first, I did this every break time for several weeks. Occasionally I needed to phone a carer, but after these initial problems I settled down to the course without problem. The first day I went without needing a crisis break, I was jubilant! I completed the course and got more pleasure from *that* fact than I did from the course itself.

Jane then referred me for additional therapy with Stephanie, a sensory-motor psychotherapist who worked with my

logic, emotions and body to help me understand the physio-
logical processes behind the panic attacks. I learnt of how
adrenaline affected the brain's chemistry to set up the fright,
fight, flight response. She explained post-traumatic stress
disorder and how that worked and having learnt about these,
I had a further weapon in my armoury to help me remain calm
and in control. I began to monitor the number of panic attacks
I was having each day, what I did to combat them, and what
activities relieved them. Then, when I got them down to four
per day, I began to grade them in terms of severity, length and
so on, using a reducing count – ten was most severe. Over five
months, the attacks reduced from sixty per cent graded ten, to
just one per cent graded ten. After seeing Stephanie once a
week for six months, I could manage my panic levels well and
so stopped seeing her.

More alters began to leave, to go to the safe place where the
youngsters were. With these older ones, it was calming. They
left when they were ready to go and it felt right. There wasn't
the kind of turmoil I felt when the youngsters left, perhaps
because these alters had suffered no abuse. They simply glided
away like so many candles drifting on a river's currents.

Not all the alters have left. There are still others, some of
whom I'd not been aware of until after my breakdown, who will
have more to say before they leave. I continue to use strategies to
cope with them; for example, when they speak with me in
public. I wear a headset similar to that used by iPod or mobile
phone users, so that if I suddenly start speaking, people simply
assume that I am on the phone. Also, if I do switch, it is for such
brief periods that it is no longer a problem.

Of course for every plus, there is a minus. If I needed any
proof that my alters were influencing my ability to function, it
came when I finally began to reintegrate them. For example, I

now have to get used to fatigue and I can no longer do as much as I did before. My reaction times have slowed dramatically as I work towards my goal of finally being one person. However, I have to accept these things because I know they are a sign that I am more like everyone else than I have ever been. Having only a few alters to deal with all my life's baggage is making me more of a whole and rounded individual and less of a super-efficient, continually energetic but also somewhat odd and extremely fragmented person.

In many ways, I was lucky. Lucky because, even though I was prematurely having to leave the job I loved, I had been able to do it until well into middle age. I was lucky because many people with MPD have catastrophic break-downs when they are young adults on the threshold of their independent lives. I was lucky because in addition to the job I loved, I married, produced three beautiful children who are my greatest pride, and, when my marriage failed, I got a second chance at love and found the most wonderful man. I can look at my life fairly dispassionately now, and make this kind of assessment but, for most of my life, despite the comments to the contrary, I never felt as though I had made a success of anything but my children. My enforced retirement reinforced that feeling, because there was just so much more that I could do, so much more I *had* to do.

But I had just one body and so many alters inhabiting it that I had stopped counting their numbers. I simply had no idea how many we were in the end. I had just one soul to go with the one body and having to share them with so many others put me on a one-way track to physical and mental breakdown.

I know that even when I am fully integrated I will probably

still talk to myself. However, I am much more confident now and continue to undertake many new challenges, including further short college courses. I have a full social calendar, meeting friends regularly and undertaking many of the household tasks that I once couldn't do.

I still see members of my care team regularly and I still have therapy once a week. I continue to use various strategies, such as GPS in the car, which helps me to find my way home if I should feel lost. I am so grateful to everyone who was around when I went through meltdown and who helped me emerge safe and well on the other side. I am especially grateful to my dear husband who has stuck with me throughout all the worst times. He has been a complete wonder and he continues to be my most marvellous supporter and hero.

There is one person in my life with whom I will never truly be able to say I am at peace but, even with my mum, I know that I am making progress. I do, inevitably, think about the people that set me on the awful path to breakdown. Of my grandfather and my father and the other men who caused such unforgivable harm to the child that I was, I will waste no more time. However, I know, and not simply from my own reactions to my children, that a mother's most basic instinct is to protect her children. Mine didn't. If only she could have controlled her own demons long enough to show us even the smallest amounts of love, things might have been very different.

As I think briefly about her, I am reminded that today she remains a sad and lonely woman. Although I am never comfortable in her presence, I cannot abandon her. What would it make me if I did? With that thought, I can square my shoulders and face my future with hope, pride and compassion. Despite all they did to destroy me, I am still here. Strong, and getting stronger every day, and part of that strength comes from the compassion and understanding I feel for the woman who gave birth to me. It's a struggle, always, but I am proud of what I have achieved . . .